Emma Lundgren Jörum teaches Political Science in the Department of Government, Uppsala University, Sweden, where she also received her PhD. She also teaches Middle Eastern and Turkish history and politics in the Department of Linguistics and Philology at the same University. She has lived and worked extensively throughout the Middle East.

'Emma Lundgren Jörum's analysis of the policies of borders and territories in Syria becomes increasingly relevant at a point in time where regional borders again are put into question: there will be new "terrritories lost", new refugees, and new unresolved conflicts. Jörum's book helps us to understand why Syria and other states in the Levant have found it so difficult to come to terms with their shape on the map.'

Volker Perthes, Director of the German Institute for International and Security Affairs and author of *The Political Economy of Syria Under Asad* **(I.B.Tauris)**

'This impressive work of erudition and scholarship provides essential clues to understanding the deadly regionalisation of the Syrian uprising of the 2010s.'

Elizabeth Picard, Director of Research at the Institut de recherches et d'études sur le monde arabe et musulman, at the Centre national de la recherche scientifique, Aix-en-Provence

BEYOND SYRIA'S BORDERS

A HISTORY OF TERRITORIAL DISPUTES IN THE MIDDLE EAST

EMMA LUNDGREN JÖRUM

Paperback edition published in 2017 by
I.B.Tauris & Co. Ltd
London • New York
www.ibtauris.com

Hardback edition first published in 2014 by
I.B.Tauris & Co. Ltd

Copyright © 2014 Emma Lundgren Jörum

The right of Emma Lundgren Jörum to be identified as the author of this work has been asserted by the author in accordance with the Copyright, Designs and Patent Act 1988.

All rights reserved. Except for brief quotations in a review, this book, or any part thereof, may not be reproduced, stored in or introduced into a retrieval system, or transmitted, in any form or by any means, electronic, mechanical, photocopying, recording or otherwise, without the prior written permission of the publisher.

Every attempt has been made to gain permission for the use of the images in this book. Any omissions will be rectified in future editions.

References to websites were correct at the time of writing.

ISBN: 978 1 78453 973 3
eISBN: 978 0 85773 780 9
ePDF: 978 0 85772 512 7

A full CIP record for this book is available from the British Library
A full CIP record is available from the Library of Congress

Library of Congress Catalog Card Number: available

Typeset by Newgen Publishers, Chennai

For my Syrian friends. It breaks my heart to see what you are going through.

CONTENTS

Acknowledgements   xi
List of Maps   xiii

1. Introduction   1
   The relevance of the book   2
   Disposition   3
   Theorising territories and borders   3
   Sources   5
   A note on terminology   7
   Translation and transliteration   8

2. The consolidation of the territorial state and the political development of the Syrian Arab Republic   9
   From Ottoman provinces to French mandate:
      The old world comes to an end   10
   Allied administration of Geographical Syria:
      Frustrated hopes of Arab independence   11
   The Paris Peace Conference and Arab attempts
      to establish 'facts on the ground'   13
   The imposition of mandates, 1920   15
   The territory of the Syrian Arab Republic takes shape   15
   The internal consolidation of the Syrian territory   17
   Striving for the independence of what? The nationalist
      movement and the Syrian territory   21

	The Syrian post-independence territory	25
	Post-independence political developments	28
	Political developments in post-independence Syria	29
	Bringing a fragmented territory together: Post-independence state building	34
	The beating heart of Arabism: Defining the state	39
	The external consolidation of the Syrian state: International and regional relations	43
3.	**'We are not strangers here': Syrian policy towards Lebanon**	**53**
	The National Bloc's 'Syria first' strategy	54
	Syrian policies towards Lebanon, 1947–1974: Decades of tension	57
	Syrian policies towards Lebanon during the War, 1975–1990: Mediation, military intervention and the establishment of Syrian hegemony	61
	Wartime indications of Syrian lack of respect for Lebanese sovereignty	67
	The 1989 Taif Agreement	68
	Syrian policies towards post-war Lebanon, 1991–2005: Securing continued Syrian control	69
	Bashar al-Asad takes over	72
	Syrian withdrawal: When?	74
	Syrian policies towards Lebanon, 2005–2010: The fall and rise of Syrian influence	77
	Syrian-Lebanese relations in the post-withdrawal period	81
	Questions regarding the Syrian-Lebanese border	82
	Syrian rhetoric on the post-withdrawal period	84
	Conclusions: Syrian policies towards Lebanon: Irredentism or something else?	85
4.	**From forgotten to stolen territory: Syrian policies towards Hatay**	**89**
	From possible partition to Turkish annexation	91
	Syrian reactions to the loss of Alexandretta	93
	Early independence: Syrian policies, 1946–1969	93

Syrian policies towards Hatay, 1970–1998 96
The 1998 turning point in Syrian-Turkish relations 98
Bashar al-Asad takes over: No claims, no
    recognition continues 100
Syrian maps after 2003 105
The Syrian uprising: Hatay resurfaces 106
Conclusions: Syrian policies towards Hatay 110

5. **The Golan Heights: From the Arab to
the Syrian Cause** 113
Syrian policy towards the Golan Heights, 1967–1990 115
Negotiations with Israel, 1991–2000 118
Bashar al-Asad takes over 127
Work on the ground: Beyond war and negotiations 129
Activities across the disengagement line 131
Conclusions: Syrian policies towards the Golan Heights 134

6. **Conclusions** 137
Possible explanations for differences in
    Syrian policies towards Lebanon, Hatay and
    the Golan Heights 141
Prospects for the future? 148

Notes 151
References 173
Index 205

ACKNOWLEDGEMENTS

Many people have contributed to this book in different ways. The multidisciplinary *Borders, Boundaries and Transgressions* research project on borders in the Middle East was what first led me to think about Syrian maps. Ever since our very first research meeting in Aleppo, the members of this project, Inga Brandell, Åsa Lundgren, Annika Rabo, Tetz Rooke and Roberta Micallef, have provided me with the intellectual framework needed for this study on Syrian policies towards territories lost. For this I am grateful. I would also like to especially thank Elizabeth Picard and Volker Perthes who read earlier versions of this book, shared their deep knowledge of Syrian and Lebanese politics and society and generously offered suggestions for improvement. Friends and colleagues at the Department of Government, the University of Uppsala, have provided inspiration and support. The Turkish, Syrian and British scholars who took part in the conference on Syrian-Turkish relations held at the University of St Andrews in July 2011 offered useful comments on my research on Hatay and extremely inspiring discussions on Syrian-Turkish relations in general. Thank you! Thank you also to Lars Wåhlin who drew the maps, Åsa Arbjörk who copy-edited the text and Maria Marsh for being such a patient and encouraging editor.

The year I spent at the Institut Français d´Études Arabes de Damas proved invaluable once I decided to go into research (and for lots of other reasons). A special thank you to Maher al-Charif and Hassan

Abbas for interesting discussions, encouragement and great teaching skills.

Nothing would have been possible had I not had the support of family and friends. You know who you are, thank you for your exceptional support in times of trouble. Last, but never least, thank you and love always to Felix, Fabian and Felicia – my everything.

LIST OF MAPS

Map 1 The Occupied Enemy Territory Administrations for the temporary administration of Geographical Syria after the cessation of World War I military operations   12

Map 2 The French mandate in the early 1920s with the outlines of the previously autonomous Ottoman region of Mount Lebanon and the Golan Heights, occupied by Israel in 1967, marked   20

Map 3 Syria and surrounding states 1946   24

CHAPTER 1

INTRODUCTION

When socialising a population to a specific territorial space there is probably no tool more efficient than the map. The precise image of territorial limits projected by maps, combined with our perception of these as correct representations of reality make them effective instruments for communicating the 'true' extension of a state. The point of departure of this book is the territorial shape of the Syrian Arab Republic, as presented on official Syrian maps. Included as parts of the national territory are two areas no longer under de facto Syrian control: the Golan Heights, occupied by Israel since 1967, and Hatay (in Arabic *liwa iskandarun*), annexed by Turkey in 1939. Not included is an area Syria has often been accused of attempting to annex and over which it has exercised considerable political influence: Lebanon. All three areas were originally included in French Mandated Syria, created on the basis of the British-French Sykes-Picot agreement and given international legitimacy with the installation of the League of Nations mandate system following World War I. Even though the Golan was the only area that ever formed part of the post-1946 independent Syria, all three areas remain, in some way, present in the official Syrian discourse on the extension of the national territory. In both words and actions Syria signals that its relations to these three areas are stronger and different from those to other areas outside of its borders and/or control. It is clear that – from an official Syrian point of view – these three areas were unrightfully detached from Syria. At the same time it is also obvious that Syrian aims and priorities with regard to them differ.

This book explores and analyses change, consistency, similarities and differences in Syrian policies towards Lebanon, Hatay and the Golan Heights over time. The aim is to conclude what Syrian goals are with regard to these three territories and if Syrian views of them have changed over time. The book also seeks to suggest why certain territories lost remain on the agenda as something that needs to be regained while others do not. Furthering our understanding of the dynamic relationship between territory and state is thereby an overarching aim of this study.

The relevance of the book

Within political science, much effort has been made to theorise state and nation building in various types of states and in different contexts. Territory, which is a necessary component of both state and nation building and a crucial precondition for any state to exist, has nevertheless largely been taken for granted. This study of Syrian policies towards territories lost suggests that the relationship between territory and state is dynamic and may change over time. Although the focus of this study is the territoriality of the state and the different policies it produces, readers with a mere empirical interest in Syria and the Middle East will also benefit from it. Despite its relatively small size and few natural resources, Syria has played a central role in Middle Eastern politics for decades. With regard to the Arab-Israeli conflict, it is widely recognised that while no major Arab-Israeli war will be fought without Egypt, no durable peace can be concluded without Syria. Syria is also considered an important actor with regard to the future of Iraq and, in view of its close relations to Iran, the Gulf Area as a whole. At the time of writing, there are fears that the civil war raging in Syria will have severe consequences in its neighbouring states and it can be concluded that Syria remains of utmost importance for regional stability.

Syrian politics are constantly debated and have often been described as mysterious, incomprehensible and confusing. Analyses in media produce contradicting images and there is disagreement on how to interpret Syrian actions, goals and motives. While this study is set within a general theoretical discourse on territory, boundaries and borders, it also seeks to advance our understanding and knowledge of a state that is largely under-studied. Arab border and territorial conflicts have so far been examined foremost with regard to the Arab-Israeli conflict. In addition, this book includes an Arab-Turkish and an Arab-Arab case. It gives comprehensive overviews of Syrian-Israeli, Syrian-Lebanese and Syrian-Turkish relations over time and constitutes the first comparative study of Syrian policies towards Lebanon, Hatay and the Golan Heights.

Disposition

The remainder of this introductory chapter will be dedicated to the theoretical and methodological considerations guiding this book. Chapter two gives a background to the development of the Syrian Arab Republic from the fall of the Ottoman Empire to date, its state- and nation-building processes as well as its foreign relations. Chapters three, four and five examine Syrian policies towards Lebanon, Hatay and the Golan Heights, respectively, each ending with a short discussion of Syrian views of these territories over time. These three chapters are followed by a concluding chapter containing a summary and comparison of the results as well as a discussion of possible explanations as to why certain territories remain important to regain while others seem to fall into oblivion.

Theorising territories and borders

Probably because a precisely defined territory is so essential to modern statehood, it has long been taken for granted within political science. As Ian Lustick has pointed out, dozens of scholars have tampered with and modified different parts of Weber's much cited definition of the state as 'a human community that (successfully) claims the monopoly of the legitimate use of physical force within a given territory' (Weber 1919, cited in Lustick 1993:3). They have thereby opened up for new research questions of great interest. Few have, however, reflected upon the 'givenness' of the territory. This has by definition excluded questions about the construction and maintenance of both the territory and the borders of emerging and established states. It has also excluded questions concerning the implications of changes in borders (Lustick 1993:3–4). By way of illustration, Barry Buzan, in his much cited *People, States and Fear* claims that the physical base of the state 'simply exists' (1991:70), and the five volume *Encyclopaedia of Political Science* (Kurian, Alt, Chamber, Garett, Levi & McClaim 2011) does not even have an entry for territory.

Following the end of the Cold War, borders and territories have been increasingly problematised (although to a lesser extent within political science). Borders and territories are now largely perceived as institutions and processes that both demarcate and negotiate the state and its territory, population and identity. Borders can be drawn, demarcated, defended, disputed, moved, ignored and violated, and their significances can change (Anderson & O'Dowd 1999:593, Paasi & Newman 1998, Wendt 1999:212). In Jackson's words: 'Borders are what states – and people – make of them and that may change over time' (Jackson 2002:157). This is also the theoretical point of departure of this book: there are no natural borders and therefore no natural – or 'given' – territory to a state. Based on Lustick's (1993, 2001) and White's (2000) works on the degrees of importance different territories may hold for a state, the fundamental premise of this book is that territories lost are not necessarily equally valued. Some territories lost may be perceived as unquestioned parts of the national territory and a founding part of the very identity of the state. They are therefore deemed necessary to regain. Others may become seen as a place apart and can, when circumstances are right, be renounced. As the importance of a territory may change over time, it may start as a territory important to regain. Depending on developments internationally and within the state to which it originally belonged, the territory in question could with time come to be seen as a place apart and possible to let go of. It is also conceivable that the importance of a territory lost could move in the opposite direction. At the time of its loss, the state to which it originally belonged may not have perceived

INTRODUCTION 5

it as a necessary part of the national territory. However, depending on political or economic developments it may, with time, be seen as increasingly important to regain.

Sources

A number of different sources have been used in the compilation of this book. Official Syrian discourse has been studied mainly in media interviews with Syrian officials and speeches held by decision makers, foremost the Presidents. Speeches by the first President of independent Syria, Shukri al-Quwatli, have been collected in the volume *Shukri al-Quwatli yukhatib ummatahu* (Shukri al-Quwatli speaks to his nation) (Beirut, 2001). The next Presidents for whom speeches have been systematically collected are Hafez al-Asad (1971–2000)[1] and Bashar al-Asad (2000–). Unless otherwise specified, all speeches by and interviews with Hafez al-Asad have been retrieved from the CD-rom *Khutub wa-kalimat wa-tasrihat al-sayyid al-rais Hafez al-Asad 1966–2000* (Speeches, announcement and statements by President Hafez al-Asad 1966–2000), consisting of 1086 documents and compiled by the National Information Center in Damascus. Speeches by and interviews with Bashar al-Asad have, unless otherwise specified, been retrieved from www.presidentassad.net, a website maintained by Syrian journalist and Syrian Arab News Agency (SANA) correspondent Muhammad Abdo al-Ibrahim. While all documents for the 2000–2005 period consist of transcripts of speeches and interviews, starting 2006 some of the documents are only summaries. Although unlikely, topics covered in the original speeches could therefore have been left out of the documents. References to speeches have been placed in endnotes because of their long titles. For documents concerning Lebanon in the pre-1970 period, the Lebanese collections *Al-alaqat al-lubnaniyyah as-suriyyah 1943–1985: waqai bibliyughrafiyyah, wathaiq* (The Lebanese-Syrian Relations 1943–1985: Bibliographical Proceedings, Documents) vol 1 and 2 (1986), two collections of official documents, letters and press citations, put together by the Lebanese Markaz at-tawthiq wa-l-buhuth al-lubnaniyyah (The Center for Lebanese Documentary Evidence and Research) have been extensively used. Because of their long titles, in the text these two volumes are referred to as *Al-alaqat* only. The least well-known case, Hatay, proved to also be the most sensitive one. Syrian silence on Hatay in combination with the fact that the limited research done on the academic level almost exclusively focuses on the 1920–1939 period (i.e. the mandate period and the French-Turkish negotiations over the future of the area) made sources on this case the most difficult to find. Here, some inferences have been drawn on what Syrian officials did not say or do. With regard to the Golan Heights, the period of Syrian-Israeli negotiations has been described and retold by several of the actors directly involved. Accounts of the negotiations are included in the autobiographies of former US President Bill Clinton and former US Secretary of State Madeleine Albright. The US envoy to the Middle East 1988–2000, Dennis Ross, as well as Israeli negotiators Uri Savir and Itamar Rabinovich have also published their understandings of the negotiation process. All of these have been used. Syrian chief negotiator Walid al-Muallim gave his view of the negotiations in a 1997 interview in the *Journal of Palestine Studies*, which has been extensively used for press clippings, speeches and interviews regarding the peace process. With regard to both the Golan Heights and Lebanon, numerous UN reports, resolutions and letters have served as sources. These have been obtained through the DagDok database, created and maintained by the Dag Hammarskjöld Library at Uppsala University, Sweden.

While the autocracy and closed nature of the Syrian Arab Republic presents a researcher with difficulties, in some aspects it has also facilitated the research process as Syrian media can be taken as mouth pieces for the regime. Analyses and reports on Syrian politics in the media of other Arab states have been sparsely used as they are still, as Rabinovich concluded in 1972, generally more important as indicators of these states' relations with Syria than as reliable sources of information on Syrian politics (Rabinovich 1972:xvi, see also Jörum 2006). They have therefore been used only when containing interviews with Syrian decision makers. The Lebanese press has periodically been an exception to 'the Arab media' as Lebanon has allowed a freedom of the press unparalleled in other parts of the Arab World. With the heavy Syrian influence exercised over Lebanese media during the

INTRODUCTION 7

1976–2005 period, it was not automatically considered a reliable source for this period. Lebanese daily *The Daily Star* (www.dailystar.com.lb) was, however, extensively used with regard to developments in Syrian-Lebanese relations during the post-2005 period. For the post-2000 era, news reporting and press were used for all three areas. The websites of the BBC and the websites of al-Jazeerah and al-Arabiyyah were of particular importance. Chapter two is meant to give the reader an overview of research so far conducted on domestic and international aspects of the Syrian Arab Republic. Unlike the chapters containing the three case studies, this chapter is therefore mainly based on secondary sources.

All maps were drawn by PhD Lars Wåhlin especially for the research informing the ideas culminating in this book. Maps 1 and 2 are largely based on written sources as it was not possible to find maps clearly specifying the post–World War I administrative divisions of Geographical Syria or the exact borders of the statelets created within mandated Syria. These maps are thereby in their own right a contribution to studies of the post-Ottoman divisions of the area.

A note on terminology

In this book, Syria and its official name the Syrian Arab Republic will be used interchangeably for the post-1970 period. Geographical Syria includes the area situated between the Mediterranean Sea to the west, the Taurus Mountains to the north, the Syrian desert to the east and the Sinai desert and peninsula to the south, i.e. roughly today's Syria, Lebanon, Jordan, Israel, the West Bank and Gaza. French-mandated Syria will be used to denote the territory within which the French mandate was established in 1920. Lebanon prior to 1946 will be called Greater Lebanon. The Golan Heights and the Golan will be used interchangeably. Hatay is the Turkish name of the province annexed in 1939. In Arabic it is known as liwa iskandarun (sometimes liwa iskandarunah). Prior to the Turkish annexation it was internationally known as Alexandretta. This name will be used for the pre-1939 period while Hatay will be used after, except in direct quotations that contain the Arabic name.

Translation and transliteration

All translations from Arabic and Turkish are my own. Transliteration of Arabic has been done in order to facilitate reading. Diacritical marks, ayns and hamzahs have therefore been omitted. I am well aware of the fact that this way of transliterating will not be a source of joy for linguists. It will, however, hopefully make the text more accessible to readers who are not familiar with Arabic script (while readers with a reasonable command of Arabic will be able to identify the words anyway).

CHAPTER 2

THE CONSOLIDATION OF THE TERRITORIAL STATE AND THE POLITICAL DEVELOPMENT OF THE SYRIAN ARAB REPUBLIC

The following chapter will provide the reader with an introduction to the creation of what is today known as the Syrian Arab Republic. It serves as an empirical overview of previous research done on Syrian territorial integration, the development and creation of a national identity, domestic political developments, as well as the development of the foreign policy context within which Syria is situated. The aim is not to give a detailed historical account of these issues but rather to set the frame for understanding Syrian policies towards territories lost. In order to generate an adequate understanding of Syrian policies over time, the starting point is to acknowledge that Syria was, following its independence in 1946, what Cederman refers to as 'an emergent actor' (1997:22). It started out as a recently created state, poorly integrated territorially and in terms of population, with borders that had no correspondence to pre-war realities. The first part of this chapter traces the formation of the territory presently constituting Syria from World War I until independence in 1946. This was a period when Arab nationalist ambitions and European plans for the region clashed. The borders of what today constitutes Syria were drawn from scratch and a number of possible outcomes with regard to these borders were plausible. Two of the three territories included in the present study were, as a result of French mandate policy, lost during this period. The second part of the chapter will provide an overview of the development of post-independence Syria from 1946 until today. As Syria – like the Middle East in general – remains largely under-studied this chapter is not 'complete' in the sense that it fully covers Syrian state building and internal and external consolidation. It rather sums up – and seeks to analyse – what research has so far concluded.

From Ottoman provinces to French mandate: The old world comes to an end

When World War I broke out in the summer of 1914, the area which today constitutes the Syrian Arab Republic had been part of the Ottoman Empire for approximately 400 years. The Allied campaigns on Ottoman territory resulted in the occupation of the (mostly) Arab provinces in 1917–1918 and the division of these provinces into mandated areas under French and British control. Several over-lapping and contradicting agreements and documents fixed what power should be awarded control over which region. *The Husayn-McMahon correspondence* in 1915–1916 resulted in an agreement whereby an Arab revolt within the Ottoman Empire would be initiated by Sharif Husayn, the Guardian of the Holy Muslim places in Mecca and Medina, in return for British recognition of and support for Arab independence. The exact borders of the future independent Arab state were not agreed upon but Husayn was given British assurance of recognition of Arab independence to the east of the Damascus-Aleppo line, provided that this Arab state turned exclusively to Britain for advice and assistance. The Arab revolt was declared by Husayn in June 1916 but the mass rising he had predicted did not happen. His expectation to be joined by at least 100,000 Arab troops – about a third of the Ottoman Army – failed to come true and in the end his army consisted of a few thousand men (Fromkin 1989:219). A disappointment to Britain, the

The Consolidation of the Territorial State 11

Husayn-McMahon correspondence and the Arab revolt nevertheless had important post-war implications for Geographical Syria – roughly today's Syria, Lebanon, Jordan and Israel/Palestine. At the same time, Great Britain had negotiated the so-called *Sykes-Picot Agreement* with France. According to this agreement, Geographical Syria would be divided into five different zones. Britain and France would each get two of these and the fifth one, Palestine, would be placed under international administration. The Sykes-Picot Agreement was never fully implemented but in the end served as the basis for the final Anglo-French settlement of their post-war conflicting views of what the best solution for the former Ottoman provinces would be.

Allied administration of Geographical Syria: Frustrated hopes of Arab independence

In the beginning of October 1918, Arab forces under the leadership of Sharif Husayn's son Faysal entered Damascus as part of the Allied campaign to occupy geographical Syria. By the end of the month it had been conquered. Even though the troops led by Faysal had taken part in the campaign, the majority of the fighting had been done by British forces. Geographical Syria was therefore placed under the authority of the Commander in Chief of the British army, General Allenby (Lalonde 2002:89). Awaiting the Peace Conference in Paris, which would decide the future of the area, Britain delegated the authority over Geographical Syria to three semi-civilian Occupied Enemy Territory Administrations (OETA), set up as a temporary solution. OETA South, which later became the British mandate of Palestine, was placed under a British Chief Administrator. OETA West covered the coastal strip from a point between Tyre (in today's Lebanon) and Acre (in today's Israel) to the north and included the today Turkish areas of Adana, Mersin and Hatay. It was placed under a French Chief Administrator. This latter, French-administered zone thus included one of the three areas (Hatay) the Syrian policy towards which is examined in this book and parts of another (Lebanon). OETA East, finally, was placed under Faysal as Chief Administrator and stretched from the Hejaz in the south – today's Saudi Arabia and the location of Mecca and Medina – through today's Jordan and north to include most of today's Syria and the eastern parts of today's Lebanon. Its northern border remained undefined until Ottoman forces withdrew, and in January 1919 an OETA North under French control was established in Cilicia (Lalonde 2002:92–93). Chief Administrators were not to consider their respective territories consolidated or in any way a sign of what could be expected in a future peace settlement with the Ottoman Empire. Nevertheless, Faysal and the members of his administration considered themselves, and acted as if they were, the rulers of an Arab state whose final territorial extension would include all of Geographical Syria, not only the part currently within

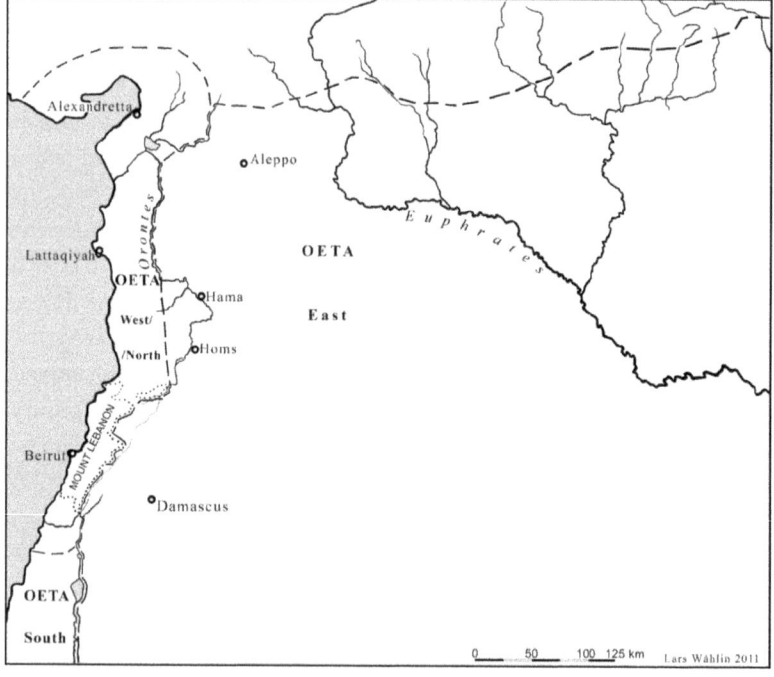

Map 1 The Occupied Enemy Territory Administrations for the temporary administration of Geographical Syria after the cessation of World War I military operations.

THE CONSOLIDATION OF THE TERRITORIAL STATE   13

OETA East (see for instance the King-Crane Commission Report 1922:22).

The Paris Peace Conference and Arab attempts to establish 'facts on the ground'

In January 1919 the Paris Peace Conference opened and brought up the question of the defeated Ottoman Empire. The stage was set for conflict. Great Britain had invited Faysal to take part in the conference as a representative of 'the Arabs'. He demanded that the conference recognise the Arabic-speaking population south of the Iskenderun-Diyarbakır line as sovereign peoples and that the peace conference take formal measures to explore the wishes of the populations concerned. An American commission, the King-Crane Commission, was sent to examine public opinion in the region. Its report, which gave strong support for a united Geographical Syria under Faysal, was disregarded in the subsequent decision making and not published until 1922. Based on the Husayn-McMahon Correspondence, the aim of the Arab administration in OETA East was to consolidate an Arab state and present the European powers with a *fait accompli* rather than wait for a European decision on who should rule the former Ottoman (mostly) Arab provinces. A civilian administration was put into place and General Allenby recognised Damascus and other centres in OETA East as part of 'the Allied Arab state' (Russell 1985:43). Awaiting the King-Crane Commission, the Arab administration in OETA East turned to organising elections for a Representative Assembly and orders were issued to all OETAs to participate. As elections for the Representative Assembly were not allowed in the French and British administered OETAs, these sent representatives chosen on the basis of petitions signed by voters (Zamir 1991:411, Khadduri 1951:138 note 1) and formed part of the resulting Assembly. The Assembly, known as the National Congress, in which representatives who were not prepared to accept anything but complete independence for the whole of Geographical Syria dominated, met in Damascus on 20 June 1919, and declared itself the legally representative body for all of Geographical Syria, i.e. all OETAs. In the beginning of July 1919, the National Congress presented the King Crane Commission with the so called Damascus Program whereby its minimum demands were made clear: complete political independence of Geographical Syria with Faysal as constitutional monarch. All French claims in the area were rejected and so was any partition of Geographical Syria (Antonius 1938:440–442). Although the results presented by the King-Crane Commission were never taken into account by the Peace Conference, these remained the demands of the National Congress until its dissolution in 1920. On 7 March 1920 the Syrian National Congress declared full independence and the dissolution of the different OETA zones with Mount Lebanon as an autonomous province (Zamir 1991:406–419). Faysal was proclaimed constitutional monarch (Russell 1985:134–135) and his administration went from being called the 'Arab-Syrian Government' to 'the Kingdom of Syria' (Ma'oz 1972:395). A few days later the first Syrian cabinet, including ministers from all OETA zones, was formed.

The constitution drafted for the new state did not mention its exact borders (Khadduri 1951:139). Although the declaration of independence made clear that the new state was meant to include both today's Lebanon and Israel/Palestine, Faysal had seemed willing to compromise with regard to both. In 1919, Faysal and Chaim Weizmann, Zionist leader who in 1949 became the first President of Israel, 'mindful of the racial kinship and ancient bonds existing between the Arabs and the Jewish people', had agreed to collaborate in the encouragement of Jewish immigration to Palestine and the development of the country (Antonius 1938:437–439). Since this agreement was to come into force only provided the Arabs be given independence in accordance with Faysal's demands at the conference in Paris, it eventually came to nothing. It nevertheless led Palestinian leaders to accuse Faysal of selling Palestine in order to secure his own kingdom (Khoury 1987a:222). With regard to Lebanon, Faysal presented a number of possible solutions. His final bid, as evident in the declaration of independence, was nevertheless that all of today's Lebanon should be included in the Kingdom of Syria, with Mount Lebanon as an autonomous region.

The imposition of mandates, 1920

The 1920 declaration of independence, the formation of a government and the drafting of the constitution were all declared null and void by France and Great Britain. Instead, the San Remo conference in April 1920 decided that the newly conceived mandate system, in accordance with article 22 in the Covenant of the League of Nations, should be applied to the former Ottoman provinces. The mandate over the northern part of Geographical Syria (today Syria and Lebanon) was given to France and the mandate over the southern part (today Jordan and Israel/Palestine) was given to Great Britain, roughly reflecting the division established in the 1916 Sykes-Picot agreement. This was rejected by the National Congress.

Following an armistice agreement with the Turkish Nationalist Forces in Cilicia in May 1920, France no longer had to fear a two-front war and could focus on the OETA East zone. It presented Faysal with an ultimatum whereby a number of pro-French measures must be taken or France would invade. Faysal's acceptance failed to reach the French authorities in Beirut before deadline (Tauber 1995:36) and French troops advanced on inland Geographical Syria. On the 25 July 1920, they entered Damascus and expelled Faysal.[1] The era of the French mandate had begun.

The territory of the Syrian Arab Republic takes shape

Geographical Syria had, under the Ottoman period, been divided into four *vilayets*:[2] Aleppo, Damascus, Mosul and Beirut. The French-British partition of Geographical Syria in 1920 did not correspond to this administrative division. The creation of new borders resulted in the obstruction of traditional trade routes and impeded the passage of goods and people. Most of the external borders of French mandated Syria were established through a series of agreements in the early years of the mandate period. Already in June 1920, France and Great Britain had decided on a border between French mandated Syria and British-mandated Palestine (Fromkin 2001:441). The border was fixed in an agreement in February 1922 and slightly modified in 1923, following the report of a Border Commission. It was demarcated in 1930 (Longrigg 1958:141 note 4, 257). Although not a point of major conflict at the time it was drawn, this 1923 border has, as we shall see in chapter five, become central in Syrian-Israeli negotiations over the Golan Heights.

In May 1920 Great Britain and Faysal's OETA East administration had decided on a temporary border between Geographical Syria and Iraq. Largely due to the efforts of Iraqi officers in Faysal's administration in Damascus, the Sanjak of Dayr el-Zor, which during Ottoman times had been subordinated directly to Constantinople had been included in OETA East instead of in Iraq (Tauber 1991:378). This border was confirmed in an Anglo-French agreement of December 1920 and partly demarcated the following year. Due to disagreements between France and Britain demarcation was halted, and the League of Nations decided the final location of the border in 1932. It was finally demarcated in 1933 (Longrigg 1958:257). The Jordanian-Syrian border had been roughly decided upon in 1920, was defined in an agreement in 1930, demarcated in 1932 (Kirkbride 1956:82) and slightly amended in 2005 (Wieland 2006:69).

The frontier with Turkey created greater difficulty. The only area where the World War I French occupation met any serious military resistance was in Cilicia (OETA North). The armistice agreement mentioned above was followed by the signing of a French-Turkish peace agreement, the Franklin-Bouillon Agreement in October 1921, whereby France evacuated Cilicia. The Franklin-Bouillon Agreement stipulated that the region of Alexandretta would remain within French-mandated Syria but with an autonomous status. Turkish would be an official language, and 'the inhabitants of Turkish race' would enjoy all facilities to develop their culture. In the Turkish-Allied final peace treaty, the Lausanne Treaty of 1923, the border separating Turkey from the region of Alexandretta was confirmed. In 1939, after years of French-Turkish negotiations, France agreed to a Turkish annexation of Alexandretta, then renamed Hatay. Syrian policies towards this territory are described and analysed in chapter four.

Most of the border between Turkey and French-mandated Syria was drawn along the Baghdad railway. In May 1926 France agreed to minor

The Consolidation of the Territorial State 17

adjustments in the areas of Killis and Payas. Condemned by Syrian nationalists and questioned by the Permanent Mandates Commission, the adjustments were defended by France as a long-awaited beginning of the demarcation of the border (Longrigg 1958:173). Finally, in 1929–1930, the eastern part of the Syrian-Turkish border was delimited and demarcated and, as the result of a compromise, about 1,000 square km of the disputed Jazirah region was added to Syria (Hourani 1946:57, Longrigg 1958:255).

The internal consolidation of the Syrian territory

We have now seen how World War I brought about the demise of the Ottoman Empire and thereby the destruction of the political order hitherto known to its southern provinces. Both Arab and Kurdish plans and hope for independence were frustrated. As new borders were drawn, Geographical Syria was divided into four new states: Syria, Jordan, Lebanon and Palestine. We now move on to the internal consolidation of the Syrian territory. This was the outcome of two opposite forces: the French mandate policy striving for further partition of mandated Syria and the nationalist movement initially seeking the unification of all of Geographical Syria but gradually settling for less.

The creation of the internal borders of the French-mandated territory

As the partition of Geographical Syria meant the obstruction of traditional trade routes and the enforced separation of territories hitherto integrated, the new borders drawn also brought areas previously not integrated together. For instance, the two major cities Damascus and Aleppo had both been capitals in neighbouring provinces during the Ottoman period. They had been administered through identical institutions and had both answered to Constantinople, but their political and economic orientations had taken opposite directions. Aleppo had strong trade links towards the north and the east, from which it was now cut off by the Syrian-Turkish and the Syrian-Iraqi borders. The port of Iskenderun was its outlet to the sea. Damascus, on the other hand, was oriented towards Palestine and Beirut, the port of the latter serving as its outlet. While the dominant feeling in Damascus at the time of the establishment of the French mandate was pan-Arab, the dominant feeling in Aleppo was rather pro-Turkish (Gelvin 1998:82–83). Aleppo and Damascus both aspired to become capital of the French-mandated Syria. Aleppo was larger, yet the French choice fell on Damascus.

The other regions that came to form French-mandated Syria were no more prone to integration. For instance, the south-western fertile plateau of Hawran was home to one of Syria's so called compact minorities, the Druze. Having immigrated to the Hawran from Mount Lebanon in the 1860s, they constituted 85 per cent of the Jabal Druze (the Druze Mountain) inhabitants. Despite several centralising attempts, the Druze had managed to retain almost complete autonomy throughout Ottoman rule (Salih 1977:252). Although the Druze community had resisted submission to external powers, it was internally divided (Bokova 1988:215). This was a fact that both the French-mandate authorities and later Syrian regimes tried to take advantage of in their attempts to integrate the area into their respective systems of rule. The coastal mountain district behind Lataqiyah and Tartous had a population of about 300,000 inhabitants out of which another compact minority, the Alawites, formed the majority (Antonius 1938:526). Like Jabal Druze, this area had been largely autonomous within the Ottoman Empire, even though Ottoman control had increased since the nineteenth century (Hourani 1946:134). The north-eastern Jazirah-region, which had been cut off from its natural commercial centre in Diyarbakır by the new Syrian-Turkish border was sparsely populated. Originally home to Arab bedouins and Kurdish tribes (Velud 1991:212–227), it gradually became the settlement ground for Kurds and Armenians from Turkey and, in the 1930s, Assyrians from Iraq (Longrigg 1958:212, Boghossian 1952:35–36). By the mid-1930s about 150,000 people had moved into this region (Seale 2010:350). As we shall see below, the largely non-Arab character of the Jazirah region turned it into an issue of concern for the Syrian-post independent regimes.

As evident above, the political and economic integration of what now became Syria proper was low at the time of the establishment of the French mandate. French mandate policy did not improve matters. Between August and December 1920, mandated Syria was gradually divided into five parts. At the end of August 1920, the French-mandate authorities created Greater Lebanon through the addition of the four coastal cities of Beirut, Tyre, Tripoli and Sidon and their hinterlands as well as the four eastern *qadhas*[3] of Rashaya, Hasbaya, Baalbek and Biqaa – all of which had belonged to the vilayet of Damascus – to Mount Lebanon (Zamir 1991:406). In September 1920, the remaining part of the vilayet of Damascus was proclaimed the State of Damascus (Khoury 1987a:58). The part of the vilayet of Aleppo that ended up on the Syrian side of the Turkish-Syrian border was proclaimed the State of Aleppo. Al-Saghur and two frontier *nahiyas* were added to the qadha of Alexandretta, which was promoted to the status of *sanjak*. It was nominally placed under the State of Aleppo with its autonomy intact (Longrigg 1958:126). The autonomy was confirmed in the 1921 French-Turkish peace agreement where one of the articles, as mentioned before, specified Alexandretta's special regime, safeguarding Turkish language and culture. After years of French-Turkish negotiations Alexandretta was annexed by Turkey in 1939.

The Sanjak of Dayr el-Zor was also placed within the State of Aleppo (Khoury 1987a:58). So were the Bedouin tribes in the northeastern region. These were, however, encouraged to set up their own nation and were placed under the military authority of the French *Contrôle Bédouin*, meant to control nomadic migration and settle disputes (Chatty 2010:33). In 1932 the Sanjak of al-Jazirah was constituted within the State of Aleppo. The French undertook widespread sedentarisation of al-Jazirah and provided tribal chiefs with money in order to assure loyalty and safe passage (Thomas 2003:539–542). As in other parts of Syria, France relied on a divide and rule strategy, playing different tribal chiefs off against each other and giving government positions to supporters of the mandate (Hanna 2004:466, Neep 2012:167–168). The region of Jabal Druze was proclaimed a Druze State in 1921, and the coastal region was proclaimed an Alawite State in 1922. By 1922 all five parts had thereby been declared states, albeit with different internal arrangements.

Throughout the mandate years, France carried out several territorial and legal changes to these states. In 1922 a Syrian federation, governed through a Federal Council, was created out of the State of Damascus, the State of Aleppo and the Alawite State. It was dissolved in December 1924 and replaced by the State of Syria, composed only of the States of Damascus and Aleppo (Hourani 1946:173). From the end of 1924, French-mandated Syria was therefore divided into four units: Greater Lebanon, the State of Syria (i.e. the former states of Damascus and Aleppo, including the autonomous sanjak of Alexandretta), the Alawite State and the Druze State. Due to nationalist pressure and for financial reasons, the Druze and the Alawite States were incorporated into the State of Syria in 1936

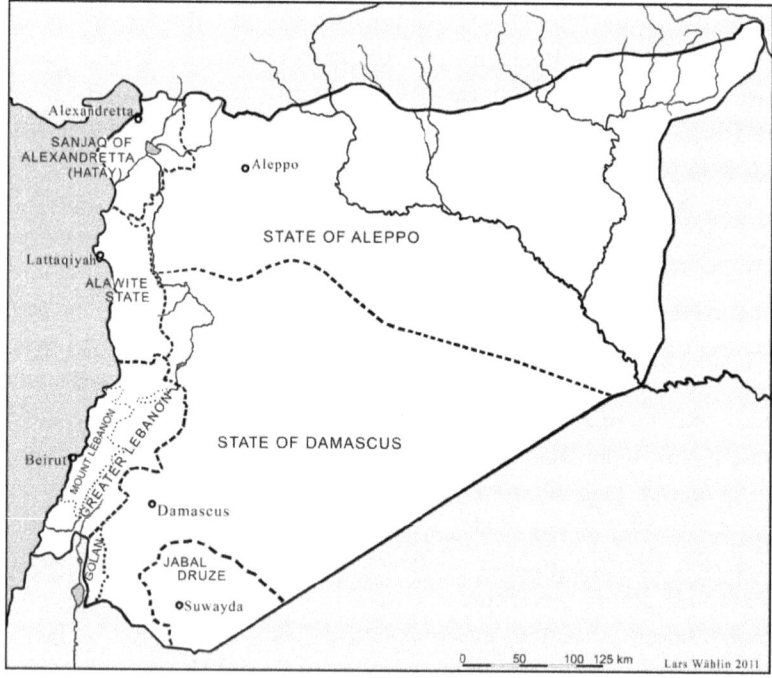

Map 2 The French mandate in the early 1920s with the outlines of the previously autonomous Ottoman region of Mount Lebanon and the Golan Heights, occupied by Israel in 1967, marked.

(Balanche 2006:36, Bokova 1988:214), only to be removed in 1939 and then again incorporated in 1942 (Hourani 1946:173). In 1937, direct French rule was established over the Sanjak of Jazirah due to disturbances and local demands for separation (Fuccaro 2004:586). The one French-orchestrated division that did not change was the first one to be carried out – the creation of Greater Lebanon. Although bound to mandated Syria through the French-mandate budget, the *Intérêts Communs*,[4] and an extensive network of cross-border family ties, it was never included in any of the different territorial combinations the French authorities experimented with. In 1946, Greater Lebanon gained independence as the Republic of Lebanon and the creation of Greater Lebanon had thereby led to the imposition of another external border. At independence in April 1946 the Syrian Arab Republic thus consisted of French-mandated Syria minus Greater Lebanon and Alexandretta. Syrian policies towards these two areas are described and analysed in chapters three and four respectively.

Striving for the independence of what? The nationalist movement and the Syrian territory

The partition of Geographical Syria into different mandates and the further partition of French-mandated Syria into smaller states created tension between the French mandate authorities and the Syrian nationalist movement. The main goal of the nationalist movement, to secure Syrian independence, remained the same throughout the mandate period. However, in order to understand the consolidation of the Syrian territory, it is important to note that the object of this independence changed with time. The original notion of Geographical Syria as the 'true' extension of Syria was gradually replaced by the idea of the reduced, French-mandated Syria. This was partly an effect of facts on the ground; borders had been established and practiced and a national, Syrian economy had developed (Khoury 1987b). It was also the result of power struggles within the national movement. Proponents of Geographical Syria and mandated Syria fought each other in a struggle where the advocates of mandated Syria came out victorious. The 1925–1927 Great Revolt, the longest and most far reaching of the uprisings that the establishment of the French mandate gave rise to, may be seen as a watershed in the nationalist movement's conception of the Syrian territory. It shifted the balance of power within the movement as prominent leaders of the revolt and strong advocates of the unity of Geographical Syria were killed or exiled by the mandate authorities. The national movement was from then on monopolised by the National Bloc (*al-kutlah al-wataniyyah*) which in practice increasingly accepted the smaller, French-mandated version of Syria.

Khadduri (1951:140) and Khoury (1987a:20) point to the 1925–1927 revolt as the origin of new forms of interaction between the nationalist movement and the French authorities. The nationalist movement, seeing that it could not win, gave up armed struggle and the French mandate authorities, seeing that military means would not root out resistance, instead resorted to diplomacy and a tentative development of local Syrian politics. The National Bloc, created at a nationalist conference in Beirut in 1927, was a loose coalition of urban upper class men with different ideological outlooks and economic interests. Due to the lack of a proper 'Syrian' identity they could all agree upon, they united under the banner of the lowest common denominator – Arab nationalism. In anticipation of the mandate power's departure they dedicated themselves to a strategy of 'honourable cooperation' (Khoury 1987a:241) as opposed to armed struggle. As part of the new French approach, elections for a Constitutional Assembly for the State of Syria (i.e. the State of Aleppo and the State of Damascus, united into the State of Syria since 1924) were held in 1928. The National Bloc, which held the majority in the Assembly, formulated its first Syrian constitution the same year. According to the draft constitution, Syria was an indivisible and fully sovereign political unit within its natural borders (Khadduri 1951:141), and the partition of the former Ottoman Arab provinces after World War I was denounced as 'meaningless' (Khoury 1987a:263). These formulations were changed by the mandate authorities to state only that Syria (with no reference to its borders) was an indivisible political unit (Khadduri 1951:144). The original notion of natural borders and the denunciation of the partition are nevertheless important as they imply an original National Bloc ambition to unite the whole of Geographical Syria and not just mandated Syria. Even so, with time the National Bloc came to concentrate on securing unity of, and independence for, French-mandated Syria only. This is indicated by the fact that the National Bloc discouraged political activities regarding areas outside of mandated Syria. This was particularly evident in the case of Palestine, which within the Geographical Syria context constituted 'southern Syria', but which now clearly did not fall under the National Bloc's perceived area of responsibility. When the 1936–1939 Arab Revolt broke out in Palestine, the National Bloc therefore did not lend its support but showed – as had the Faysal Administration in its time – a clear 'Syria first' priority.[5] This would not have been the case had Geographical Syria still been the only acceptable frame of reference for a future independent Syria.

The conclusion of the 1936 Syrian-French Treaty, meant to lead to independence within three years, constituted the National Bloc's major political success. However, as the treaty was never ratified by the French parliament, countdown to independence came to nothing and the popularity of the Bloc waned. Both the treaty negotiations and the treaty itself were still of considerable importance with regard to the process of delimiting the Syrian territory. Not only did the treaty negotiations set off the conflict over Alexandretta (see chapter four), it also largely established the National Bloc's readiness to accept Greater Lebanon as a separate state (see chapter three). The negotiations and the conclusion of the 1936 treaty thereby reveal not only a changed focus from Geographical Syria to mandated Syria but even to a *reduced* mandated Syria. This is further confirmed by the fact that President Shukri al-Quwatli, when delivering his Independence Day speech in 1946, elaborated extensively on French mandate policies but made no reference at all to territories lost or French-orchestrated changes to the Syrian borders.

Britain strove for a unification between Syria and Iraq and managed to get Syrian President al-Quwatli to reluctantly sign a secret agreement whereby he accepted unification with Iraq in exchange for British assistance in obtaining independence from France (Zamir 2010:798). This indicates that the main priority of the

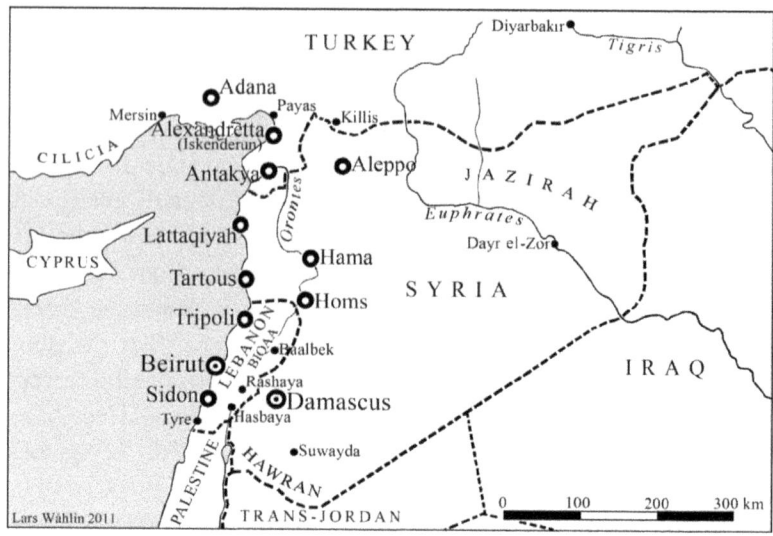

Map 3 Syria and surrounding states 1946.

Syrian National Bloc was independence from France and that this superseded the importance of specific territorial borders. However, once independence had been obtained, the focus on, and the necessity of, maintaining independence within the present borders was the main priority. Even though the National Bloc established the transformation of 'Syria' from Geographical Syria to mandated Syria and eventually a reduced mandated Syria, Khoury and others have pointed out that popular sentiment in Syria remained focused on a larger Arab entity and that nationalist leaders had to balance local Syrian self-interest with an at least verbal commitment to the larger pan-Arab cause (Khoury 1987c:325, Barnett 1998). The necessity to formulate Syrian goals and ambitions in terms of a larger Arab interest has remained a recurring feature in Syrian verbal policies ever since. From the early 1960s, this feature was increasingly underpinned by the doctrines of the Baath Party, which came to power in Syria in 1963 and the ideology of which denounces all borders currently dividing the Arab World.

The Syrian post-independence territory

Geographical Syria has, with the exception of the 1949–1954 reign of Adib al-Shishakli, not been an issue pursued by the different regimes in power since independence. The idea of Geographical Syria has instead been championed by other actors. In 1946 the unification of Geographical Syria, referred to as Greater Syria, was officially declared a principle of Jordanian foreign policy. The Syrian government was not impressed and president Shukri al-Quwatli stressed that the Hashemite Greater Syria plan was contrary to Syrian national aspirations (Seale 1965:11–15). Landis argues that the Syrian government's fear of King Abdullah's plan to unite Geographical Syria into one state even guided Syrian strategy during the 1948 Arab-Israeli war (Landis 2001:8). While the central government was eager to maintain Syrian territorial integrity, both the Druze and the Alawites supported the Greater Syria scheme, as this was seen as a possibility for them to retain their particularities in a context where Arab nationalism was not dominated by a Sunni Muslim version of Arab history (Landis 1997:16, 164). When King Abdullah was assassinated in 1951, Jordan abandoned its ambitions for unification with Syria. The possibility of an Iraqi-Syrian unification, however, remained alive well into the 1950s as the Aleppo-based People's Party strove for unification with Iraq. This possibility intensified the already existing geographical tensions within Syria. As Damascus dominated politics and state institutions, Aleppo and northern Syria as well as the peripheries Jazirah, Dayr el-Zor and Jabal Druze, turned to Iraq as a counterweight. Damascus, leaning on Egypt for support, saw any type of coordination with Iraq as a threat to its own standing (Landis 1998:381). It also severely intensified political tension as several of the military coups that Syria went through 1949–1958 were directly connected to the question of unity with Iraq.

Another champion of the Geographical Syria idea was the Syrian Socialist National Party (SSNP). Founded by Antun Saada in Beirut in the early 1930s, this party promoted the idea that there was a distinct Syrian nation inhabiting roughly the area of Geographical Syria.

It was at the peak of its popularity on the eve of World War II (Torrey 1964:58). Saada was executed in Lebanon in 1949 and in the mid-1950s the party was outlawed in Syria (Ma'oz 1972:401) due to its rivalry with the Baath Party. In 2005 the SSNP was again given permission to function in Syria. Its reappearance as a legal party has not changed Syrian foreign policies and should not be understood as a change in the official perception of the state borders. It is nevertheless an important acknowledgement of the strategic importance Geographical Syria holds for the regime and, in addition, an important recognition of the decreasing importance of pan-Arabism as opposed to a more narrowly defined Syrian identity.

Syria under Hafez al-Asad was often, particularly after its 1976 intervention in Lebanon and efforts to create a united front against Israel through the coordination of Syria, Lebanon, Jordan and the Palestine Liberation Organisation, accused of striving for the unification of Greater Syria (see for instance Pipes 1990:100–106, Hinnebusch 1999:61). Al-Asad was asked about this on numerous occasions and always denied any interest in reviving the Greater Syria scheme.[6] Nothing indicates that the efforts by Hafez al-Asad dedicated to creating a united front in the Levant were anything beyond precisely that: an effort to coordinate forces and secure a policy towards Israel that would safeguard Syrian interests.

The 1958–1961 United Arab Republic

Despite recurring talks of unity with Iraq, the unity that finally materialised was that with Egypt in 1958. Syria then ceased to exist as an independent state and became the northern province of the United Arab Republic. The unification of Egypt and Syria has been explained in different manners. Seale (1997:54–55) and Hinnebusch (2002a:146) point to Syria's external relations as the major driving force. Torn between the Aleppo-Iraq and the Damascus-Egypt axes and pressured to opt for or against the Baghdad Pact, the Syrian government ultimately sought Egyptian protection. Others point to the domestic situation. Heydemann (1999) holds that class struggles and economic issues within Syria led to unification, while Landis stresses

THE CONSOLIDATION OF THE TERRITORIAL STATE 27

the lack of a common sense of identity and political institutions dedicated to upholding Syria's integrity (1997:25). Kienle, in his study of Syrian and Egyptian rhetoric with regard to the union, points in a similar direction arguing that Syrian official discourse tended to define the inhabitants of Syria as members of a community stretching beyond the Syrian territorial borders. This community sometimes included all Arab states and sometimes Geographical Syria only (Kienle 1995:53). Although Egyptian domination was one of the main causes for the Syrian secession coup of 1961, according to Kienle the UAR and Egyptian President Naser enjoyed support in Syria to such extent that the secessionists still felt compelled to defend their move in terms of Arab unity (1995:54–55). After its resurrection as an independent state, Syrian regimes have made verbal commitments to unity on several occasions,[7] but these have never been translated into practice. Kienle (1995:54), Mufti (1993) and Hinnebusch (2002) all see this as a result of Syrian state building, where internal stability has decreased the attraction of what Mufti refers to as 'defensive unionism' (1996:7).

Traces of Syria as part of something bigger remained in the Syrian constitution until 2012. Until then Syria had been referred to as a republic but also as a region (*qutr*), part of the Arab Homeland. The idea of Syria as a region is closely connected to the Baath party ideology, which holds that the entire Arab World should constitute one state. One of the demands protestors voiced during the early phases of the 2011 uprising was the omission of the special status afforded the Baath Party as 'the leading party in the society and the state' in article 8 of the 1973 constitution. When the new constitution was adopted in February 2012, this article had been removed and so had all references to Syria as a region.

While the present-day Syrian borders are officially referred to as created by imperialism, there is scholarly agreement that the existence (if not the exact location) of these borders are now accepted and a narrower national identity relating to the Syrian Arab Republic has emerged.[8] Territories treated as lost are thus not those territories that together with present-day Syria constituted Geographical Syria (i.e. Jordan, Lebanon and Israel/Palestine) but those that were within the French-mandated Syria of 1920 but are no longer under Syrian control.

Post-independence political developments

We have now traced the formation of the Syrian territory from World War I until today and seen that the original ambition by Syrian nationalists to unite the British- and French-mandated parts of Geographical Syria into one Arab state was replaced by a focus on the territory within the borders of the French mandate. In exchange for independence, the National Bloc was – as seen above – prepared to show flexibility on the exact location of the borders. The next part of this chapter will be dedicated to the post-independence political development, domestically as well as in terms of Syrian international relations. Scholars on Syrian politics tend to adhere to one of three dominating readings of Syrian state building and policies. The driving force behind Syrian politics is then identified as either a sectarian struggle where religious minorities and the Sunni Muslim majority compete for power; a geographically based struggle between the geographical centre and the periphery of Syria; or a class-based struggle between an economic and social elite on the one hand and workers and peasants on the other. In essence the three approaches overlap as the traditional economic elite is Sunni Muslim and urban based, while the traditionally poorer religious minorities are of rural origin.

As has often been pointed out, the domestic and foreign policies of states are deeply intertwined. Syria is no exception to this rule. On the contrary it is a most illustrative case. As the domestic situation prior to 1970 was characterised by great instability, so was Syrian foreign policy. While scholars focusing on pre-1970 domestic developments have referred to Syria as 'a case study of political instability' (Lerner 1958:264) and 'the world's most unstable state' (Rubin 2007:27), scholars dedicated to regional and international relations prior to 1970 have characterised Syria as 'a pinball in the political game' (Wieland 2006:159) and 'a political football, kicked back and forth between rival Arab and international actors' (Seale 1997:51). Domestic changes in Syria following the Baath take-over and especially since the 1970 take-over of Hafez al-Asad were so great that Perthes points out that the concepts and categories appropriate for understanding the pre-Baath era are rendered useless when applied to the Syria of the 1990s (Perthes 1995:1). The increasing domestic stability following the 1970 coup was mirrored in regional and international relations. Consequently, in Hinnebusch's words: 'no other Arab state has [...] proved so adept at exercising power out of proportion to its natural endowments or so resolute in ensuring that its interests could not be ignored' (Hinnebusch 2002a:141). Kabalan likewise concludes that Hafez al-Asad turned Syria into a regional actor whose role exceeded its economic and military weight and that this role eventually became its major commodity as Syria is often seen as the key to stability or instability in the region (2010:41).

Political developments in post-independence Syria

At independence, Syrian politics were dominated by the same Sunni Muslim urban bourgeoisie that had constituted the political, economic and religious elite since Ottoman times. Consisting of the (male) members of a group of urban Sunni upper class families, they exercised their power through the 'politics of notables', whereby they mediated between local society and a distant ruler (Khoury 1987a:xiii). The National Bloc, which had led Syria to independence, did not survive the move to a position of leadership within an independent state. Torn by internal quarrels, it split in 1947. Two new parties were formed: the National Party (*al-hizb al-watani*) which was closest to the original National Bloc and the People's Party (*hizb al-shaab*) (Seale 1965:29). While the National Party was Damascus based (Moubayed 2006:304), the People's Party represented mainly business interests in Aleppo (Perlmutter 1969:828). These two parties thereby reflected the Damascus-Aleppo rivalry pointed to above. The National Party and the People's Party ensured the continued dominance of the traditional urban elite in Syrian politics until the late 1950s, and as sons replaced their fathers within the political hierarchy, the urban upper class managed to retain political power and influence within a narrow group of families.[9] Their freedom to pursue their own interests gradually decreased as of 1949. A series of military coups secured a position for the army where it always had the final word in politics and civilian politicians interested in pursuing their careers had to adapt to this new reality. Political instability reigned. As Torrey's overview shows, during the nine years between the first coup in 1949 until union with Egypt in 1958, Syria had 25 governments, two of which lasted less than a day (Torrey 1964:405–415). As pointed to above, geographical rivalry within Syria at least partly explains this instability as several of these coups were connected to the question of unity with Iraq. Because Aleppo, prior to the mandate, had been oriented not only towards Turkey but also towards Mosul and Baghdad, the Aleppo-based People's Party strove for unification with Iraq (Seale 1965:30, see also Sluglett 2002:288–289). Despite several far-reaching plans, unification never materialised. According to Seale, this was the result of several factors: nobody on either side wanted it enough; most Syrians did not want a monarchy, and each time Iraq had supported a coup in Syria, the Syrian newcomers to power found it wiser to accept funds and support from all sides (Iraq, Egypt and Saudi Arabia) than to align with Iraq only (Seale 1997:167).

The Baath Party, which had first scored success in the 1954 elections, secured key posts in government in 1956. This contributed strongly to the 1958–1961 union with Egypt as the Baath Party held the view that union with Egypt would guarantee Syrian security. Although union meant the dissolution of all Syrian political parties – an Egyptian precondition for unification – regional Baath members in Lataqiyah, Dayr el-Zor and Hawran remained secretly organised and came to play a dominant role in the party apparatus following the March 1963 military coup by mainly minority Baathist officers (van Dam 1997:22).

The Baath party takes over

The 1963 Baath Party coup marked the beginning of a radical change within the Syrian military. Due to French recruitment policies and their own understanding of the armed forces as a way for social advancement, members of the rural minorities had long been overrepresented in the army. They had, however, mainly dominated the lower ranks (Bou-Nacklie 1993:652, Batatu 1999:157). As the 1963 coup was followed by purges of Sunni Muslim officers, vacant posts were made available to members of the rural Alawite, Druze and Ismaili minorities (Van Dam 1997:31). In turn, further intra-regime conflict ousted many of the Druze and Ismaili officers. Alawites, replacing them, therefore became heavily overrepresented within the officer corps (Batatu 1999:173). Because the military was such a dominating component within Syrian politics, the Alawite overrepresentation was transferred into this arena. Although the first post-1963 governments were careful to put up a Sunni 'facade', the take-over by Hafez al-Asad in 1970 put an end to this as he was the first Alawite to rule Syria without a Sunni front man. His take-over further ended another unstable period characterised by rapid regime changes and intra-regime struggles between two factions within the Baath party. Having remained in power ever since, the Baath Party had its special role in Syrian politics and society inscribed in the Syrian Constitution in 1973. Although its ideology in reality heavily coloured Syrian policy 1963–1966 only, it has remained one of the defining features of Syrian rhetoric. As mentioned above, the party's special status was omitted from the constitution in February 2012.

The al-Asad era: Increasing domestic stability

The Hafez al-Asad take-over, known as the Correction Movement (*al-harakah al-tashihiyyah*), set Syria on a less radical course. Unlike the regime he overthrew, Hafez al-Asad saw clear advantages in separating rhetoric and action. He de-ideologised Syrian politics (Hinnebusch 1991:387) and, in Lobmeyer's words, turned Baathism 'into a reservoir for propagandist phrases' (Lobmeyer 1995:184, cited in Wieland 2006:109). In power for 30 years and the object of a heavy state-orchestrated personality cult (see for instance Wedeen 1999), he ruled Syria with an iron fist as the head of what Drysdale & Hinnebusch refer to as the Middle East regime with the poorest human rights record, rivaled only by the Iraqi Baath regime (1991:11). During the reign of Hafez al-Asad Syria was transformed into a highly centralised authoritarian presidential system with the military and bureaucracy playing dominant roles. The scope of state control over society was expanded and efforts were made to build and transform institutions that largely account for the stability and longevity of the post-1970 regime (Perthes 1995:133–135, Drysdale & Hinnebusch 1991:133, Hinnebusch 1990:145–149). Perthes, Hinnebusch and Heydemann all point to the Hafez al-Asad regime's continuation and development of the previous Baathi strategy of organising the population into corporatist, regime-dependent popular and professional organisations with the aim of representing, mobilising and controlling the members. The trade unions and the Peasant Union stand out as the most important vehicles (Perthes 1995:170–171, Hinnebusch 1990:197, Heydemann 1999:196–197). The al-Asad regime further opened up possibilities for Baath Party membership to the masses, with the ambition of broadening the regime's support base. Likewise, in 1972 the al-Asad regime established the National Progressive Front (*al-jabhah al-wataniyyah al-taqaddumiyyah*), which allowed for a limited number of co-opted political parties to function within the political system under Baath leadership (Perthes 1995:136). There is scholarly agreement that neo-patrimonialism and clientelistic networks and dependencies played a major role in the stability of post-1970 Syria (Hinnebusch 2001:84–85, Balanche 2006:7). Perthes points out that not only do these networks tie strategic groups to the regime and create a supportive base for it within groups which would otherwise oppose it, they also serve to create fragmentation within these groups, thus making a unified opposition more difficult (Perthes 1995:181).

During Hafez al-Asad's regime socialism was in reality – although not officially – replaced by state capitalism. A period of economic liberalisation (*infitah*) in the 1980s, described and analysed in detail by Perthes (1995), resulted in an extraordinary growth of the private sector. Although cautious and of an ad hoc nature, reforms allowed the state bourgeoisie, the new commercial bourgeoisie and parts of the old commercial bourgeoisie that al-Asad had gradually let return to business as part of an earlier *infitah* following his take over, to gain financially and strengthen the bonds tying these groups together (Perthes 1995:32, 254, Haddad 2012). According to Haddad, by the late 1990s the Syrian economy had gone from a state-controlled planned economy to a fully fledged *capitalisme des copains* where businessmen and decision makers were often both policy makers and policy takers. Individuals and families with ties to the president became increasingly wealthy while the rest of the population, including the peasants and workers the Baath Party had once favoured, were largely locked out from possibilities of economic advancement. Haddad concludes that during the reign of Bashar al-Asad, the economic and political elite have largely become one and the same (2012). This was partly a return to the state of things prior to the 1963 Baath take-over.

Hafez Al-Asad's position was seriously undermined in the late 1970s and early 1980s following the Syrian 1976 intervention in Lebanon. Inflation, elite corruption and nepotism, the overwhelming power of the security services and opposition to the intervention (Perthes 1995:137) all resulted in a wave of political assassinations, the victims of which were almost exclusively Alawites (Van Dam 1997:72). The Muslim Brotherhood claimed responsibility for the violence and was duly punished. A 1980 attempt on al-Asad's life was revenged by the massacre of all 550 Muslim Brotherhood members then held at Palmyra prison (Van Dam 1997:105) and the efforts to extinguish the Syrian branch of the Brotherhood resulted in, among other things, the battle for Hama in 1982. This battle could, according to Van Dam 'be distinguished from earlier confrontations by their unprecedented level of violence, bloodshed and destruction' (1997:111). Membership in the Muslim Brotherhood has since then been punishable by death. In 1983 the regime was further challenged, this time from within, by Hafez al-Asad's brother Rifaat al-Asad (Van Dam 1997:120–121). From the mid-1980s on, there were no serious threats to al-Asad's regime and Batatu concluded in 1999 that his position was 'guaranteed' for lack of a credible alternative and a widely shared fear that should his regime fall, sectarian strife and chaos were both possible and probable outcomes (Batatu 1999:277–278).

When Hafez al-Asad passed away in June 2000, he was replaced by his son, Bashar al-Asad, groomed for the presidency since 1994. A constitutional amendment and a referendum were meant to add legitimacy to the change, which has been characterised as 'quasi-monarchical' (Perthes 2004:7). Changes clearly took place: most of the 'old guard' forming part of his father's regime were retired and replaced by younger successors in 2000. Perthes stresses that this was mainly 'system maintenance', adapting to new circumstances while keeping the power within desired groups of the population (Perthes 2004a:26). The first year of Bashar al-Asad's rule, known as the Damascus Spring, brought the release of political prisoners and the establishment of discussion forums and human rights organisations. However, the spring soon turned into harsh winter with steadily increasing repression (George 2003). Despite numerous prophecies regarding his imminent downfall, Pace & Landis concluded in 2009 that Bashar al-Asad had proven a more capable ruler than most analysts had initially given him credit for (2009:138). They further argued that Bashar al-Asad was safe in his position, strengthened by events in Iraq as the violent aftermaths of the 2003 invasion 'taught a new generation of Syrians to appreciate the stability and security of rule by a strong man' (2009:138–139). To this should be added the points he scored on the popular level both in Syria, and in the Arab World generally, by denouncing the 2003 invasion of Iraq. While the Syrian civil war[10] puts these conclusions into question, it also clearly shows the capability of the regime to resist both peaceful demonstrations and armed rebellion. The limited number and relatively low level of regime defections indicates a tightly knit regime nucleus which perceives its survival as closely tied to that of Bashar al-Asad.

Bringing a fragmented territory together: Post-independence state building

As we have seen, at the imposition of the French mandate in 1920, Syria was deeply fragmented. Due to French mandate policy, this was still the case at independence in 1946. Seale's often cited description of the first Syrian post-independence parliament is illustrative: parliament consisted of members out of whom 'some spoke only Kurdish or Armenian, others only Turkish; some wore a *tarbush*,[11] others a *kafiyeh*;[12] townsmen and beduin' (Seale 1965:32). Fearing to loose their political and economic privileges the members of the National Bloc had no socio-economic program to speak of and had neglected the rural areas (Khoury 1987a:286, Balanche 2006:41). While Khoury sees this as the outcome of the leadership's urban origin, resulting in a complete lack of ambition beyond the four cities Damascus, Aleppo, Homs and Hama (1987a:267), Balanche adds that the chronic domestic instability strengthened this attitude as it ruled out possibilities of working out development strategies (Balanche 2006:5). However, as Landis points out, the abolition of the territorial division established by France and the unification of the territory (except Greater Lebanon and Alexandretta) inevitably brought the areas and communities outside of these four cities into Syrian politics (Landis 1997:31), albeit not in a manner anticipated by the urban Sunni political and economic elite. Emphasising the unity of Syria and its inhabitants, the first post-independence government abolished communal representation in the parliament, introduced under the French mandate (Ma'oz 1972:399). It further directed efforts at suppressing Alawite and Druze ambitions for autonomy. While successfully dealing with the former, it was unable to do so when it came to the Druze. These resisted until the 1954 clampdown by military dictator Adib al-Shishakli (Landis 1997:168), who is pointed out as the first large-scale state and nation builder in post-independence Syria (Ma'oz 1972:399).

State building under the Baath

The second big state building project was initiated by the post-1963 Baathi regimes. Scholarly agreement holds that their role in 1963–1970 state building can hardly be overestimated. They directed efforts at developing new industries as well as nationalising existing ones. They also continued the redistribution of land, initiated during the UAR (Garzouzi 1963:83, Heydemann 1999:109–117), thereby destroying the economic base of their rivals for power – the traditional Sunni elite.[13] The Baathi regimes structured the national economy through five-year plans, developed infrastructure and extended education and health care into the traditionally neglected rural areas (Balanche 2006:7, 61, Drysdale 1981). While Hinnebusch shows that workers and peasants benefited from these policies and provided the regime with support (Hinnebusch 2002b:54), Drysdale holds that the rural periphery, and the religious minorities, benefitted (Drysdale 1981). This goes to show to what extent the class based, center-periphery and sectarian reading of Syria's political development overlap. Heydemann argues that corporatist structures, initiated under al-Shishakli and developed during the UAR and in the post-1963 period, made sure these new social forces, mobilised and radicalised, were kept in control and provided the channels for continued authoritarianism (Heydemann 1999).

One of the intra-regime conflicts leading up to the take-over of Hafez al-Asad in 1970 concerned priorities. Should Syria focus on a domestic socialist revolution, or prioritise state consolidation and the struggle against Israel? Al-Asad advocated the latter option and once in power, slowed down or ended socialist reforms pursued by the Baathi regime since 1963. He brought land reform to an end and moved to broaden the support of the regime by introducing business friendly policies, thereby giving the ousted merchant and industrialist class a stake in the regime (Perthes 1992:55–56, Batatu 1999:327, Ismail 2009:15). This alliance was not entirely stable, mainly due to the fact that Alawite domination within the regime never ceased to diminish its legitimacy in the eyes of the predominantly Sunni business class. Especially the Aleppo and Hama business class largely supported the Muslim Brotherhood during its bloody confrontation with the regime in the late 1970s and early 1980s (Ismail 2009:16), while the Damascus-based merchants were suspected of secretly doing so (Batatu 1999:208). Economic liberalisation, initiated in the late 1980s and early 1990s and continued under Bashar al-Asad, has caused the alliance between the regime and Sunni merchants to weaken. As individuals and families with mainly family ties to regime members have been favoured in processes of privatisation, a new economic elite has come to rival the traditional business class. According to Ismail, this can be seen as a mere conflict between a new and old business class. Alternatively, as this new elite is mainly Alawite, it can be seen as sectarian rivalry (2009:20–21).

The Consolidation of the Territorial State 37

While Van Dam concludes that Baathi efforts to suppress tribal, regional and sectarian loyalties have failed (1997:143), Balanche argues that this was never the goal. On the contrary, he stresses that the post-1963 regimes have been careful not to upset traditional ethnic, tribal or religious boundaries (Balanche 2006:14–15, 41, 71, and 136). Instead, the ambition of the Baathi regimes have been to strengthen their own power and secure their control over society through a well-developed clientelism (Balanche 2006:4, 7). This was also, according to Balanche, the goal of the territorial integration pursued by the Baathi regimes, especially since the take-over of Hafez al-Asad in 1970. Van Dusen concluded in 1972 that then recent development programs had not greatly diminished regional divisions and subdivisions (Van Dusen 1972:123). He identified nine agro-cities (Damascus, Aleppo, Hama, Homs, Latakiyah, Qunaytrah, Suwayda, Der'aa and Dayr el-Zor) serving as the focus for regional loyalty and the centre of a network of villages. Communication between the agro-cities was described as minimal and communication between the capital, Damascus, and the villages went through the agro-city of the village in question (Van Dusen 1972:124). The regime of Hafez al-Asad set out to change this regional fragmentation. By 1990 the goal of connecting every Syrian village directly to Damascus by asphalted road had been reached (Balanche 2003:151). Balanche holds that the centralisation of the state around Damascus, with the goal to subordinate and weaken Aleppo, was an early Baath policy (Balanche 2006:57, 112). This has to be understood within the context of the 'traditional' geographical rivalry between Aleppo and Damascus, which now had the additional impetus of the Alawite-dominated regime installed in Damascus versus the traditional Sunni business class based in Aleppo. Furthermore, Balanche argues that although understanding territorial integration policies in terms of security may appear as 'géopolitique fiction', the security-related paranoia of the Syrian regimes explains much of the sometimes illogical network of communications and is also an important explanatory factor for many of the problems caused by the geographical location of certain industries (Balanche 2006:59, 123). Perthes, on the other hand, adds that apart from 'the personal interests of members of the regime elite', such dysfunctionalities are mainly the outcome of regime failure to thoroughly prepare investments and investigate actual needs (Perthes 1995:44).

Although the Syrian regime is dominated by Alawites, the Alawite community as such is not in power. Membership in the Alawite community does not guarantee access to the regime or possibilities to enrich oneself (Balanche 2006:165, Perthes 1991:82, Goldsmith 2012:4, 13). The Alawite community in general – and to a lesser extent other minority and rural communities (van Dam 1997:140) – has nevertheless benefitted from the post-1963 regimes. In return for its support, it enjoyed material benefits such as public investments in the mainly Alawite coastal area, education and employment possibilities (Balanche 2006:142, 65–168, Drysdale 1977, Drysdale 1981). As ordinary Alawites are mostly found within the public sector and the lower ranks of the army, both of which have ceased to be effective paths for social advancement, economic liberalisation has limited the possibilities of the average Alawite (Balanche 2006:143, 272). Balanche, Van Dam and Goldsmith argue that in spite of this, the regime owes large part of its still intact Alawite support to fears of what a Sunni take-over could bring in terms of religious and social persecution (Balanche 2006:284, 287, van Dam 1997:97, 149, Goldsmith 2012). With increasing reports of sectarian strife in the context of the ongoing civil war and the failure of oppositional groups, organizations and coalitions to seriously address Alawite fears of the future (Lundgren Jörum 2012:30) the Alawite 'by default' support of the regime can not be expected to decrease. Balanche argues that the fact that the Alawite region has been favoured with regard to investment, but still largely been kept as a region apart, could be explained by a similar fear harboured by the regime itself. A somewhat isolated Alawite region would then serve as a safe(r) haven where Alawites could retire (Balanche 2006:285). This idea is rejected by Perthes (1995:185).

The fact that politically sensitive positions within the army and security services have been, and still are, reserved for Alawites adds to what van Dam characterises as a 'vicious circle with no apparent way out'; regime dependence on those same tribal, regional and sectarian loyalties, the existence of which it denies (van Dam 1997: 103,

143–145). Balanche concluded in 2006 that the different communities were still largely 'worlds of their own' and that it was therefore not possible to speak of Syria as a nation state. Instead it should be seen as an institution organising a defined territory which it controlled in its entirety and had managed to integrate through a well-developed network of communications (Balanche 2006:281). As a consequence of the civil war, by August 2012, the Syrian territory in reality encompassed three entities – a government controlled one, a rebel held area and the in practice autonomous Kurdish region.

The beating heart of Arabism: Defining the state

Since independence, Islam and Arabness (*uruba*) have to varying degrees formed the basis of the state-driven Syrian national identity. As in most cases where the territorial state precedes the development of a national identity, the choice of an efficient and inclusive Syrian identity was not self-evident. As Landis puts it: 'Sunnis, Shiites, Druze, Alawites, Ismailis, Kurds, Jews and Christians found it a good deal easier to agree that they were not Frenchmen than to agree on what it meant to be Syrian. The creation of Syria did not mean the creation of Syrians' (Landis 1997:39). Although the National Bloc rhetorically stressed an Arab, and in practice gradually a Syrian, nation and state to both the French mandate authorities and the League of Nations, Khoury points out that the Bloc's message to the population was not purely secular. Islamic symbolism and invocation was used in order to mobilise support (1987a:218). While this combination had the potential to attract the single largest community, the Arabic-speaking Sunni Muslim community (about 60 per cent of the population, Van Dam 1997:1), the tendency to fuse Arab and Sunni Islamic history was a problem for Arab Christians, Jews and the heterodox Alawite, Druze and Ismaili minorities as this interpretation of Arab history did not fully include them. Nor did it include non-Arab communities such as Kurds, Turkmen, Armenians, Syriacs and Assyrians, the latter three being neither Arab nor Muslim. With the rise of the Baath party to power in 1963 – with its secular ideology and the shifting centre of gravity from the Sunni Muslim to the heterodox minority communities – Islam was increasingly removed from the picture and Arabness became the focus of the national identity.

Arabness as a defining feature of the Syrian state, has led to attempts at re-defining communities and territories that do not fit into this image. The first President of independent Syria, Shukri al-Quwatli, proposed the transfer of Druze from the over-populated and poverty-stricken Jabal Druze in the south to the largely Kurdish, Assyrian and Armenian north-eastern Jazirah region (Landis 1997:386). This would have been a way of arabising this region while at the same time geographically fragmenting the Druze community. In 1949, President Husni al-Zaim, the first in a long line of military coup-makers, maintained regime focus on the Jazirah as a problematic region for the Arabness of Syria. Al-Zaim, himself of Kurdish descent, offered to settle approximately 300,000 Palestinian refugees there in exchange for financial compensation and a peace deal with Israel (Shlaim 1986:68–69). Apart from securing good money, this was another attempt at the arabisation of the Jazirah region. The deal offered by al-Zaim never materialised and the large influx of Palestinian refugees into Syria was handled quite differently. Adib al-Shishakli, one of al-Zaim's successors, implemented policies aimed at the creation of a homogenous Arab-Muslim state. Among other things, he issued orders that only Arabic could be spoken in public, all signs were to be in Arabic and cafés and restaurants were only allowed to carry Arab names. Although implemented all over Syria, these policies had greatest effect in the more linguistically and culturally heterogeneous northern parts, where they were resisted and met with public protests. In addition, religious leaders of minority communities were not allowed to address public meetings outside of their own places of worship (Seale 1965:135), further indicating the special status of Sunni Islam.

The preoccupation with the Arab character of Syria deepened during the union with Egypt, during which those who did not fit into the 'national ideal' were not only defined as problematic but as the enemy (Tejel Gorgas 2006:122). In 1962, the post-UAR secessionist regime again sought to arabise the northeastern Kurdish territories through repressive measures. One hundred-twenty thousand Kurds were stripped of their Syrian nationality and many of them lost the right to their property, which was seized by the government and used to settle Arabs in the area (Tejel 2008:51). The official policy of the Baath party has been to forcibly assimilate the Kurds in Syria into the 'Arab nation' (Tejel Gorgas 2006:122), whereby their cultural and linguistic rights remained denied. A policy formulated in 1963 included plans for the re-location of Arabs into the Kurdish areas and the expulsion of Kurds from these same areas into the Syrian interior. The resettlement plan was initiated in the early 1970s with the construction of model farms in the north-eastern Kurdish areas. An estimated 4,000 Arab families settled in the area as a result (Tejel 2008:62). Arabness as the defining feature of the national identity also resulted in changes of toponyms that indicated religious or ethnic particularism.[14]

Following the 2003 invasion of Iraq, the Kurdish question became more visible in Syria. As some of the territories with a Kurdish majority in Syria are adjacent to the autonomous Kurdish region in northern Iraq, they were increasingly seen as possible candidates for separatist mobilisation. About a month after the Syrian uprising began in March 2011, Bashar al-Asad issued a decree whereby between 150,000 and 300,000 Kurds would be given Syrian citizenship (BBC 7 April 2011), rectifying the results of the 1962 census. As the uprising turned into a civil war and government forces partly withdrew from the Kurdish areas, some of these territories in practice became autonomous. While the outcome is still uncertain, it can be concluded that no matter what the final solution to the war in Syria will look like, it will no longer be possible to ignore the Kurdish question (nor that of other minorities).

Not all non-Arab communities have been handled the same way. While the Armenians were also subject to denial of linguistic and cultural rights during the 1950s and 1960s, repression eased significantly after the 1970 Hafez al-Asad take over (Migliorino 2006:102–113). While the difference in policies towards the two groups in the post-1970 era may be striking, it is hardly surprising. The Armenian community is much smaller – it is estimated at 90,000 (Migliorino 2006:99), while the Kurdish one is estimated at about two million (ICG report 136 2013:3) – and thereby poses less of a challenge to the Arabness of Syria. More importantly, unlike the Kurds, the Americans do not pose a threat to the territorial integrity of Syria.

Hafez al-Asad, after his take-over, upheld the focus on Arabness, rather than Islam, as the central feature of the state-driven national identity. For instance, the 1973 Constitution effectively denied the existence of non-Arab communities in Syria by stating that the inhabitants of Syria are part of the Arab nation. At the same time, the official name of the state was changed to the Arab Republic of Syria. None of this was changed in the constitution adopted in February 2012. With regard to religion, the Hafez al-Asad regime made efforts in recognising the 'red lines' and securing some degree of Islamic legitimacy. For instance, in 1970, the Supreme Islamic Shia Council in Lebanon recognised the Alawites as Shia Muslims (Batatu 1999:219). Likewise, the original draft of the 1973 Constitution was changed as one such red line had obviously been crossed.[15] Kedar further argues that the Syrian state-controlled media pictured Hafez al-Asad and continues to picture Bashar al-Asad as devote Muslims, publishing pictures of them attending public prayer during Ramadan and reporting on the *Id al-Fitr* holiday greetings they receive(d) from Muslim state leaders and religious personalities (Kedar 2005:89– 100, 268–269). Following the bloody years of confrontation with the Muslim Brotherhood, Hafez al-Asad further began to curry his speeches with Islamic greetings and occasional quotations from the Qur'an (Van Dam 1997:96). Balanche points out that although Arabness is what theoretically should bind together all Syrians, the post-1970 regime has nevertheless made sure that ethnic identities within the Sunni majority (for instance Arab, Kurdish, Circassian or Turkmen) remain vivid in order to divide it. While Valter sees the choice of a Kurdish mufti of Syria, Ahmad Kuftaro (1964–2004), as proof of Kurdish participation in Syrian politics (2002:70), Balanche and Tejel, on the contrary, argue that this choice was made in order to decrease his legitimacy as a leader among Sunni Arabs (Balanche 2006:284, Tejel 2008:66).

The external consolidation of the Syrian state: International and regional relations

Regional politics after independence were dominated by the Hashemite (i.e. Iraqi and Jordanian) and Egyptian rivalry for Arab leadership. Both sides understood that to control Syria – the centre of Arabism – or at least enjoy its support, would ensure a dominant position in the region. According to Seale, Syria was so crucial to Arab leadership that during the 1940s and 1950s, to have an 'Arab policy' was equal to having a plan for Syria (Seale 1965:1). As we have seen, the Hashemites had ambitions for a larger Kingdom already during the mandate period and continued to strive for the incorporation of Syria after independence. Egypt, on the other hand, did not want a strong Hashemite state and with support from the Hashemite longtime foe Saudi Arabia, sought to block any move in that direction. Syria, not strong enough to push an agenda of its own, was tugged by both sides.

A number of developments during the 1950s drove Syria closer to Egypt. The tug of war over the Baghdad Pact in the mid-1950s included two British and US planned coups for regime change in Syria. Both were uncovered prior to execution, and as one of them had involved Iraq and the other Turkey (both pro-Western states at the time) (Kaylani 1972:20, Seale 1997:54), they caused Syria to distance itself from both. In 1955, Syria instead formed a military alliance with Egypt (Seale 1997:53). The Suez Crisis of 1956 added to the popularity of Egyptian president Naser in Syria and the climax of Egypt's influence in Syria was the 1958 unification between the two states. This union lasted until the Syrian secession coup of 1961 and was followed by deep Syrian-Egyptian enmity.

Despite structural and ideological similarities, Iraq had gradually turned into Syria's Arab arch enemy. The conflict between them had many roots. Disagreement over regional policies was one, disputes over pipelines and water another (Drysdale 1992:350–352), and they were each ruled by rival branches of the Baath Party. Although attempts at reconciliation were occasionally made in the hope of creating a Syrian-Iraqi axis, different outlooks and ambitions turned into personal enmity between Hafez al-Asad and Iraqi President Saddam Hussein in the early 1980s. Both engaged in proxy wars against the other, harboured each other's exiled dissidents and waged an ideological war against the other. In 1997 relations eased as a result of economic needs on both sides (Kandil 2008:444). After his take-over in 2000, Bashar al-Asad continued to open up to Iraq (Hinnebusch 2010:13, Perthes 2004:107), and Syria was its main supporter during the run-up to the 2003 US-led invasion.

Syrian-Turkish bilateral relations hovered between chilly and tense throughout the period from Syrian independence in 1946 until the beginning of the 2000s. This was due to several factors. The Turkish-Syrian border constituted the border between NATO and a country with strong connections to the USSR and the two neighbours held radically different views of the Baghdad Pact. Further, there were conflicts over water allocations, where Syria accused Turkey of both withholding water and letting polluted water into Syria through its Southeastern Anatolian Project (Kushner 1999:6). Other points of tension were Syrian support for the PKK and ASALA, according to Turkey a way of exercising pressure with regard to the conflict over water (Çarkoğlu & Eder 2001b:41). There was also a historical luggage from the final years of the Ottoman Empire, resulting in mutual suspicions of hostility and unreliability. Further, Turkey was the first Muslim country to recognise Israel in 1948. While Turkey largely went along the Arab line in its policies towards Israel after the Suez War of 1956 (Soysal 1994/95:69–70), Turkish-Israeli relations gradually improved during the 1990s. Several Turkish-Israeli agreements on military cooperation were signed (Inbar 2001:115). After the 1998 October Crisis, which put an end to Syrian support of the PKK, Syrian-Turkish relations gradually improved, especially so after the take-over of Bashar al-Asad. Between 2000 and 2004 there were more than 45 ministerial visits between Syria and Turkey (*Arabicnews.com* 30 October 2004). In the light of simultaneously improving Turkish-Israeli relations and the failed Middle East peace process, Syria became increasingly eager to maintain good relations with Turkey. Syria went from being one of the fiercest condemner of the Turkish-Israeli agreements (Mu'awwed 1998:242) to saying that 'If we are able to better our relations [with Turkey] parallel to the improving relations between

Israel and Turkey, it will be a good step for us.' (*Turkish Daily News* 6 July 2000). While Turkish-Israeli relations later deteriorated, Syrian-Turkish relations continued to develop. With the invasion of Iraq in 2003, the question of a possible Kurdish state in northern Iraq further united Syria and Turkey as it, according to President al-Asad, 'made the danger direct and similar' to both (al-Jazeerah 1 May 2004). Turkey's new 'zero problems with neighbours' policy further helped reformulate its approach in trying to solve contentious issues with Syria. Turkey thereby helped ease Syria's international isolation after the 2003 invasion of Iraq. Syria, in return, helped ease the isolation of Northern Cyprus (Moubayed 2013:74). With the outbreak of the Syrian uprising in 2011, bilateral relations again turned sour. The Turkish government hosted a number of Syrian oppositional conferences, served as a basis for both armed and unarmed oppositional groups and organizations and as a hub for the smuggling of arms and money to rebel groups within Syria. Turkish Prime Minister Erdoğan called for Bashar al-Asad to step down (Reuters 22 November 2011) and Bashar al-Asad described Erdoğan as a liar and an opportunist (Ulusal TV 5 April 2013). Syrian-Turkish relations were, at this point, worse than ever.

Cold War, superpower relations and regional alliances

The Cold War certainly had an impact on every region of the world, but the Middle East was particularly affected. Because of its strategic location, oil resources and the fact that the two superpowers chose to back opposite sides in the Arab-Israeli conflict, US-USSR rivalry was more intense here than elsewhere. Over the Cold War years, the Middle East saw several violent superpower confrontations by proxy as well as occasional risks of real US-USSR confrontation. During the 1973 October War, USA even declared its (so far) last nuclear alert (Halliday 1997:10). While the US had formed close ties with Israel, Saudi Arabia, Iran and Turkey, the USSR developed relations with a number of nationalist military regimes in the Middle East. Syria was one of these. The USSR offered long-term, low-interest development loans, scholarships and technical assistance (Seale 1965:259). More importantly, it also broke a Western arms embargo on Syria.

In Hinnebusch's words, over the years arms 'arrived in formidable quantities at minimal costs' (1991:386). Although Syria became the most important Soviet ally in the Middle East, Seale has described the Syrian-Soviet relationship as a 'dialogue of the deaf'. Initially this was a relationship of convenience where both sides, despite different motives, agreed on the goals: to keep Western influence and military pressure out of the region (Seale 1997:49). As the years passed, they began to differ with regard to goals – Syria wanted arms of a quality and in a quantity that would allow an Arab military victory over Israel, and the USSR was looking to keep the status quo (Vassiliev 1993:102). The relationship was further strained by the fact that Syrian regimes were suspicious of communism and refused Soviet interference in their rule (Seale 1997:55–56). The 1966 coup, which led to the most radical and leftist-oriented government Syria had ever had, nurtured Soviet-Syrian relations but also spelled out their differences. The radicalism of the regime was among the factors bringing on the Six Days War, a development clearly not wanted by the USSR (Vassiliev 1993:102). The war resulted in the Israeli occupation of the Golan Heights, Syrian policies towards which will be analysed in chapter five.

Hafez al-Asad, taking power in 1970, quickly moved to a more pragmatic policy. Widely recognised as an able and strategic leader with a high potential for patiently advancing the interests of his regime while, when necessary, adapting to changing circumstances, he managed to counter balance the two super powers for much of the 1970–1991 period. Dependence on the USSR initially decreased during the Hafez al-Asad reign but with Egyptian president Sadat's gradual move out of the Soviet sphere, al-Asad's bargaining position was strengthened, and he was able to extract a considerable amount of military aid from the USSR (Freedman 1991:144–146). The 1973 October War, aimed at regaining Syrian and Egyptian 1967 losses, resulted in USSR-Syrian friction as the Arab states blamed the failure on the quality of Soviet arms and Soviet countered by pointing to Arab incompetence (Seale 1997:57). Al-Asad continued the Syrian tradition of refusing the status of a Soviet vassal state. Although the USSR had had air and naval facilities in Syria since the 1960s, they were never turned into Soviet bases (Freedman 1991:146), and al-Asad refused to sign a Treaty of Friendship and Cooperation until 1980 (Hinnebusch 1991:402). This was a time when the Syrian regime not only faced domestic difficulties – as seen above – but adversity also dominated in the regional and international arenas. The 1974–1975 Israeli-Egyptian armistice agreements Sinai I and II had in practice removed Egypt from the equation of the Arab-Israeli conflict. In 1979, Egypt concluded the first Arab peace treaty with Israel. A huge disappointment to al-Asad, who staunchly believed in a united Arab front as the only way of defeating Israel, the Camp David peace treaty resulted in the Arab isolation of Egypt. The following year, Iraq attacked Iran and became entangled in a war that was to last until 1988. Criticising Iraq for wasting resources on issues not related to 'the highest Arab goal' (i.e. the liberation of Israeli-occupied Arab land) and forcing Iran – which through its 1979 revolution had joined the radical anti-Israeli camp – to do the same, Syria supported the latter. This largely isolated Syria in the Arab world and deprived it of Arab financial aid (Kandil 2008:438–439). This was compensated for by Iranian oil (Kabalan 2010:27) and Iranian support in a for Syria crucial arena: Lebanon. As a result of the outbreak of the second Lebanese civil war in 1975, Syria invaded the following year in order to impose order and block developments negative for Syria (see chapter three). The above mentioned 1980 Treaty of Friendship and Cooperation with the USSR then came in handy as it implied a Soviet re-arming of Syria. Al-Asad thereby moved closer to his goal of achieving strategic parity with Israel. Although the Treaty of Friendship and Cooperation stipulated consultation in times of crisis, al-Asad's regime demonstrated freedom of action and obstructed Soviet policy on a number of occasions (Freedman 1991:194–196).

Syrian relations to USA have been marked by tension mainly due to disagreement over Israel. USA broke its diplomatic relations with Syria in 1967. They were restored in 1974 as a result of the Syrian-Israeli disengagement treaty (see chapter five). Accused of hosting militant Palestinian groups, Syria was added to the US State Department list of states sponsoring terrorism in 1979. Of the four states currently included (Syria, Cuba, Iran and Sudan), Syria thereby has the longest history on the list. The inclusion of Syria on the list led to a series of US sanctions. The US ambassador was again withdrawn from Syria in 1986 over the Hinnawi-affair but returned the following year after the Syrian expulsion of the Palestinian Abu Nidal group and Syria's assistance in obtaining the release of a US hostage in Lebanon (ICG report 83 2009:2).

The post–Cold War period: Peace talks, Gulf Wars and Lebanese dissidence

With the waning power of the USSR, its reluctance to provide military and economic aid, and Gorbatchev's move to normalise relations with Israel (Kandil 2008:433), Syria needed to seek new alignments. Opportunity to adapt to changing circumstances presented itself with the 1990 Iraqi invasion of Kuwait. As the US needed Syria in order to gain legitimacy for its UN-led coalition to free Kuwait in 1991, Syria joined in against its principal Arab enemy. This move resulted in generous and much needed economic aid from Arab Gulf states and a considerable amount of international goodwill. Syria then agreed to participate in the Arab-Israeli peace talks, which began in Madrid in October the same year (see chapter five). Reported on by Robert Fisk as an extremely hateful gathering (2006:383–385), it nevertheless developed into bilateral talks that ended with a Jordanian-Israeli peace treaty in 1994 and the secret Israeli-Palestinian negotiations leading to the 1993 Oslo Accords. After the dissolution of the USSR in December 1991, the US continued as the Syrian-Israeli broker until the last round of (failed) talks in 2000.

The early 2000s saw renewed trouble for Syria. Shortly prior to the take-over of Bashar al-Asad, the main Syrian argument for maintaining its military presence in Lebanon was removed with the Israeli withdrawal from southern Lebanon in June 2000. Furthermore, as the Syrian decision to participate in the coalition against Iraq in 1991 had led to a US green light – or at least a blind eye – to Syrian hegemony in Lebanon (el-Husseini 2012:26), the decision to stand with Iraq in 2003 had the opposite effect. The US now challenged the Syrian presence in Lebanon and added new sanctions to the ones in place since 1979. It also accused Syria of selling arms to Iraq and allowing volunteer

THE CONSOLIDATION OF THE TERRITORIAL STATE   49

fighters to cross the Syrian border into Iraq in order to join the resistance (Hinnebusch 2010:14). The US began funding Syrian exiled opposition groups (Kandil 2008:437) and there was talk of US plans to instigate regime change in Syria. Following the assassination of Lebanese former Prime Minister Rafiq al-Hariri in February 2005, the US again withdrew its ambassador to Syria, which was widely blamed for Hariri's murder. International pressure mounted. Syria found itself increasingly isolated and therefore moved to improve relations with Russia. All forms of cooperation had been frozen since Yeltsin had begun pressuring Syria to settle its debt, and although Putin was initially accommodating to Syrian approaches, he soon chose to prioritise relations with Israel (Kandil 2008:433). Syria further turned to China (Salloukh 2009:161) and deepened relations with its regional allies Iran, Hizbullah and Hamas (Hinnebusch 2010b:16–17). In February 2005, Syria and Iran formed a united front, vowing to support each other diplomatically and militarily in case of a US or Israeli attack (BBC 17 February 2005). Analysts who had initially predicted that the Bashar al-Asad takeover would result in a Syria gravitating towards the West, were thus disappointed.[16]

The Syrian decision to stand with Iraq against the US-led coalition in 2003 has been explained in different ways: while some have pointed to the inexperience and incompetence of the new Syrian president Bashar al-Asad (see for instance Salloukh 2009:161, Rubin 2007:5), Hinnebusch sees the Syrian stand as a result of its Arab nationalist identity and regional role, institutionalised especially under Hafez al-Asad (Hinnebusch 2010:3). Kabalan dismisses identity and instead points to domestic needs (Kabalan 2010:30–31). Regardless of different interpretations of this decision, it cannot be disputed that, motivated mainly by economic factors, Hafez al-Asad had started to mend fences with Iraq in 1997 (Kandil 2008:444). Increased trade with Iraq and especially Iraqi oil outside of UN control brought enormous economic benefits for Syria. In 2001–2002, Syrian profits from this deal accounted for 15 per cent of the state budget (Perthes 2004b:107). This source of income was cut off following the 2003 invasion. In 2006 Syria and Iraq restored diplomatic relations and Syria had thereby recognised and legitimised the Iraqi regime change.

Out of isolation, 2006–2010

With the visit of Tony Blair's top advisor to Damascus in late 2006, Syria's isolation began to break. The large number of European diplomats and later US high-level congressional visits that followed as well as French president Sarkozy's visit to Syria in September 2008 showed that Syria had come in from the cold. The Obama Administration abandoned George W. Bush's recipe of isolation and punishment as the best way to deal with Syria and instead sought to engage it. As part of this new approach, in mid-2009 the US announced its intention to appoint an ambassador to Syria. Syrian relations with Saudi Arabia, strained since the murder of Rafiq al-Hariri, improved the same year when King Abdallah visited Damascus. The EU-Syrian association agreement also seemed to be back on the agenda. These negotiations had been initiated in 1998 with the goal of facilitating and increasing Syrian-EU trade. Bashar al-Asad had speeded up negotiations, seeing the agreement as a way of adapting the Syrian economy to international standards (Perthes 2004:101–102). When ready for ratification in 2004, it was blocked by the EU over a clause on weapons of mass destruction and EU insistence that Syria cooperate fully with the Hariri investigation (Zorob 2009:148). Bashar al-Asad in March 2010 commented on the renewed possibility of reaching an agreement that it first has to be clear 'in what direction the EU is moving', stressing that he had not been impressed by EU policies during the Bush era (Hammargren 2010). By the outbreak of the 2011 uprising the agreement had been negotiated by remained unsigned. Due to developments in Syria, the process was subsequently frozen.

Back into isolation in 2011

Following the outbreak of the Syrian uprising in March 2011, the EU, the US, the Arab League and Turkey imposed sanctions on Syria. As the uprising turned into civil war, a number of states, including most EU and Arab League members, broke off diplomatic relations. In November 2011 the Arab League further suspended Syria's membership, and in August 2012 the Organisation of Islamic Cooperation followed suit. In March 2013 the Arab League allowed the National Coalition for Syrian Revolutionary and Opposition Forces, formed in November 2012, to represent Syria within the organisation, and several states recognised the Coalition as the sole legitimate representative of the Syrian people. Although supported by Russia, China and Iran and to a lesser degree by Lebanon and Iraq, the Syrian regime is at the time of writing (May 2014) more isolated than ever before.

CHAPTER 3

'WE ARE NOT STRANGERS HERE': SYRIAN POLICY TOWARDS LEBANON

As seen in chapter two, throughout 1920–1946, France put mandated Syria through a number of permutations and administrative changes. The first territorial change carried out, and the only one to remain constant throughout the mandate period, was the creation in 1920 of Greater Lebanon. In 1946 it became independent as the Republic of Lebanon. It consisted of the area known as Mount Lebanon with the addition of Beirut and the three coastal cities of Tripoli, Sidon and Tyre and their administrative hinterlands. Also added were the four inland districts of Rashaya, Hasbaya, Baalbek and the Biqaa, making it stretch over a total of 10,452 km² (Seale 2010:321). Mount Lebanon, which had enjoyed a period of autonomy during the final years of the Ottoman Empire (1864–1915), had a majority population of Christian Maronites. The rest of the areas included in the new state had a Muslim majority, except Beirut which was evenly mixed (Khoury 1987:57). The four coastal cities had all belonged to the Ottoman *vilayet* of Beirut while the four inland districts had belonged to the *vilayet* of Damascus. Mount Lebanon and the coast had been part of the interim Arab administration OETA East for a week only (Zamir 1991:406) but the four inland districts had remained within this administration until the establishment of the French mandate. Faysal, throughout his reign 1918–1920, repeatedly brought up the question of the coast and Mount Lebanon with the British but was indecisive with regard to his position on the issue. He vacillated between accepting an independent Mount Lebanon, an autonomous Mount Lebanon with extended borders (including the coast) provided it was economically and politically linked to his Syrian kingdom, to finally insisting that both the coast and Mount Lebanon were inseparable parts of Syria. He exercised pressure through bans on grain export from inland Syria to the French administered OETA West and redirected transit trade from Beirut to Haifa in order to demonstrate the dependence of Mount Lebanon and the coast on the interior (Zamir 1991:408–419). Once Faysal had been ousted and the mandate established, not only did Mount Lebanon and the coast remain separate from the rest of French-mandated Syria. In addition, as mentioned above, the four inland districts from OETA East were added to them to create Greater Lebanon. The creation of Greater Lebanon caused outrage within the Syrian nationalist movement, working for the unification of all of French mandated Syria. Throughout the 1920s, the efforts of the Syrian nationalist movement to reverse the French move were foremost focused on the four inland districts. It also repeatedly raised claims to the coastal city of Tripoli, which remained a militant anti-Greater Lebanon stronghold throughout the mandate period. Among other things, a Syrian delegation handed a petition to the League of Nations demanding that the areas annexed to Mount Lebanon in 1920 be returned to Syria (Atiyah 1973:127). Still, the perception of all of Greater Lebanon and the rest of the French mandate as one was indicated by the fact that the National Bloc was formed at a nationalist conference in Beirut. The conference included delegates from different parts of Greater Lebanon and National Bloc branches were set up in the areas of Greater Lebanon that the Bloc felt it should focus on: the coast, which had been part of the French administered OETA West 1918–1920 and the eastern part which had until 1920 administratively belonged to the 'Syrian Kingdom' (OETA East) (Seale 2010:228).

The National Bloc's 'Syria first' strategy

At a National Bloc conference in 1932, it was decided that Mount Lebanon could 'decide her own fate' (Khoury 1987a:263), a strong indication that this area was not perceived as a necessary part of Syria. During the years to follow, it was made clear that the rest of Greater Lebanon was not necessarily part of Syria either. In 1935, the National Bloc was prepared to renounce all claims to areas within Greater Lebanon except Tripoli in return for the Christian Maronite Patriarch's support for independence for both Syria and Greater Lebanon. The Patriarch did not accept the Syrian claim to Tripoli and the agreement therefore came to nothing (Atiyah 1973:141). In February the following year, the National Bloc in Syria made clear that it would recognise the separate existence of Greater Lebanon provided that the Maronites joined the struggle for Lebanese independence from France (Chaitani 2007:10–11).

The same year, the French initiated negotiations with the Syrian National Bloc and the Lebanese Constitutional Bloc, with the aim of concluding a French-Syrian and a French-Lebanese Treaty meant to lead to the independence of both Syria and Greater Lebanon within three years. During these negotiations the Syrian National Bloc went from demanding that either the areas annexed in 1920 should be 'reunited' with Syria or that Greater Lebanon remain intact on condition that it was economically and politically linked to Syria, to in practice renouncing all demands with regard to Greater Lebanon in exchange for a treaty promising independence for Syria. This 'territorial abandonment' of Greater Lebanon by the Syrian government encouraged the emerging tendency among the Muslim population within the annexed areas towards the acceptance of the Greater Lebanon entity. This, in combination with the fact that the Maronites had begun to demand complete independence from France opened up for a rapprochement between the Muslims and the Maronites, eventually resulting in the 1943 Lebanese National Pact. It is worth noting that Syrian Prime Minister Jamil Mardam Bey (1936–1939) helped get the internal Lebanese rapprochement and co-operation on the way (Atiyah 1973:176) and that the Syrian government sent representatives to Lebanon, urging Sunni Muslim leaders to end the demonstrations that had broken out in protest of the signing of the French-Lebanese agreement (Zamir 1999:200–201, Seale 2010:348). The National Bloc thereby encouraged Muslim acceptance of the Lebanese entity within its 1920 borders, indicating that the National Bloc itself had accepted these borders.

Despite the implicit recognition of Greater Lebanon in the 1936 treaty, messages stemming from Syria during the following years were mixed. Already at the signing ceremony Syrian President Hashim al-Atasi announced a desire to form a federation with Lebanon, thus indicating that a complete separation of the two states was not desirable (Zamir 1999:201). In 1937, faced with emerging Turkish ambitions to separate Alexandretta from Syria (see chapter four), Syria again raised claims to the coastal town of Tripoli as compensation for the Iskenderun port it was to lose (Guilquin 2000:144, Zamir 2000:219) and in a 1939 article President al-Atasi talked of Beirut as part of 'our country'.[1] However, formal written recognition of Lebanon's separate existence came in the early 1940s; in January 1942 the Lebanese Foreign Ministry announced that it had received a letter from the Syrian government recognising Lebanon as an entity separate from Syria (*Al-alaqat* vol 1 1986:29).

On 1 October 1943, Lebanese Prime Minister Riyad al-Sulh, presented the Lebanese parliament with the formulas on which the Lebanese National Pact was based. This unwritten compromise agreement has received attention mostly for its consocialism, regulating power sharing between Lebanon's dominating confessional groups. However, this domestic pact also contained clear instructions for the nature of Lebanese-Syrian relations; Syria would support Lebanon's independence and Lebanon would refrain from becoming 'a beachhead or corridor for imperialism' against Syria (Khalidi 1989:378 note 1). This idea of Syrian recognition of Lebanese independence in exchange for (or the avoidance of) certain policies continued to guide Syrian actions towards Lebanon during the entire period studied.

In 1944, both Syria and Lebanon were founding members of the Arab League, the charter of which explicitly specifies the recognition of Lebanon within its 1920 borders. The Syrian declaration of war on the Axis Powers in 1945 repeats the Syrian recognition of Lebanon within the borders stipulated by the Arab League charter.[2] Prime Minister Faris al-Khoury stated in April 1945 that Syria had renounced its claims in Lebanon on the condition that Lebanon remain an Arab state, independent of any foreign control (Chaitani 2007:27), thus repeating the basic idea inherent in the National Pact. Finally, in 1946, when the French troops left Syria and Lebanon and full independence was gained, Syrian President al-Quwatli, in his speech on Evacuation Day 17 April 1946, expressed joy that 'Lebanon has won what we have won' (i.e. independence).[3] The letter of recognition the Syrian government had sent in 1942 was thereby confirmed on several occasions throughout the 1940s.

Syrian policies towards Lebanon, 1947–1974: Decades of tension

Syrian-Lebanese relations after independence were characterised by tension. This was initially most evident in the economic ties between the two states. The *Intérêts Communs*[4] left to Syria and Lebanon by France constituted a constant problem until March 1950 when the customs union was terminated (Seale 1965:94, Picard 2002:70). Conflict over monetary policy and restrictions of imports were so harsh that in newspapers on both sides of the border it sometimes even overshadowed the 1948–1949 Arab-Israeli war (Chaitani 2006:91–93). During the decades following independence, Syria showed an ambition to decide the nature of Syrian-Lebanese economic relations and, quite naturally, strove to gain as much as possible from these relations. Syria made several suggestions for the continuation and improvement of the economic unity with Lebanon and the 1940s, 1950s and the 1960s saw several rounds of negotiations in order to reach economic agreements acceptable to both sides. Unable to attain this, Syria also presented proposals for agreements whereby trade and financial regulations would be coordinated and responded to Lebanese refusals by numerous closures of its border, periodical banning of trade with Lebanon, increased fees on Lebanese air and ground transit trade and a periodical prohibition for Syrians to spend holidays in Lebanon (*Al-alaqat* vol 1 1986:1, 14, Chaitani 2006:107). Although tension was most evident with regard to financial matters, additional points of contention emerged with time. In April 1949 Syrian President Husni al-Zaim convinced Antune Saada, founder of the SSNP (see chapter two) to plot a coup in Lebanon. Even though al-Zaim had reportedly told an American diplomat in Damascus that 'Lebanon should belong to Syria' (Moubayed 2006:352), his attempt to realise a change of governments in Beirut should not be seen as an endeavour to incorporate Lebanon into Syria. Rather, it was a pre-emptive strike in order to remove Lebanese Prime Minister Riyad al-Sulh, whom al-Zaim suspected of plotting his own downfall. In exchange for Lebanese support for his government, al-Zaim later handed Saada over to the Lebanese authorities (Seale 1965:70, 94, Moubayed 2006:352). Shortly after the extradition, al-Zaim signed an economic agreement with Lebanon ending a long period of dispute (Seale 1956:71).

The Lebanese free press constituted an irritant to several Syrian presidents and governments. Syrian reactions consisted of formal protests and demands that the Lebanese Government control Lebanese media.[5] Furthermore, over the years, Syrian political dissidents and refugees sought and found refuge in Lebanon and several successful as well as abortive coups against Syrian regimes were planned from Lebanon, causing further tension (Weinberger 1986:82). Lebanese dissidents likewise sought refuge in Syria[6] and in the late 1950s Lebanon accused Syria of ordering bombings in Lebanon.[7] Political conflict reached its climax in 1958 when civil war broke out in Lebanon. The Lebanese Government accused Syria, then part of the UAR, of infiltration and the training and arming of rebellious groups. These accusations were denied by Syria and the UN observer group dispatched to Lebanon failed to verify the smuggling of arms into the country (Yearbook of the United Nations 1958:36–48).[8] Further, in 1958 the Lebanese Ambassador to Spain complained that the UAR Embassy in Madrid was distributing a book that claimed Lebanon to be a Syrian district and several well known Lebanese writers to be Syrians (*Al-alaqat* vol 1 1986:204).

The Lebanese civil war ended, but political tension with Syria did not. After Syria's withdrawal from the UAR, Syria instead accused Lebanon of providing a base for Egyptian anti-Syrian Nasserist agitators and spies. A case in point was the written note the Syrian Minister of Foreign Affairs handed to his Lebanese counterpart in December 1961. It contained a clear reference to the link between Lebanese independence and Syrian security inherent in the 1943 National Pact. Accusing Lebanon of permitting anti-Syrian propaganda and activities coordinated by the Egyptian Embassy, the note stated that, 'so far Syria has shown respect for the independence of Lebanon [...] Syria is obliged to take the necessary measures to protect its own security and hope to find help and brotherly co-operation in the Lebanese government' (*Al-alaqat* vol 1 1986:216). To counter the anti-Syria activities by the Egyptian Embassy, Syrian Prime Minister Bashir al-Azmah proposed the establishment of Syrian-Lebanese diplomatic relations in August 1962. Fearing that Lebanon would turn into an Egyptian-Syrian battle ground, Lebanese Prime Minister Rashid Karami rejected the suggestion.[9]

Another occasional point of tension was the lack of border demarcation. Of the three steps generally carried out as part of any border determination – the allocation of a certain territory to a state, the description of the border in a written document and the actual marking on the ground – only the first was carried out when Greater Lebanon was created.[10] Although Syrian-Lebanese border commissions to solve ambiguities were formed on several occasions, complete demarcation was never carried out and this allowed for border-related conflicts. Today, the most significant result of the lack of proper demarcation is the currently disputed status of the Shebaa Farms, a 14 km long and two km wide area consisting of agricultural properties. Although located within Syria on maps since 1920, for all practical purposes it was considered part of Lebanon by both French mandate officials and local residents (Kaufman 2002:584). In 1955, Syria constructed a military post there and forced inhabitants to take Syrian citizenship (Kaufman 2002:591). In attempts to settle the issue both Lebanon and Syria had made official requests to France in 1947 to provide them with all cartographic information, and did so again in 1960–1963. France failed to meet their requests (Kaufman 2002:589–590). A Syrian-Lebanese Border Commission then decided in 1964 that the border should be set according to farmers' land ownership and Shebaa was therefore Lebanese. Kaufman, however, reports that Syria still had physical control of the area in 1967. When the area was occupied along with the Golan Heights by Israel in June 1967, it was treated as Syrian territory by both Syria and Lebanon, as well as by Israel and the UN (Kaufman 2002:591). Not until the withdrawal of the Israeli army from southern Lebanon in June 2000 did the disputed status of the area resurface.

The take-over of Hafez al-Asad in 1970 initially eased Syrian-Lebanese relations. An agreement of free movement of goods and people was reached, a Permanent Lebanese-Syrian Committee was established in order to handle economic and political bilateral problems (Seale 1988:171), and a 1967 border commission was re-activated (Weinberger 1986:112). One of Hafez al-Asad's ambitions with regard to the Arab-Israeli conflict was to create a single front extending from Lebanon to the port of Aqaba in Jordan (Avi-Ran 1991:7), where the frontline states and the PLO would coordinate their actions and strategies under Syrian leadership. In such a united front, Lebanon's military weakness was a liability as, in case of war, an Israeli attack on Syria through Lebanon would be a possibility. Syria therefore wanted the Lebanese government to agree to the entry of the Syrian army into the eastern part of Lebanon (the Biqaa, next to the Syrian border) (Avi-Ran 1991:8). This did not happen and Lebanon's geographical position and military weakness remained a security concern for Syria. This perception would become increasingly evident during the years to come.

Throughout the 1946–1973 period Syria and Lebanon concluded (at least) 27 agreements within different areas such as communication, financial matters and cooperation on tourism. Being inter-state, they all contained implicit recognition of Lebanese statehood and independence. In 1973, relations deteriorated again due to Lebanese-Palestinian fighting in Lebanon. As during earlier rounds of Lebanese-Palestinian fighting, Syria supported the Palestinians. Furthermore, to the annoyance of the Lebanese Government, the Palestinian fighters active in southern Lebanon received regular supplies from Syria which encouraged their activities against Israel from across the Lebanese border. The presence of Palestinian fighters in Lebanon, and their attacks on Israel bringing retaliation affecting Lebanese civilians, underscored the latent tensions in Lebanese society, eventually constituting one of the catalysts for the second Lebanese civil war, 1975–1990.

Syrian policies towards Lebanon during the War, 1975–1990: Mediation, military intervention and the establishment of Syrian hegemony

Much has been written on the second Lebanese civil war and Lebanese, Syrian, Palestinian, Israeli, US and others' actions, reactions and interactions with regard to it. The objective here is not to give an account of the war itself. This section will instead focus on Syrian verbal and non-verbal policies during the Lebanon war and how these relate to the Syrian attitude towards Lebanese independence.

Throughout the 1975–1990 civil war, Syrian policy was characterised by attempts to reconcile two different roles: that of objective mediator trying to find the lowest common denominator between the different Lebanese warring factions in order to put an end to the war and that of interested party trying to make sure the final solution was in line with Syria's interests and goals. Even though changes in circumstances required changes in policy – from mediation and indirect intervention to direct military intervention and several changes of allies – Syrian goals remained constant throughout the war: to put an end to it in a way that would keep Lebanon from in any way enabling Israel to threaten Syria, to keep the balance of power between the warring factions – as opposed to ensure the complete victory of one side – to keep Lebanon united as one state within the Arab camp and to safeguard the existence of the Palestinian guerillas in Lebanon. From the outbreak of the war in April 1975 until the end of that year, Syria assumed the role of mediator while simultaneously supplying military assistance to the Lebanese National Movement (LNM), a loose coalition of anti-establishment, leftist forces. In January 1976, when a partition of Lebanon along sectarian lines (an idea entertained by and prepared for by some Maronite leaders, see for instance Fisk 2003:120) seemed a possible outcome of the fighting, Syrian Foreign Minister Abdul Halim Khaddam made clear that Syria would not permit such a development:

> Lebanon was [once] part of Syria, and we will restore it in case of any attempt at partition. And it has to be clear that this does

not mean the four districts and the coast only [the areas annexed to Mount Lebanon in 1920], it means Mount Lebanon as well. Lebanon will either be unified or it will be restored to Syria.[11]

Syria intensified its dual roles. Mediation efforts were stepped up with a delegation of Syrian officials meeting with representatives of the LNM and traditional Muslim leaders in Aramoun, Lebanon. During this meeting Khaddam spelled out Syria's goals: a unified Arab Lebanon with a continued Palestinian presence without 'erroneous Palestinian behaviour'.[12] The LNM demanded that a new President be elected and Hafez al-Asad later said that he had spoken to President Suleiman Franjieh who had 'agreed to step down'.[13] The LNM further asked for changes in the Lebanese constitution but these were turned down by Syria.[14] The Syrian mediation, with a clear flavour of negotiations as Syria simultaneously tried to secure its own interests, resulted in the never implemented Damascus Agreement. Al-Asad commented on it as containing 95 per cent of what the warring factions demanded. Syria had added to the document the specification that Lebanon was an Arab state 'because none of the parties had said that they wanted this included',[15] a clear indication of how Syria's mediation efforts included measures ensuring that Syrian goals were met. The Lebanese President announced the contents of the Damascus Agreement to the public. Among other things, he pointed to 'responsible freedom' for the press, which would have to contribute to the 'realisation of national unity and the strengthening of Lebanon's Arab and international relations'.[16] Although not spelled out clearly, this was without doubt another Syrian demand resulting from annoyance with some Lebanese papers' criticism of Syrian policy in Lebanon.

Syrian military intervention in Lebanon

The negotiations resulting in the Damascus Agreement were coupled with military intervention by proxy as the Syrian sponsored Palestinian Liberation Army (PLA) crossed into Lebanon in response to a Maronite offensive. The intervention through the PLA was, according to al-Asad, carried out at the repeated requests by the LNM and without prior knowledge of Lebanese President Franjieh.[17] In response to the shift that then took place in the balance of power between the Maronite dominated pro-establishment and the Muslim and leftist anti-establishment forces, Syria switched to direct intervention, this time on behalf of the pro-establishment. On 1 June 1976, Syrian troops crossed the Lebanese border, distributing leaflets saying that Syria had been invited by President Franjieh to come and help Lebanon (Fisk 2003:82). That Syria had been asked to intervene 'by legitimate Lebanese authorities' has always been maintained by Syrian officials.[18] However, even though he later defended the intervention, former President Franjieh denied that he had had any knowledge of the intervention in advance. Neither had new President Elias Sarkis, elected in May 1976 (Weinberger 1986:211). In the absence of evidence that legitimate authorities actually did ask for Syrian help, the June 1976 intervention has been classified as illegal by several authors (Weinberger 1986, Pogany 1987, Thompson 2002:72). However, a 2004 UN report, as well as the UNIIIC report of October 2005, confirm the Syrian version (S/2004/777 2004:1, S/2005/662 2005:5).

Syria has, from 1976 until today, described its intervention in Lebanon as an altruistic and successful effort to help its neighbour, based on national duty and the special Syrian-Lebanese relations stemming from history, geography and family ties.[19] A reading of Hafez al-Asad's speeches and interviews during the war years 1975–1990 shows that he recognised the interdependence of the security of Lebanon and Syria and that especially the Biqaa region was important to safeguard Syrian security.[20] He denied, however, that Syrian security had anything to do with the Syrian intervention in Lebanon. The war itself was, according to Hafez al-Asad, the result of a conspiracy.[21] When specified, the goal of this conspiracy was to cover up the 1975 Sinai Accord and later the Camp David Accord of 1979, crush the Palestinian guerrilla[22] and obtain the partition of Lebanon into smaller states.[23] Al-Asad also made clear that Syrian and Lebanese interests were the same,[24] that a majority of the Lebanese were in favour of Syrian policies in Lebanon,[25] and that 'a solution to Lebanon's problems does not come from the [Mediterranean] Sea and not from outside the borders of Lebanon and Syria',[26] thus making clear that Syria had to be part of the solution in Lebanon. The independence of Lebanon was continuously emphasised by President Hafez al-Asad[27] and he stressed that Syria had no other interests in Lebanon except peace and stability.[28]

Syrian troops: Under the command of whom?

While it is unclear whether Syria intervened on its own initiative only or if Syria was invited by Lebanese actors, the Syrian intervention was given legitimacy through the creation of the Arab League Deterrent Force (ALDF) in October 1976. A peace keeping force initially meant to replace the Syrian troops in Lebanon, the ALDF first ended up with a Syrian majority and later with Syrian troops only.[29] Continuously pointing to the legitimacy of the Syrian presence – based on the invitation of the Lebanese government and the Arab League ALDF resolution – President al-Asad stressed that the Syrian troops were placed under Lebanese command and that the final decision on the whereabouts of the troops, including their withdrawal, was up to the Lebanese. Nevertheless, Syria refused at least four demands by Lebanese governments for Syrian redeployment and withdrawal.[30] During the 1982 Israeli siege of West Beirut, the Lebanese government, which until then had requested renewals for the ADFL mandate at each expiration – although occasionally after negotiating with Syria – even terminated the mission and asked for the withdrawal of all non-Lebanese forces (Pogany 1987:145). Syrian president al-Asad argued that this would place Syrian troops on a par with Israeli forces in Lebanon and instead insisted that a Syrian withdrawal should be negotiated between the Lebanese and Syrian governments after an Israeli withdrawal (Pogany 1987:145). This became the basis of the compromise eventually endorsed by the 1982 Arab League resolution on the matter. The mandate was declared terminated at Lebanon's request, but negotiations between the Lebanese and Syrian governments would decide 'the adoption of measures in the light of an Israeli withdrawal from Lebanon'.[31]

A withdrawal of Syrian forces could thus not be discussed prior to an Israeli withdrawal. This was a policy Syria continued to pursue until 2005.

The 1983 Lebanese-Israeli Treaty, the 1985 Tripartite Agreement and the 1985 National Union Front document

On 17 May 1983, the Lebanese government under President Amin Gemayel reached an agreement with Israel, whereby the northern border of the latter would be secured in exchange of an Israeli withdrawal from Lebanon. This was in all but name a peace agreement between Israel and Lebanon. However, Israel added a side letter which said that it would not withdraw from Lebanon until Syria and the PLO had withdrawn. Syrian President al-Asad's reaction was: 'This agreement will never be implemented' (Boykin 2002:306), and it never was. Lebanese President Gemayel commented on the Syrian objection expressing hope that Syria would respect the Lebanese government's right to make its own decisions and not interfere in Lebanon's internal affairs.[32] Syria argued that the Israeli-Lebanese agreement had turned Lebanon into an Israeli protectorate, torn apart its unity, violated its sovereignty and severed its links with the Arab homeland[33] and, pointing to the Arab League resolution 314[34] of 1950, requested sanctions against Lebanon. Syria demanded a halt to all kinds of transactions and the severance of political and diplomatic relations with the authorities in Beirut, the suspension of the membership of the authorities in Beirut in the Arab League and all institutions working within its framework.[35] It should be noted here that although the resolution Syria pointed to talks of measures against the state and its subjects, Syria demanded sanctions against the government only, thus opening up for relations and contacts with Lebanon and Lebanese representatives as long as they were not within Gemayel's camp. While the original resolution talks of breaking with the subjects of the state in question, Syria called for the provision of all kinds of aid to the Lebanese people in their struggle to recover Lebanon's unity and independence. Nor did Syria, as stipulated by the resolution, close its border with Lebanon. The help required for the 'Lebanese people' and Syria's omission of the closure of the border opened up for a continued

Syrian presence and activity in Lebanon. Al-Asad later said that the 1983 Lebanese-Israeli treaty had put unacceptable restrictions on Lebanon and threatened Lebanon's independence and freedom as well as the security of Syria and the Arab Nation.[36] He claimed that with Syrian help the Lebanese people had stopped its implementation.[37] Earlier statements that Syria would accept anything the Lebanese legitimate authorities decided[38] thus came to nothing.

Throughout the 1980s, Hafez al-Asad emphasised a new National Pact as the only possibility to end the war.[39] Two Syrian attempts were made to negotiate such pacts. Neither of them were implemented but both are important as they clearly show the Syrian ambition to establish an influence, legitimised in writing, in Lebanon. The 1985 Tripartite Agreement, negotiated with the heads of the three major warring Lebanese militias dedicated an entire chapter (out of five) exclusively to Syrian-Lebanese relations as the common interests of the two states 'require a high degree of coordination in all fields': security, economy, education and media. Syrian preoccupation with the weakness of Lebanon's defence was evident: 'Lebanon cannot be allowed to be the gateway through which Israel may attack or threaten Syria'. Therefore an agreement had to be reached for the deployment of Syrian military units 'at certain points in Lebanon, to be decided by common military committees'. The treaty further stipulated that all disturbance of bilateral relations stemming from Lebanese media must be stopped and that Lebanese media had to rise to 'a high degree of patriotic and national [pan-Arab] responsibility'.[40] Likewise, the National Accord, negotiated with a number of Lebanese political and religious leaders (the so-called National Union Front) the same year, included specific instructions for bilateral relations:

> the real expression of Lebanon's Arab identity is its distinctive relationship with and decisive and unchangeable link to Syria. [...] this requires, for the good of Lebanon, that our distinctive pan-Arab relationship be given a legal basis. It must be reflected in co-ordination and integration agreements in various areas, with special emphasis on defence, security, foreign policy, education and the economy.[41]

Both agreements stress the Arab identity of Lebanon and the necessity for a Lebanese pan-Arab foreign policy, reflecting the Syrian fear that Lebanon might leave the Arab camp. The emphasis on the Arab identity of Lebanon, as well as the sections on Syrian-Lebanese relations were largely reproduced in the 1989 Taif Agreement that eventually put an end to the war.

Wartime indications of Syrian lack of respect for Lebanese sovereignty

Syrian troops in Lebanon took upon themselves tasks that were not connected to peacekeeping and that create doubt concerning Syrian respect for Lebanese sovereignty. For instance, after entering Beirut in 1976 Syrian troops occupied the offices of several Lebanese newspapers critical of Syrian policy in Lebanon, arrested at least two journalists and imprisoned them in Damascus (see Fisk 2003:96, Sherry 1997). Five Lebanese newspapers were shut down (Middle East Watch 1997:1). The freedom of the Lebanese press, an irritant to Syrian regimes since independence, thus continued to be subject to Syrian efforts to control anti-Syrian reports (as seen above, an attempt to legitimise this control in writing was made in the 1985 Tripartite Accord). Earlier that year, Syrian forces had begun arresting Lebanese citizens and stateless Palestinians in Lebanon. One of the earliest examples was the founder and leader of the Lebanese Arab Army, a dissident Sunni Muslim faction of the Lebanese National Army, which had disintegrated along sectarian lines in March 1976. He was brought before a military court in Damascus charged with acting against Syria and aiming at obstructing Syrian efforts to end the fighting in Lebanon (Weinberger 1986:192). Disappearances of Lebanese citizens and stateless Palestinians residing in Lebanon at the hand of the Syrian security service continued throughout the war as well as the post-war period (Sherry 1997).

Due to the lack of a parliamentary quorum, the 1988 Lebanese presidential elections could not be carried out. Retiring President Amin Gemayel then claimed adherence to the constitutional provisions of succession in the case of no election and appointed the

Commander of the Lebanese Forces, General Michel Aoun, as Prime Minister to head a transitional military government. This move was not accepted by the already existing government. During attempts to solve the conflict and organise new elections, Syrian Foreign Minister Khaddam declared that every presidential candidate would have to present a written manifesto for approval (Hanf 1993:271), clearly indicating that no presidential candidate could run in the election without a green light from Syria.

The 1989 Taif Agreement

In May 1989 the Arab League decided to create a Tripartite High Commission with the task of facilitating the election of a Lebanese President and promote political reforms, ensure the liberation of Lebanon from the Israeli occupation and the evacuation of other non-Lebanese forces.[42] None of these other non-Lebanese forces were specified but would inevitably include Syria. The first version of the National Reconciliation Document was not accepted by Syria as it not only failed to specify Syrian-Lebanese relations but also talked about the withdrawal of Syrian troops. This was unacceptable, according to President al-Asad, as it made Syria appear as an occupier.[43] Disagreement between the Commission and Syria on time frames for withdrawals and areas to withdraw to, as well as disagreement on the formulation of Syrian-Lebanese relations, led the Commission to declare that it had failed because of the Syrian stand.[44] Giving it another try, the Commission invited all members of the last elected Parliament (1972) still alive to gather in Taif, Saudi Arabia, to reach an agreement on national reconciliation. The Document of National Understanding, more commonly known as the Taif Agreement, which emerged out of this session did not represent a radical departure from earlier attempts to reform the Lebanese political system and many of its features had been part of both the 1976 Damascus Agreement and the 1985 Tripartite Agreement. Like both the 1985 Tripartite Agreement and the National Union Front document, the Taif Accord formalises Lebanon's relations with Syria, emphasising their special relationship and stresses the need for coordination and cooperation.

The Taif Accord points to the necessity of bilateral agreements in all areas, in a manner that accomplishes Syrian and Lebanese interests within the framework of their sovereignty and independence. The Accord further stipulates that neither state, under any circumstance, be allowed to constitute a threat to the other.[45] The Accord was rejected by General Michel Aoun on the grounds that it did not call, even in principle, for a Syrian withdrawal from Lebanon (Hanf 1993:590). His rejection sparked another round of warfare resulting in a Maronite-Maronite war ending with Syria ousting General Aoun in October 1990. The Taif Agreement was also criticised by other actors on the Lebanese arena such as Hizbullah, Amal and the PLO but the strong regional and international support the agreement enjoyed ensured its survival (Nasrallah 1994:134). The Lebanese era of *Pax Syriana* had begun.

Syrian policies towards post-war Lebanon, 1991–2005: Securing continued Syrian control

According to the Taif Agreement, the Syrian forces would, during a period of two years, assist the Lebanese forces in establishing the authority of the Lebanese state over its territory. The Syrian forces would then redeploy to the Biqaa area and, if necessary, other points to be determined by a joint Lebanese-Syrian military committee. Following this, the two governments would conclude an agreement to 'determine the strength and duration of the presence of Syrian forces in the above-mentioned area and to define the relationship between these forces and the Lebanese state authorities.' The two-year period passed with no Syrian redeployment. It should be noted that while the agreement stipulated redeployment, it made a complete Syrian *withdrawal* a question to be negotiated between the two states, not something that Lebanon could decide unilaterally. It should also be noted that it was not up to the Lebanese government to decide the size of the Syrian forces nor under whose command they would function. The agreement thereby had a built-in guarantee for a continued Syrian military presence within Lebanon's borders should Syria insist on staying. Hanf reports that the Commission had made major concessions to accommodate Syrian views (1993:581) and an indication of this can be found in Hafez al-Asad's comment, 'We support the Taif agreement and nobody should doubt our commitment to it. Had we not been committed to it, the agreement would not exist.'[46]

In accordance with the Taif Accord, a large number of bilateral agreements were signed between Syria and Lebanon and a constantly strengthened co-operation, under the slogan 'One people in two states' (*shaab wahid fi dawlatayn*), was the main characteristic of Syrian-Lebanese relations during the 1990–2005 period (a sarcastic version of this slogan was later used by Lebanese critics of the Syrian regime during the Syrian uprising; *thawrah wahidah fi dawlatayn*, 'One revolution in two states'). The first, and most significant, agreement was the 22 May 1991 Lebanese-Syrian Treaty of Brotherhood, Cooperation and Coordination. This treaty stipulated that Lebanon and Syria should 'work to achieve the highest level of coordination and cooperation in all political, financial, security, cultural, scientific and other fields in a way that would ensure both brotherly states' interests within the framework of each state's sovereignty and independence'. It also states that 'The correlation between the two states' security necessitates that Lebanon will not constitute a threat to Syria's security and vice versa'. It further specifies the Arab identity of both states.[47] In order to fulfill the cooperation stipulated by the treaty, the Syrian-Lebanese Higher Council, consisting of the Presidents, Vice-Presidents, Prime-Ministers and Speakers of Parliament of both states, was formed.[48] Between 1991–2005 the Treaty of Brotherhood, Cooperation and Coordination was followed by 39 other treaties regulating bilateral relations with regard to defence, social affairs, economy, education, health care etc.[49] These agreements and treaties clearly specify that Lebanon and Syria have a shared history, common interests and a shared destiny but also that they are two separate, independent states. As Perthes points out, these agreements were not solely in Syria's interest – Lebanon also had an interest in for instance the unhindered exchange of goods – but their implementation and sometimes lack of complete implementation still reflected the power relationship between the two states to Syria's advantage (Perthes 1996:32). In addition, the agreements established a firm legal framework within which Syria could exercise control over

Lebanon. Syria had thereby successfully established a long term influence and had managed to have it legitimised through these bilateral agreements.

Syrian influence was also evident in areas not covered by official agreements. For instance, Syria had the final word on candidates for political posts and on political decisions (see for instance Norton 1991:457, Thompson 2002:91, Hanf 1993, el-Khazen 2003:613, Salloukh 2005:20, el-Hosseini 2012:17). In the parliamentary elections that took place regularly after the conclusion of the Taif Agreement, the common denominator of the political parties banned from acting freely in Lebanon was their opposition to Syrian hegemony and their demands for a balance in Syrian-Lebanese relations (el-Khazen 2003:613). There were numerous indications of direct Syrian interference in order to secure the election of the 'right' members of parliament and thereby also the election of the 'right' President, Prime Minister and cabinet (Norton 1991:457, Zisser 2001:142, el-Husseini 2012:18). For instance, the designation of Omar Karami as Prime Minister in 1990 was announced in the Syrian press two days prior to his formal nomination (Norton 1991:466). In 1995, when President Elias Hrawi's term ended, Syria managed to have the Lebanese constitution amended and have his term extended for another three years. There were also reports of gerrymandering serving pro-Syrian candidates as the result of new electoral laws, imposed in violation of the electoral law laid down in the Taif Agreement, and Syrian intervention in the formation of candidate lists and alliances. For instance, in 1998 Émile Lahhoud was allowed to run for President after another Syrian-backed amendment of the constitution opened up the possibility for public employees to stand for office. Syria further interfered in appointments within the military and government decisions in Beirut needed a green light from Damascus (Picard 2002:191–192).

Lebanese criticism of Syria was effectively silenced. For instance, the September 1991 Lebanon-Syrian Defence and Security Agreement banned 'all military, security, political and media activity that might harm' either state.[50] In 1993 Human Rights Watch reported that a dozen politicians, journalists and scholars critical of Syria had been assassinated in Lebanon since 1989 and by 1993 Lebanese media 'was forced to toe a Syrian-drawn line' (Middle East Watch vol 3, no 2:24). In 1997, Human Rights Watch further reported that the only TV and radio stations licensed to broadcast news and political programs were those that were not critical of Syria (Human Rights Watch 1 April 1997) and that Syrian security forces operated inside Lebanon, taking Lebanese and stateless Palestinians into custody either inside Syria or in one of the at least five Syrian detention facilities within Lebanon (Sherry 1997:3, see also ICG Middle East Report 86 2009:6). Further, the 1991 Amnesty Law, which freed the different militia leaders from the responsibility of war crimes committed prior to March 1991, was applied to all but Samir Geagea, leader of the Lebanese Forces militia. Geagea, who was charged with murder of political opponents during the war and sentenced to four life sentences, was the only militia leader still in Lebanon who had refused to participate in elections or governments supported by Syria (Picard 2002:165).[51] In mid-2005, Soutien aux Libanais Detenus Arbitrairement (SOLIDA) estimated that at least 200 Lebanese prisoners were being held in solitary confinement in Syria, without having been brought to trial (SOLIDA 2005:2).

Syria was also in control of Lebanese foreign policy, and this was particularly evident with regard to the Arab-Israeli peace process. In 1994, Hafez al-Asad declared that Lebanon and Syria would, provided their demands were fulfilled, sign simultaneous peace agreements with Israel.[52] In December 1999, US President Bill Clinton asked al-Asad to let the Lebanese-Israeli peace negotiations resume. Al-Asad answered that the Lebanese 'preferred to resume talks with Israel only after some headway had been made between the Syrians and the Israelis' (Ross 2004:545–546). Lebanon was thus not trusted to manage its own peace negotiations with Israel.

Bashar al-Asad takes over

When Hafez al-Asad passed away in June 2000 he was replaced by his son Bashar al-Asad. As part of his preparation for the presidential post, Bashar had gradually been given responsibility for the so-called Lebanon portfolio and part of his inauguration speech was dedicated to this subject. 'We consider our relationship with the brother state Lebanon to be a role model for the relationship that should exist between any two Arab states, but this model is not yet perfect. It still requires efforts in order to become exemplary and in order to realise our shared interests in the way that both of us aspire to.'[53] Asad later explained that the most beneficial part in the Syria-Lebanon relationship was the mutual coordination of policy, in terms of decision making and execution, but that his immediate responsibility ended at the border.[54] This indicates his wish to continue in his father's footsteps: maintaining Lebanon as a separate state but ensuring that it behaves in line with Syrian interests.

Israel's decision to withdraw from southern Lebanon (occupied since 1978) in May 2000 was the starting point for an increasingly outspoken, largely Christian, Lebanese opposition to Syrian hegemony in Lebanon. There was talk of 'creeping annexation' and a 'Syrianisation' of Lebanon.[55] These critics saw the Israeli withdrawal as the removal of the last Syrian excuse to maintain a military presence in Lebanon. Open opposition and demands for a change in Syrian-Lebanese relations increased despite arrests and government attempts to stop them (Human Rights Watch 26 April 2000, el-Khazen 2003, al-Jazeerah 13 March 2001). President al-Asad commented on the opposition by stating that,

> whatever happens in Lebanon, whether Syria did right or wrong, the responsible person is a Lebanese [...] When there is no Lebanese problem there will be no Syrian problem in Lebanon. If there is no serious Lebanese wish to solve the problems, Syria can not do a thing no matter how much they blame her or any other state.[56]

He thereby pointed to one of the advantages of the Syrian 'behind the scene' control over Lebanon; the possibility of denying responsibility when things go wrong.

Syrian interference with regard to the 2004 presidential elections was widely discussed in Lebanese press (see for instance *al-Nahar* 17 June 2004, Hatoum 2004). Pro-Syrian Lebanese President Émile Lahhoud's term in office was to expire in November that year. In September the UN Security Council had adopted resolution 1559 declaring its support for a free and fair electoral process, in accordance with Lebanese constitutional rules and without foreign interference (S/RES/1559 2004). The next day, the Lebanese Chamber of Deputies had approved Constitutional Law 585, thereby extending President Lahhoud's term by three years. The law stated that, 'for one and exceptional time, the mandate of the current President of the Republic will be renewed to three additional years that should end on 23 November 2007'. The Lebanese government informed the Security Council that this amendment was made in accordance with Lebanese constitutional rules (S/2004/777 2004:6). The amendment was widely contended in Lebanon and was followed by the resignation of five Lebanese ministers, including Prime Minister Rafiq al-Hariri. The sponsors of resolution 1559 held that the extension of President Lahhoud's term in office was the result of a direct intervention by Syria (S/2004/777 2004:6). Both the Syrian and Lebanese governments denied this. President al-Asad expressed surprise at the fact that the 'same people and states' that had endorsed an extension of Hrawi's presidential term in 1995 opposed an extension in 2004 and said that if the question of accepting an extension or not was based on who was President, this was a clear interference in domestic Lebanese affairs.[57] Political tension rose and additional numbers of political figures joined the traditionally Christian movement of opposition to Syrian hegemony in Lebanon. By early February 2005, all the major groups except the Shia formed part of this opposition. The assassination of former Prime Minister Rafiq al-Hariri in February 2005 further increased the split between supporters and critics of Syria. The two major blocs that came to dominate Lebanese politics after the assassination were the pro-Syrian 8 March coalition and the anti-Syrian 14 March coalition. They were both named after the dates of their huge demonstrations in Beirut in support of, or in opposition to, Syria in March 2005.

Syrian withdrawal: When?

Since its military intervention in 1976, Syria repeatedly stressed that its military presence in Lebanon was temporary only. A final date for a complete withdrawal was never given and conditions for such a withdrawal changed over time. Up until the Israeli invasion in 1982, the Syrian answer as to when withdrawal would take place had been 'When the legitimate Lebanese authorities ask us to'.[58] When Syria was asked to withdraw, conditions had changed as Israel had now entered Lebanon. After the Israeli invasion the answer was 'We are prepared to do whatever the Lebanese government asks us to after an Israeli withdrawal'.[59] On 18 June 2000, when the UN concluded that Israel had withdrawn from southern Lebanon and fully complied with Resolution 425, Syria and Lebanon together claimed that the withdrawal had not been complete since the Shebaa Farms were still under Israeli occupation.[60] Syria stayed, but four redeployments and partial withdrawals from different parts of Lebanon took place between June 2001 and July 2003. What is new during this period is an explicit recognition of the necessity to keep Syrian troops in Lebanon for the protection of *Syrian* security. When asked about a timetable for a complete withdrawal Bashar al-Asad answered that this

> depends on the regional situation, especially [withdrawal from] the Biqaa region because when Israel entered Lebanon in 1982 it came within 20 km from Damascus and Damascus was threatened. So the presence of the Syrian and Lebanese armies in this region is necessary for this reason. But we are no longer present deep inside Lebanon, we are no longer present in the Lebanese cities (al-Nasf 2004).

Starting 2003 Syria saw increasing international pressure for a complete withdrawal. In December 2003, the US Congress passed the *Syria Accountability and Lebanese Sovereignty Restoration Act*, followed in May 2004 by the imposition of US sanctions.[61] The UN Security Council resolution 1559 of September 2004 had not only called for free and fair presidential elections in Lebanon but also for the withdrawal of all remaining foreign forces from Lebanon. Although the resolution did not explicitly mention it, it was obvious that the resolution was aimed at Syria. This was later explicitly confirmed in *The Report of the Secretary General pursuant to Security Council resolution 1559*, which stated that apart from the United Nations Interim Force in Lebanon (UNIFIL), the only significant foreign forces deployed in the country were Syrian (S/2004/777:4). The Syrian government submitted letters to the Security Council and the UN Secretary General in response to the initial draft resolution, declaring any discussion of the draft in the Security Council a dangerous precedent that makes the council 'a tool for illegal interference in the internal affairs of independent and sovereign member states.' (A/58/883). Similarly, Lebanon rejected any discussion on Syrian-Lebanese relations in the Council (A/58/879).

Following the passing of the resolution, Syria redeployed approximately 3,000 troops south of Beirut. According to the Syrian Government, 14,000 Syrian troops then remained in Lebanon. The majority of these were stationed near the Syrian border. Further withdrawals would be determined by the security situation in Lebanon and the region, and through the Joint Military Committee established as a result of the Taif Agreement. The Lebanese Government claimed that its goal was a complete withdrawal of all foreign forces but that the fragile security situation in the region made it difficult to establish a timetable for the full withdrawal of the Syrian troops. The Syrian Government, likewise, informed the UN that Syria and Lebanon were actively discussing the nature and extent of the Syrian deployment in Lebanon but that it could not provide the UN with numbers and timetables for any future withdrawal (S/2004/777:4). Lebanese vice Prime Minister Issam Fares defended the Syrian presence in front of the UN General Assembly saying that Syrian forces were in Lebanon as the result of a request by the Lebanese government but that the Israeli ones (in the Shebaa Farms) should be immediately withdrawn.

Syrian Information Minister, Mahdi Dakhlallah, interviewed on Al-Jazeerah's Open Dialogue (*Hiwar Maftuh*) show in October 2004, recognised that Syria had an influence in Lebanon but said that there was no such thing as Syrian hegemony over it. He asked whether the opposition would be able to criticise Syria openly if Syria had really controlled Lebanon and continued

> Have you ever seen a state controlling another state helping in strengthening the institutions of its army [...] in order for them to be the base of national sovereignty and independence? Have you ever seen a state controlling another state reinforcing the existence of the state as a strong institution [...]? Syria and Lebanon

have common interests through historical ties, but right now the common danger is the danger that the so-called Arab-Israeli conflict will be solved at the cost of Syria and Lebanon.

Asked to comment upon allegations of Syrian interference in Lebanese domestic affairs, Dakhlallah answered: 'Nobody denies that there are problems in the relations but we must judge this relationship within the frame of the currently present dangers. Syria did not enforce any political system or any political solution upon Lebanon' (Al-Jazeerah 23 October 2004). President Bashar al-Asad repeated what Syrian officials had said since the 1970s:

> We always stress the sovereignty of Lebanon, and whenever we are asked about the Syrian forces in Lebanon we say that their presence is temporary and not infinite. The proof of this is the redeployment and the return of part of our forces to Syria. [...] we talk of a strong and independent Lebanon and we recognise its independence (al-Nasf 2004).

Like Dakhlallah, he pointed to Syrian policy as proof of Syria's presence in Lebanon being temporary only and with no ambition to integrate Lebanon into Syria:

> When a state wants to control another state it must have explicit or concealed goals. Why would Syria control Lebanon? Have we asked for money? Are there any natural resources that we want? Have we taken electricity? Have we taken water? We have not taken anything from Lebanon, we have offered blood. If we wanted to control Lebanon, why have we gradually withdrawn our forces during the last five years?[62]

Syrian policies towards Lebanon, 2005–2010: The fall and rise of Syrian influence

Due to the pressures of Security Council resolution 1559 and increasing Lebanese popular demands for a withdrawal of Syrian troops following the murder of ex-Prime Minister Rafiq Al-Hariri (and 22 others) on 14 February 2005, Syrian President Bashar al-Asad announced full withdrawal in March 2005. While stating that this withdrawal took place in order to show the world that Syria respects UN resolutions, al-Asad again stressed that the resolution as such constituted an interference in Lebanese domestic affairs. He also stressed that the Syrian withdrawal was not the end of its role in Lebanon.[63] The last Syrian soldier crossed back into Syria from Lebanon the 26 April 2005.

The Hariri Investigation Commission: From blaming Syria to silence on the Syrian role

In April 2005, UN Security Council resolution 1595 established the International Independent Investigation Commission (UNIIIC) in order to investigate the murder of al-Hariri. The first two reports by the UNIIIC, made public in October and December 2005 respectively, both pointed decisively to Syria as the main suspect. The first report concluded that the assassination could not have been carried out without the knowledge of the Lebanese security services and the approval of top-ranking Syrian security officials (S/2005/662 2005:28, 33). The report was distributed in a way that allowed journalists to track changes to the text and reveal omitted names of high-level Syrian officials, such as President al-Asad's younger brother Maher and his brother in law, Assef al-Shawkat, pointed to as directly involved in the assassination (Young 2010:139). Lebanese witnesses, among them al-Hariri's son, testified that al-Asad had threatened al-Hariri over his opposition to the extension of President Lahhoud's term in office and the UN Fact Finding Mission report stated that Syria held al-Hariri personally responsible for the adoption of resolution 1559 (S/2005/203 2005:5–9). What later developed into the 'false witnesses scandal' put large parts of the incriminating information gathered by the UNIIIC in doubt. Nine reports later, the UNIIIC ended its mission on 28 February 2008, without having solved the case. While the two initial reports had pointed to Syria as impeding the investigation (S/2005/662 2005: 9–10), the final report characterised Syrian cooperation as 'generally satisfactory' (S/2008/752 2008: 2). There was no indication that Syria remained a prime suspect. Based on Security Council resolution 1664, the case was handed over to the Special Tribunal for Lebanon (STL), which opened in The Hague in March 2009. In May the same year, the Tribunal began to focus on Syria's Lebanese ally Hizbullah as possibly being behind the assassination (Follath 2010). This was denied by Hizbullah, which made clear that it would not cooperate with the Tribunal, and pressured the Lebanese government to stop funds for the STL (al-Arabiyyah 22 July 2010). Rumours that a number of Hizbullah members would be indicted caused disturbances during summer and autumn 2010. In October the same year, Syria issued arrest warrants of 33 persons, most of them Lebanese open critics of Syria (Mallat 2010), whom it accused of having deliberately misled the UN investigation. While Bashar al-Asad and Syrian foreign minister Walid al-Muallim both said the warrants had no political importance, they were received by the March 14 Coalition as an indication of disrespect for Lebanese sovereignty (*The Daily Star* 8 October 2010, BBC 4 October 2010).

The killing of Rafiq al-Hariri was followed by a number of additional political assassinations. Between March 2005 and September 2007, eight Lebanese Ministers from the anti-Syrian March 14 coalition and journalists critical of Syrian policies towards Lebanon were assassinated. Like the assassination of Rafiq al-Hariri, these killings remain unresolved and one of the Lebanese investigators was killed in a car bomb in January 2008 (Al-Jazeerah 24 May 2009). Although many Lebanese voices accused Syria, there were no proofs and Damascus denied any involvement. In October 2007, Saad al-Hariri, Rafiq al-Hariri's son and 14 March parliamentary majority leader since the 2005 elections, claimed he had evidence that Syria was planning to assassinate both him and Lebanese Prime Minister Fuad Siniora. These accusations were – naturally – denied by Syria (BBC 31 October 2007).

The May 2008 Doha Agreement

The self-proclaimed Hizbullah 'divine victory' in the summer 2006 war with Israel served as a basis for the organisation to demand greater influence on government decision-making. Its insistence on an increased share of seats in government in order to obtain veto power[64] was rejected by March 14. The following Hizbullah sponsored downtown Beirut sit-in, demanding the resignation of the March 14 government, lasted for 18 months. In November 2007 Émile Lahhoud's extended presidential term was to expire. In the run up to the presidential elections there were accusations of Syrian interference (Bathish 2007) and disagreement between the March 8 and March 14 coalitions made the election of a new president impossible (*Svenska Dagbladet* 23 November 2007). The split between the pro- and anti-Syrian camp intensified further in May 2008 when, in a show of armed force, Hizbullah took over mainly Sunni Muslim West Beirut and the mainly Druze Chouf Mountains in response to the Lebanese government's attempt to dismantle Hizbullah's internal telecommunications system. The 21 May Doha Agreement brought a halt to the conflict, which had risked pushing Lebanon into a third civil war. As a result of the Doha Agreement, Hizbullah's – and thereby Syria's – position in Lebanon was strengthened. The package deal agreed upon in Doha, included not only the end of armed hostilities and the election of President Michel Suleiman but also the revocation of the government decision to remove the Hizbullah telecommunications system. Further, it stipulated the creation of a unity government which effectively gave the March 8 Coalition – and thereby Syria – veto-power. Included was also an agreement on national dialogue in order to promote Lebanese state sovereignty, also a victory for Hizbullah and Syria. The Doha Agreement of May 2008 thus greatly strengthened Syria's possibilities to influence Lebanese politics. The question of the arms of Hizbullah provides an example. One of the most divisive issues in Lebanon since the Syrian withdrawal had been the arms kept by Hizbullah in defiance of UN Security Council resolution 1701. At the time the resolution was passed in 2006, the March 14 Coalition had welcomed it and argued that disarmament of Hizbollah was necessary. When UN Secretary General Ban-Ki Moon in 2009 urged the Lebanese government to fully comply with this resolution, Prime Minister Saad al-Hariri made clear that the government would not move to disarm Hizbullah (CNS News 11 November 2009).

Syrian-Lebanese relations in the post-withdrawal period

Post-withdrawal parliamentary elections in Lebanon produced a majority for the March 14 coalition. The pro-Syrian opposition, March 8, was often able to block political decision making through non-participation. Ties between the March 14 majority and Syria from 2005 until 2008 were non-existent and best characterised by open hostility. Following the May 2008 Doha Agreement, a change in Syrian-Lebanese relations was increasingly evident. While Syrian President Bashar al-Asad had told UN Secretary General Ban-Ki Moon in 2007 that the establishment of bilateral diplomatic relations was impossible as long as the 'illegitimate' March 14 government was in power (Young 2010:154), in August 2008 diplomatic relations were agreed upon by Syria and Lebanon. Syria appointed its first ambassador ever to Lebanon in March 2009 (Al-Jazeerah 29 May 2009). Syrian Deputy Foreign Minister Faysal al-Mekdad commented on the opening of the Lebanese embassy in Damascus saying that it demonstrated the strong historic ties between Syria and Lebanon (Reuters 16 March 2009). Interestingly, the exact same reason had earlier been given by Hafez al-Asad for *not* establishing diplomatic relations with Lebanon.[65] Further changes in Syrian-Lebanese relations followed. Lebanese Prime Minister Saad al-Hariri visited Damascus in December 2009 (BBC 20 December 2009) and signalled further rapprochement in September 2010, claiming that it had been a mistake to blame Syria for the assassination of his father (Black 2010). In March 2010 another one of Syria's harshest critics, Druze leader Walid Junblatt, made up with Syria after publicly apologising on Al-Jazeerah's Open Dialogue (*hiwar maftuh*) show for having insulted Bashar al-Asad 'in the heat of anger' during the previous years (Al-Jazeerah 13 March 2010). Two of the most prominent March 14 leaders had thereby reconciled with their former enemy.

In July 2010 agreements of understanding within finance and security were signed between Lebanese Prime Minister Saad Al-Hariri and Syrian Prime Minister Naji al-Utri. These were the first bilateral agreements signed since the Syrian withdrawal in 2005 (Al-Jazeerah 19 July 2010). They were followed by twelve more bilateral agreements signed between July and October 2010. A thirteenth agreement, on 'media cooperation', was reported by the Lebanese press in October 2010. Contents were not specified but it was reportedly a step in 'fostering relations' between Syria and Lebanon. The Lebanese Minister of Information commented saying that there was a constant need for cooperation with Syria and that Syria could be of help in Lebanon, formulating a new Lebanese media law (*The Daily Star* 8 October 2010).

Following the outbreak of the Syrian civil war, the Lebanese government tried to keep the war on the Syrian side of the border by not supporting either the regime or the rebels. As Hizbollah sided with the Syrian regime and became increasingly involved in actual fighting on the ground in Syria and as Lebanese Sunni fighters joined the Syrian rebels, the government's policy of 'dissociation' proved difficult to uphold. This, in combination with Lebanon's lack of resources for dealing with the enormous influx of Syrian refugees, made Lebanon the state most vulnerable to spillover effects (International Crisis Group 13 May 2013).

Questions regarding the Syrian-Lebanese border

The May 2007 fighting between the Lebanese Army and the Palestinian Fatah al-Islam in Nahr al-Bared refugee camp near Tripoli brought the question of the spuriousness of the Syrian-Lebanese border to the fore. The Lebanese government brought up the issue of a Palestinian military build up in Lebanon both in the UN Security Council and General Assembly, stating that weapons were brought in from Syria (A/61/953). The Lebanon Independent Border Assessment Team (LIBAT), established in April 2007, concluded in its reports that the Syrian-Lebanese border security was insufficient to prevent arms smuggling. In response, the Security Council's forecast report for July 2007 suggested either the establishment of a sanctions committee, the reinforcement of the arms embargo stipulated in resolution 1701[66] or the expansion of the mandate of UNIFIL to include its deployment along the Syrian-Lebanese border (Security Council Report 28 June 2007:7). President al-Asad denied the accusations of arms smuggling and also rejected the idea of UNIFIL troops along the border: 'This is a declaration of war. There are only international forces between warring states and there is no reason to have them between two states that are not at war'.[67] The 2008 LIBAT follow-up report came to the same conclusion; smuggling across the Syrian-Lebanese border was still facilitated by insufficient control (S/2008/582 2008:15–16).

The delineation of the border became a point of contention after the Syrian withdrawal. While still maintaining that the Shebaa farms are Lebanese, Syrian officials announced that it was not Syria's problem to prove this.[68] Lebanese Prime Minister Fuad Siniora in April 2006 said that an agreement on the border with regard to the Shebaa farms would be a sign that Syria accepts a truly independent Lebanon. The Syrian answer was that it would be willing to demarcate the line only after an Israeli withdrawal (SC/8696 2006:3–4). In May 2006 the Security Council adopted resolution 1680, which 'strongly encourages' Syria to respond positively to the request made by the Lebanese government to delineate the common border, and UN resolution 1701 of August 2006 again called for the delineation of the border. Siniora stated in September 2007 that it would help Lebanon demand full Israeli withdrawal if Syria would help prove that the area is Lebanese (al-Arabiyyah 23 January 2006). Although Bashar al-Asad announced in October 2007 that Syria was prepared to demarcate the border even though this would only benefit Israel and hurt 'the resistance' (i.e. Hizbullah),[69] at the end of the year he repeated that an Israeli withdrawal would have to precede such a demarcation. It could only be done on the ground, he explained, and a delineation of the border on a map only was out of the question.[70] This was repeated in August 2008. At the same time, Syria agreed to demarcate the rest of the Syrian-Lebanese border (Ibrahim 2008). In spring 2009, Syrian Deputy Foreign Minister Faysal al-Mekdad, stated that Syria would move to demarcate the border with Lebanon once it had finished demarcating the border adjustments agreed upon with with Jordan in 2005 (Reuters 16 March 2009). Although both Lebanon and Syria then talked of the importance of demarcating the border in June 2010 (*Hürriyet Daily News* 16 June 2010), they failed to reach an agreement on when and how to demarcate it. Again, the Syrian reasons given were the Israeli occupation of the Shebaa Farms and Syria's ongoing demarcation of the Syrian-Jordanian border (Al-Jazeerah 19 July 2010). A Syrian acceptance to demarcate the entire border except the part concerning the Shebaa farms had thus been obtained in 2008 but no practical steps were taken to initiate it. In May 2010 Bashar al-Asad stated that a demarcation of the border was a Syrian-Lebanese matter, and as long as it was a demand from other states, Syria would not agree to it.[71] The issue of the border was raised again during the Syrian civil war when the lack of demarcation was pointed to as a reason for a number of Syrian army incursions into Lebanon (Meguerditchian 2012). The spuriousness of the border was also pointed to by Bashar al-Asad who in 2012 claimed that most weapons held by the rebels had entered through this border.[72] In this context, the March 14 coalition again brought up the issue of deploying both the Lebanese Army and the UNIFIL troops along the Syrian-Lebanese border (El Hassan 2013).

Syrian rhetoric on the post-withdrawal period

Like Hafez al-Asad had explained the 1975–1990 war in Lebanon in terms of a conspiracy, Bashar al-Asad claimed in 2006 that 'the latest events' in Lebanon (UN resolution 1559 and the assassination of al-Hariri) were attempts to cover the failure of the 'occupation forces in Iraq'. Like Hafez al-Asad had claimed that a majority of the Lebanese were in favour of Syria, Bashar al-Asad stated that a majority of the Lebanese citizens want a special relationship with Syria but that some of the Lebanese politicians serve the 'goal of the conspiracy'. There was, according to Bashar al-Asad, 'a small number of groups in Lebanon that reject Syria and the Arab solution [...] this is a temporary condition and therefore we do not consider it a real problem'.[73] Al-Asad also claimed that Lebanon had begun to abandon the Arab nation and its Arab roots and started moving towards Israel.[74] The year 2005, the year of the Syrian withdrawal, is referred to as 'a new 17 May 1983' (in reference to the Lebanese-Israeli treaty that Hafez al-Asad had managed to halt). As his father had maintained that Lebanese critics of Syria did not understand what was best for

Lebanon, Bashar al-Asad made similar claims; 'some Lebanese chose the wrong path'.[75]

Conclusions: Syrian policies towards Lebanon: Irredentism or something else?

Lebanon has long ceased to be perceived as part of the Syrian national territory. Often repeated claims that Syria never recognised the independence of Lebanon (Pipes 1990, Rubin 2007:75, Avi-Ran 1991, Hopwood 1988:24, Podeh 1999:58, el-Husseini 2012:216) are erroneous. As we have seen above, the Syrian National Bloc renounced all claims to Lebanon in exchange for independence from France in the mid-1930s. In the early 1940s, Syria formally recognised Lebanon as a separate and independent state. No Syrian government has demanded the incorporation of Lebanon into Syria since then. Syrian Foreign Minister Khaddam's statement in 1976 that Lebanon should 'return to Syria' was not, in effect, a demand for its return but an emphasis on the importance of the territorial unity of Lebanon. Syrian officials have constantly repeated Syria's respect for Lebanon's independence and sovereignty, especially since the 1976 intervention in the Lebanese civil war. However, the mere fact that Syrian officials have felt the need to constantly stress this suggests that it is not self-evident. Non-verbal policy has confirmed this as Syria more often than not aimed at controlling Lebanon and keeping it within the 'red lines' laid down by Syria. Initially evident mainly in the economic sphere, Syrian efforts to influence Lebanese politics became increasingly evident after the creation of Israel in 1948 and especially after the outbreak of the second Lebanese civil war in 1975. The 1943 Lebanese National Pact, a domestic arrangement regulating power sharing between Lebanon's dominant confessional sects, gave an early hint of Syrian-Lebanese future relations. In accordance with the trade-off spelled out in this pact, neither Lebanese independence nor sovereignty were problems for Syria as long as Lebanon did not in any way constitute a threat to Syria. However, for much of the period studied, Lebanon was perceived as a state harbouring potential threats to Syrian security. Among these threats were Egyptian anti-Syria propaganda in the post-UAR period, possible spill over effects from the Lebanese civil wars and the weakness of the Lebanese army and state – a liability in the context of the Arab-Israeli conflict.

Syrian-Lebanese coordination and cooperation were central themes in the different agreements Syria mediated and tried to implement during the civil war. They were also central to the agreement which finally (almost) put an end to the war, the Taif Agreement of 1989. Although all of these agreements were supposedly between the Lebanese warring parties and meant to end the war, they included specific regulations of Lebanese-Syrian relations, a strong indication of Syria's unwillingness to risk having Lebanon act on its own. During the 1976–2005 period, Syrian ability to control Lebanon increased through direct intervention in its domestic as well as foreign policy. Syrian interference in Lebanese elections, imposition of media censorship and arrests of oppositional individuals ensured pro-Syrian governments, willing to sign agreements and treaties increasingly tying the two states together. Syrian-Lebanese relations did therefore not conform to the Syrian description of these relations as cooperation and coordination between two equals.

Although the 2005 withdrawal was premature from a Syrian point of view, there are no indications that Syria had planned to keep a military presence in Lebanon forever. The Syrian troops, amounting to approximately 40,000 at the end of the civil war, were gradually withdrawn – although not at the pace stipulated by the Taif agreement. Neither were there indications of Syria actually trying to integrate Lebanon into Syria. While a demarcation of the border had not taken place by May 2014, the *existence* of the border was not questioned. No demographical changes were made in Lebanon. The Syrian guest workers, numbering between 250,000 and one million prior to the Syrian withdrawal, were not settlers – and Syria assisted Lebanon in the rebuilding of its army and state institutions. The 1990–2004 period was when Syria, with a heavy military presence and firmly in control of Lebanese politics, would have attempted incorporation had this been the ultimate Syrian goal. The slogan guiding Syrian policies during this time period, 'One people in two states' clearly indicates that Syria did not see Lebanon as part of its national territory and an incorporation was therefore not the goal. The goal was to protect Syrian security and, therefore, have Lebanon as an obedient vassal state. Accusations of Syrian irredentism and desires to annex Lebanon are therefore oversimplifications of the very complex relationship between the Syrian state and the Lebanese territory.

CHAPTER 4

FROM FORGOTTEN TO STOLEN TERRITORY: SYRIAN POLICIES TOWARDS HATAY

As outlined in chapter two, the border between Turkey and French-mandated Syria had been decided upon in 1921, confirmed in 1923 and demarcated in 1930. In the 1923 Lausanne Treaty, Turkey had renounced all rights and title over territories situated outside the frontiers laid down in the treaty. At the time of the establishment of the French mandate in Syria, the region of Alexandretta had been rewarded an autonomous regime within the state of Aleppo and had thereby been marked as special from the beginning. As the 1936 Franco-Syrian treaty was silent on the future of the autonomy of the region, the Turkish government raised the issue of the Turkish speaking population in Alexandretta. Although Syrian President Hashim al-Atasi eventually declared Syria's preparedness to maintain the autonomy (Honvault 2002:214), the Turkish government expressed fears that the special status given to the Turkish language and culture would not be respected and instead demanded independence for Alexandretta. France's position was that, bound by article IV in the League of Nations Mandate Treaty for Syria and Lebanon, it could not detach Alexandretta from a future independent Syria. Since the French and Turkish views were too different for an agreement to be reached, the question of the future of Alexandretta was handed over to the League of Nations in December 1936. At the end of January 1937, the League issued a report stipulating that Alexandretta would remain part of independent Syria but with the status of 'collective protectorate'; protection against foreign attack would be the responsibility of Turkey and France, while Syria would handle the foreign relations of the area (Khadduri 1946:419). As Syria's own foreign relations were exclusively controlled by France, it had no say in the matter. It nevertheless reacted to the resolution in a memorandum to the French Ministry of Foreign Affairs protesting against the League's decision. Likewise, the Parliament of the State of Syria rejected the League of Nations' decision (Honvault 2002:215) and there were strikes and demonstrations all over the country (Güçlü 1994:77, Shields 2011:78–79). Syrian Prime Minister Jamil Mardam stressed that Alexandretta was an inseparable part of Syria while Foreign Minister Saadallah al-Jabiri explained that he would be among the first to march should it be necessary to defend the area by violent means (Güçlü 1994:77). The French High Commissioner, in an attempt to calm the fury, pointed to the 'positive aspects' of the League's decision: the region would remain within the borders of Syria, the fact that it would be de-militarized would keep Turkey from occupying it and the creation of a free-trade zone in Alexandretta would benefit the whole region. But he also made sure Syrian officials understood that should they reject the decision of the League of Nations, they would also risk having to face a Turkish refusal to formally recognize the territorial integrity of Syria (Shields 2011:80). In May 1937, the League of Nations decided that an autonomous regime with a Legislative Assembly, consisting of 40 deputies representing the various communities, was to be set up in Alexandretta. Elections for this Assembly were to be held in March and April 1938 and representation was to be proportionate according to the size of each community. As Alexandretta held a mixture of different ethnic, religious and linguistic groups, and as the inhabitants did not necessarily identify with one group only, the classification of the inhabitants into different communities turned into a major conflict (Shields 2011:3).

In July 1938, France and Turkey signed a Treaty of Friendship whereby they agreed not to enter alliances or in any way assist in aggression against the other (Khadduri 1945:422). They would also together guarantee the territorial integrity of Alexandretta. According to Güçlü (1994:111), 'the Syrians' denounced the Treaty as a betrayal that sacrificed Alexandretta for a Franco-Turkish military alliance. Although the Syrian government still had no say, it was allowed to send a representative to the following official Turkish-French negotiations on the future of the region. Decisions of substance had, however, been made during secret French-Turkish negotiations (Honvault 2002:224), and the future of Alexandretta had already been decided. This was probably evident to the National Bloc government in Syria, which throughout 1937–1939 raised claims to the Lebanese city of Tripoli as compensation for Alexandretta, the location of mandated Syria's only modern port (Zamir 2000:219).

From possible partition to Turkish annexation

When the registration lists for the elections were finalized, they held a Turkish majority. Sources differ concerning whether this was the result of Turkish pressure and French-Turkish arrangements or not (see Guilquin 2000:64, Alantar 1992:275, Güçlü 2000:112, Bandazian 1967:121 note 32, Honvault 2002:217). At the same time, negotiations between a representative of the Syrian Government and the Turkish Government, for the possible division of Alexandretta, had taken place. The Turkish suggestion was that the city of Antioch would be given to Turkey, that there would be an exchange of Arab and Turkish populations and that Syria would be given the right to use the Iskenderun port. The Syrian Government could not accept that Antioch would be Turkish and refused. When Syria was later ready to accept this proposal, Turkey had already struck a better deal with France and rejected any further discussion of partition (Khadduri 1945:422, Massigli 1964:68).

The Legislative Assembly held its first meeting in the beginning of September 1938, elected an all-Turkish cabinet and adopted the Turkish name *Hatay Devleti* (the State of Hatay) for the new autonomous state, still within the borders of Syria. A good indication of the state of things, the President and Prime Minister of Hatay were at the same time deputies in the Turkish Parliament in Ankara, representing the Turkish constituencies of Antalya and Gaziantep (Güçlü 1994:113).

The Assembly passed acts adopting the Turkish criminal and civil codes and the Turkish national anthem. Turkish citizens could enter and leave Hatay without a passport or visa and the same was true for people going from Hatay to Turkey (Bandazian 1967: 130–131). Despite the monetary union with Syria, the League of Nations had decided upon, the Turkish lira was adopted as the currency of Hatay in March 1939. Hatay was, from then on, in practice controlled by Turkey (Güçlü 1994:112–113).

A French-Turkish agreement for the Turkish annexation of Hatay was signed in Ankara on 23 June 1939. At its final meeting on 29 June 1939, the Assembly of Hatay approved the annexation and dissolved itself (Güçlü 1994:126). Hatay had thereby left French-mandated Syria to become the sixty-third province of the Republic of Turkey. The secession was defended by France at the League of Nations as being necessary for the protection of Syria from Turkish aggression (Crowfoot 1942:131). Following the annexation, Turkey added the areas of Dörtyol, Hassa and Erzin to Hatay. As a result, today's Turkish province of Hatay measures 5570 km² whereas the mandated Alexandretta measured 4800 km² (Guilquin 2000:29).

As a result of the Turkish annexation, a number of demographical changes took place within Hatay. During the six months following the annexation, (male) inhabitants above the age of 18 were given the right to chose between staying and becoming Turkish citizens, or opt for citizenship within either French mandated Syria or Greater Lebanon. If opting for emigration, they were given an additional 18 months to bring their movable assets and establish themselves in their new states (Massigli 1964:213). According to Picard, almost half of the Arabic-speaking Sunni Muslims left. According to Gilquin and Picard, the annexation also produced 'an exodus of Armenians', the only community directly encouraged by the French authorities to leave and the only community to receive financial assistance (Picard 1983:51, Gilquin 142).[1] One thousand sixty-eight families from the six Armenian villages of Musa Dağ were moved to the Biqaa valley in Lebanon.[2] The descendants of these families today make up the town of Anjar (which after the Syrian invasion of Lebanon 1976 turned into the base of the Syrian intelligence forces and the control centre for the Syrian command in Lebanon. Anjar was the last town the Syrian army left in 2005.) The total number of people leaving for Syria has been estimated at 50,000, out of which 22,000 were Armenian, 10,000 Alawites, 10,000 Arab Sunnis and 5,000 Arab Christians (Khoury 1987:513).

Syrian reactions to the loss of Alexandretta

At the time of the annexation, Syrian press was deeply critical of the move, but sources on Syrian official reactions to the development of the Alexandretta issue are scarce. It should be noted that Adil Arslan, representative of the Syrian government to the largely fictitious official French-Turkish negotiations, commented on the Alexandretta issue in his diary in early 1939. He argued that Syria would need Turkish support in order to obtain independence. Therefore Syria should recognise Turkish sovereignty over Alexandretta in exchange for Turkish recognition of Syrian independence (Honvault 2002:225). Although Syria never officially recognised the Turkish annexation, a policy similar to that suggested by Arslan was pursued by both Syria and Turkey in the years to come. Syria rejected a Turkish demand for Syrian recognition of the annexation when it obtained formal independence in 1943[3] (Sanjian 1956:383) but later largely conformed to the policy Arslan had suggested. In 1946, when Syria obtained full independence, Iraq helped mediate a Turkish-Syrian deal where Syria agreed not to make any formal demands for the return of Hatay. In exchange, Turkey would recognise Syrian independence (Liel 2001:193). The problem was thus temporarily solved. In the long run, however, the lack of a formal recognition of the border created insecurity and remained an irritant in Syrian-Turkish relations until the early 2000s.

Early independence: Syrian policies, 1946–1969

A good indication of the second-degree importance of Hatay for Syrian decision makers, a reading of Syrian President Shukri al-Quwatli's speeches during the early independence period shows that he did not mention the area at all. Nor was the French decision to allow a Turkish annexation of the area among the complaints about French mandate policies Syria brought to the UN in 1946 (UN Yearbook 1946:341). Honouring its agreement with Turkey, Syria did not demand the return of the area. But at the same time it made sure its policies could not be mistaken for an indirect recognition of the new border. For instance, when Turkey offered to create a free zone in the port of Iskenderun and to grant Syrian requests insofar as they did not conflict with Turkey's own vital interests, it refused (Sanjian 1956:383).

In 1947, Syrian Prime Minister Jamil Mardam raised the issue of Hatay and suggested Turkish-Syrian negotiations in order to settle the dispute. It is unclear what kind of solution Syria was looking for, and Turkey made clear it was not interested (Soysal 1998/9:102). At the same time, a 1947 CIA document mentions rumours 'coming from Damascus' that Syria would take the case of Hatay to either the International Court of Justice or the UN Security Council. This was denied by Prime Minister Mardam. Pointing to Syrian public opinion and the Syrian nationalist press as standing in the way of a Syrian recognition of Hatay as Turkish territory, the document also stresses the fact that no Syrian government had so far made 'an energetic claim' to Hatay (CIA 28 February 1947).

With the coup of Syrian Commander in Chief Husni al-Zaim in March 1949, Syrian policy towards the Hatay question changed briefly. With ambitions to carry out reforms inspired by the Turkish model (see Moubayed 2000:35–36 and Seale 1965:58–63), al-Zaim announced during a press conference in Ankara that territorial claims to Hatay had been relinquished and that all Syrian parties advocating irredentism had been dissolved[4] (Sanjian 1956:386). Al-Zaim's reign came to an end in August the same year. So did the verbal recognition of Turkish sovereignty over Hatay, and it has not been repeated since. Al-Zaim's successor Colonel Sami al-Hinnawi made clear that Syrian public opinion did not agree with al-Zaim's policy (Sanjian 1956:385). The fact that al-Hinnawi pointed specifically to al-Zaim's policy towards Hatay but not to his attempts to make peace with Israel (see chapter two), indicates that of the two, recognising the Turkish annexation was at the time – when Syria had made territorial gains in 1948–1949 Arab-Israeli war – considered a more serious misstep.

According to Liel, Syria 'later' published maps where Hatay was shown as Syrian territory. Exactly when these maps began to appear is unclear, but they were present by the three-year reign of President Adib al-Shishakli (1951–1954). His Arab Liberation Movement Party produced maps of the Arab Homeland including not only Hatay but also a considerable amount of additional now Turkish territory. However, according to Turkey's Chargé d'Affaires in Damascus at the time, İsmail Soysal, al-Shishakli personally told him that the Hatay question was brought up for internal consumption only and that no Syrian leader neglecting the issue could expect to remain in office (Soysal 1998/9:101). Even though the Hatay question was not actively brought up by the following governments, the region remained part of Syria on Syrian maps (Sanjian 1956:388). According to Liel, Syria in 1955 again approached Turkey for negotiations over Hatay but was told by the Turkish Prime Minister Adnan Menderes not to 'play with fire' (Liel 2001:193). Again, a reading of Syrian President Shukri al-Quwatli's speeches from this period (1955–1958) shows that he did not mention the area at all.

The 1958–1961 UAR period saw increased Syrian-Turkish tension. Although this was mostly caused by Cold War-related issues, Hatay was a clear irritant. For instance in 1960, the National Union Party of the UAR adopted a resolution calling for the return of the area.[5] Yilmaz holds that Hatay became a 'national obsession' in the Syrian press during the UAR period (2006:112), but does not substantiate this claim.[6] There are no indications that the UAR interest in Hatay went beyond verbal statements, and in 1961 UAR President Naser reportedly used diplomatic channels to inform Turkey that he did not intend to challenge Turkish sovereignty over the area (Walz 1961). In 1963, the Director of Financial Planning at the Syrian Ministry of Planning published an article where the surface of Syria is specified at 185,180 square kilometers (Helbaoui 1963:698) – the surface of Syria not counting Hatay. Since the article also contains a map where Hatay is included as part of Syria the surface specified cannot be understood as a Syrian recognition of Turkish sovereignty over Hatay. Two years later, during Turkish-Syrian-Iraqi water negotiations, Syria refused to link the Euphrates and Tigris rivers to the Orontes River, which originates in Lebanon, passes through Syria and crosses into Hatay. This refusal was based on the Syrian claim that Orontes, unlike the Euphrates and Tigris, did not flow on Turkish territory (Çarkoğlu 2001a:244), a clear rejection of Turkish sovereignty over Hatay.

Syrian policies towards Hatay, 1970–1998

The early 1970s saw a shift in Syrian policy towards Hatay. The area remained on Syrian maps, but otherwise decreased in visibility. According to Soysal, the yearly 'Occupied Iskandarunah' demonstrations were banned in 1972 (Soysal 1998/9:102).[7] A reading of President Hafez al-Asad's speeches, announcements and interviews 1970–2000 shows that the area is not mentioned at all. Lucien Bitterlin, in his *Alexandrette: Le Munich de l'Orient* (1999), noted that during his interviews with Syrian President Hafez al-Asad – who dwelled extensively on the 'artificial borders drawn by imperialism' and 'the injustices done to the Arab nation' – Hatay was never even mentioned (1999:8). Likewise, during his visit to southern Cyprus a year after the Turkish invasion and occupation of the northern part of the island, Al-Asad expressed appreciation for the Cypriot 'support for our struggle against Zionism, which occupies our Arab land'.[8] Turkey was not mentioned at all. Another indication of the second-degree importance of Hatay can be found in a comment made following the Iraqi declaration of war on Iran in 1980. It is made clear that any border/territorial conflict not involving Israel had to be put on hold until the Palestine question had been solved:

> This war is diverting attention from our most important national cause. How do we look upon questions of borders? Can we settle a border conflict at the expense of an existential conflict? Where is the Arab state that does not have a border problem? If all Arab states with a border problem were to declare war, the minor [problems] would cover the major one, the Palestinian cause would have an end worse than any other issue in history and Israel would rule the region.[9]

During the 1980s and 1990s, Syrian officials occasionally spoke of Hatay as Syrian territory. In his 1988 book *Suriyah 1916–1946: al-tariq ila-l-hurriyah* (Syria 1916–1946: The Road to Freedom), Walid al-Muallim, later Syrian Ambassador to Washington, chief negotiator with Israel and since 2006 Foreign Minister of Syria, argues that Hatay falls within the 'natural borders' of Syria (1988:299–300) and that it was unjustly taken away. He does not, however, comment on events after the Turkish annexation and makes no demand for its return. A few years later, the five volume *al-mujam al-jughrafi li-l-qutr al-arabi al-suri* (The Geographic Dictionary of the Syrian Arab Region) was published. It treats Hatay as part of Syria and makes no mention of the Turkish annexation (Rooke 2006:135). Further, in 1995, as in 1965, Syria refused to include the Orontes River in Syrian-Turkish negotiations over water allocations on the basis that it was a domestic river with no connection to Turkey.[10] However, when Syrian Defence Minister Mustapha Tlas in 1997 wrote an article critisising the evolving Turkish-Israeli relations, specifically pointing to the city of Iskenderun as central to Turkish-Israeli cooperation, he did not mention that according to all Syrian maps this city was situated within the Syrian borders (Tlas 1997). The following year, Walid al-Muallim, then ambassador to Washington, appeared on an Arab American TV channel claiming that Syria would focus on Hatay once the Golan Heights had been regained (*Turkish Daily News* 8 May 1998). Straight forward as this statement seems, it should be noted that it was made during a period of tense Syrian-Turkish relations, which a few months later led to the 1998 October crisis. It should also be noted that it was made to a channel far removed from the ordinary Syrian (and Turkish) audience and not repeated elsewhere. It is therefore not likely that it mirrored actual Syrian plans for the future.

Until the late 1990s, Turkey accused Syria of encouraging high birth rates among the Arab inhabitants (Mu'awwed 1998:197). It also suspected that 'certain government circles' in Syria provided inhabitants of Arab origin with money in order to buy land in Hatay for relatives in Syria (Ömer Onhan, interview Ankara, 22 April 2002), an issue discussed by the Turkish National Security Council in April 1997 (*Turkish Daily News* 2 April 1997). Turkey further claimed that

Syria was broadcasting 'its own propaganda material' to the inhabitants of Turkey's border provinces, thus including Hatay (*Turkish Daily News* 17 June 1996). In January 1996 the Turkish National Security Council met to discuss a report on Syrian efforts to organise Arab and Kurdish 'separatist elements' in Hatay (Mufti 2003). One such separatist element Turkish security officials worried about was a new secret organization, the Popular Front for the Liberation of Iskandarun (*al-jabhah al-shaabiyyah li-tahrir liwa iskandarun*), which had reportedly formed in Hatay during the mid-1990s. According to pamphlets distributed in several cities, this front aimed at demanding linguistic and cultural rights for Arabs in Hatay and called for a halt to Turkish-Israeli cooperation. It also had the long-term goal of reuniting Hatay and Syria (Khalifah 1999). While not much more came out of this organization at the time, a militia carrying the same name appeared as a pro-regime force in the context of the Syrian civil war. The commander of this militia had, according to Turkish sources, been a leading member of the earlier organization and a link between separatists in Hatay and the Syrian intelligence service (Albayrak 2013).

Another point of contention for Turkey was Syria's acceptance of students of Arab origin from Hatay into Syrian universities. They were accepted without having to pass the otherwise mandatory entrance exams and were given scholarships to cover living expenses. These students often worked within the Turkish broadcasts of Syrian radio, initiated in 1990.[11] In October 1998, Turkish media reported that one such student had been arrested at a Hatay-Syria border crossing trying to smuggle photos of military installations in Hatay to the Syrian secret service (*Turkish Daily News* 16 October 1998). The same year, as a consequence of a decision by the Turkish Ministry of Education to no longer accept Syrian diplomas, the number of these students began to decrease.[12]

The 1998 turning point in Syrian-Turkish relations

On the Turkish side, Syrian insistence on including Hatay as part of Syrian maps became part of the perceived 'Syria package', i.e. the problems and issues that Turkey felt were increasingly worsening bilateral relations (Maliha Altunışık, interview Ankara 29 April 2002). Syria's role as the main supporter of the Kurdish separatist organisation Partiya Karkerên Kurdistan (PKK) had become increasingly evident following the end of the Cold War and when the PKK started carrying out attacks in Hatay in the mid-1990s Turkish-Syrian relations deteriorated considerably (Alantar 2000:153). In July 1998, the Turkish Prime Minister Masut Yılmaz pronounced the most severe Hatay-related warning to Syria in many years: 'those who have their eyes set on our territory are bound to go blind [...] those who print maps showing Iskandarunah as their own territory should not forget the historical realities' (*L'Orient Le Jour* 24 July 1998). Worsening relations resulted in a showdown in October 1998, followed by the signing of the Adana Agreement which put an end to Syrian support of the PKK. According to Gilquin, the Hatay question resurfaced in the Syrian press during the crisis (2000:159). However, as Guilquin does not give references and as Syrian newspaper *Tishreen*, known as 'the paper of the President', did not mention it (Lundgren Jörum 2006:183 note 38), this is doubtful. Syria thus kept domestic silence on the Hatay question. Meanwhile, papers in other Arab countries carried an interview with Syrian Information Minister Muhammad Salman at the height of the crisis, stating that 'Syria will not renounce its rights [...] the Iskandarunah question is a national cause on which one can not make concessions' (*L'Orient Le Jour* 20 October 1998, *al-Bayan* 20 October 1998).

After the signing of the Adana Agreement the question of Hatay again decreased in visibility but did not entirely disappear. The region remained on Syrian maps but Syrian officials seemed eager to avoid discussions about it. When asked about the map by a Turkish journalist, Syrian Information Minister Muhammed Salman, who less than six months earlier had stressed that Syria could not make concessions with regard to Hatay, answered: 'I do not want to comment on this subject. Whenever there is a desire to strain bilateral relations, this subject is put on the agenda' (*Turkish Daily News* 11 March 1999). During the Berlin International Tourism fair in March 2000, the Syrian delegation distributed both maps showing the border separating Hatay from Syria as a 'temporary border' and maps where Hatay was entirely included within the Syrian borders. When asked about these maps by Turkish journalists, the Syrian representatives said that the maps indicated that the people living on both sides of the border were related and that there are historical links between Hatay and 'the rest of Syria' (Micallef 2006:141).[13] Interviewed in the evening news on Turkey's NTV channel, Syrian Foreign Minister Farouq al-Shara stated in 2000 that no solution to the Hatay question was needed in order to boost bilateral relations and that Syria hoped to solve the problem in the upcoming years (*Turkish Daily News* 6 February 2000). Again, although the solution Syria hoped to reach was not specified, the message sent through these responses was that Syria did not want these maps to stir up trouble with Turkey. Nevertheless, Turkish media reported in June 2000 that in the context of the Syrian-Israeli negotiations over the Golan Heights, President Al-Asad had, during one of his meetings with US President Bill Clinton, claimed that Hatay was occupied Syrian territory (*Turkish Daily News* 15 June 2000).

Bashar al-Asad takes over: No claims, no recognition continues

With the signing of the 1998 Adana Agreement, Syrian-Turkish relations improved considerably. This was particularly evident after Bashar al-Asad took over as president of Syria in 2000. Like his father, who had not mentioned Hatay in any of his speeches, Bashar al-Asad did not mention the area in his inauguration speech (while both the Golan Heights and Lebanon were elaborated upon). Neither has he done so in any of his following speeches. The Hatay question, however, initially still constituted a problem. Although no Syrian official sources commented on Hatay, there were reports in both Turkish and Arab (non-Syrian) press on how the Syrian refusal to sign a Declaration of Principles, containing a formal recognition of Hatay as Turkish territory, stalled a further development of relations (Arabicnews.com 9 and 18 January 2001). The refusal impeded both a planned visit by President al-Asad as well as Syrian ministerial visits to Turkey (Arabicnews.com 3 October 2000 and 19 July 2001, Oruc 2000). The lack of a Syrian recognition of the border was also reported as a reason for Turkey's reluctance to join tripartite talks on the water issue with Syria and Iraq (*Turkish Daily News* 26 August 2001).

In 2001, the *Syria 2000: Geographical and Economic Yearbook* (2001), published by the National Information Centre (NICE) in Damascus, included Hatay as part of Syria on its maps, claimed that the Orontes river flows through Lebanon and Syria but did not mention that it continues into Turkey (2001:44). Nevertheless, the same year, at the Hannover Fair in June, the Syrian delegation reportedly removed its maps showing Hatay as part of Syria when Turkish authorities complained (Kemal Kirişci, interview Istanbul 30 May 2002). In 2002, Syria turned down a Turkish suggestion to jointly re-demarcate the border on the basis that it was not clear where the border should be drawn (Ömer Onhan, interview Ankara 24 April 2002). Taken together, Syrian messages thus continued to be mixed and evasive.

Turkish media continued to report on the statements of Syrian representatives concerning Hatay during visits to Turkey. In September 2001, former Syrian Ambassador to Turkey, Muhammad Said al-Bunni, assured that Hatay was not a major problem as there were no claims being taken to international court and no fighting over it (Sabriibrahimoğlu 2001). Likewise, at a conference at Istanbul's Boğaziçi University in February 2002, Syrian Deputy Minister of Education, when asked by a Turkish researcher whether Syria considered the Hatay question solved, answered: 'Is there such a question? You talk about Hatay, I don't' (Zeynep Özden Oktav, interview Istanbul 1 May 2002). When Syrian Foreign Minister Farouq al-Shara visited Ankara in February 2003, Turkish media reported that he signaled that the Hatay question was a closed chapter as far as Syria was concerned. Among other things, he reportedly stated that recently published school textbooks portrayed Hatay as Turkish territory (Galip Över 2003). Al-Shara's claim is correct to the extent that Syrian history textbooks from this period state that the area was unrightfully taken from Syria and given to Turkey. They do not call for its return.[14] However, Syrian *qawmiyyah* (approx. Arab national education) textbooks for the same period include maps where the area is clearly marked as Syrian.[15] None of these statements reported in Turkish media were mentioned in Syrian media, where silence was kept.

A former advisor to President Hafez al-Asad, George Jabbour, explained in 2003 that nobody expected Hatay to be returned to Syria but that Syria would like to have some kind of privileges in the area (thus accepting a solution Turkey had suggested following the annexation) (George Jabbour, interview Damascus 18 July 2003). But both Turkish and Syrian representatives maintained that Hatay was not discussed at all during bilateral meetings. Instead, all efforts were focused on building mutual confidence and improving bilateral relations in every possible field (Ömer Onhan, interview Ankara 24 April 2002 and Atiyah al-Judah, interview Damascus 8 July 2003).[16] One such 'improvement' was made at Syrian universities. As mentioned earlier, a point of contention for Turkey had been Syria's acceptance of students from Hatay to Syrian universities. Although the number of students from Hatay had decreased since 1998, in 2002 students of Arab origin from Hatay at Damascus university were estimated at between 100 and 200. In 2003 there were 70 such students. All new students coming from Hatay to study in Damascus that year were refused. No official reason was given[17] (Lundgren Jörum 2013:118).

Syrian policies towards people from Hatay of Arab origin indicated that they were not seen as Syrians. When coming to Syria for work or studies, they were treated as any other Turkish citizen by Syrian authorities.[18] This had not been the case in 1947 when a Syrian court freed a man of charges for crossing the border between Hatay and Syria without a passport, as no passport was needed 'when traveling inside Syria' (Sanjian 1956:385). Prior to the lifting of visa requirements in 2009, all Turkish citizens – including those of Arab origin in Hatay – had to apply for visas to enter Syria. When a special holiday regime for the Turkish-Syrian border was established in 1999, people from both sides were allowed to visit relatives on the other side. Starting 2002, the two border crossings in Hatay were included in the program (Ufuk Gökçen, interview Damascus 14 May 2002). Within the framework of this program a distinction had thus been made between Turkish citizens with relatives on the Syrian side and those without such family ties, but there were no indications that people from Hatay were treated differently from people with family ties along other parts of the border.

The 2004 turning point

In January 2004, the Syrian presidential visit to Turkey finally took place. Although some Turkish media reported that a formal recognition of the border would be pronounced during the visit (Duygy 2004), this did not happen. Al-Asad's comments regarding Hatay were not different from what other Syrian officials had repeated since the 1998 crisis, 'This issue is not a topic today. It has been on the agenda for almost 60 years. [...] With time we will be able to find a solution'. He further declared that Hatay would not be discussed during the visit (*Milliyet* 5 January 2004). Interviewed on CNN Türk, al-Asad stated that it was only natural for states to initially focus on points of agreement when trying to solve points of difference. Therefore Hatay was, at the moment, not an issue to be discussed. It would be in the future, he explained, and then it would be necessary to find a solution satisfactory to both states. Before trying to find that solution, bilateral relations would have to develop further (Syrian Arab News Agency 5 January 2004).

While not signaling any change in Syrian policy towards Hatay, it should be noted that Al-Asad's comments were reported by the Syrian news agency and one of the Syrian newspapers (*Tishreen* 6 January 2004). Although the other Syrian papers, *al-Baath* and *al-Thawrah*, did not mention his Hatay-related comments, the domestic silence on Hatay had been broken. A free trade area was planned along the Syrian-Turkish border and at the end of 2004, Syria and Turkey signed a free trade agreement which reportedly defined the borders of the two states (Stern 2005). However, the agreement later published on the homepage of the Syrian Ministry of Finance did not mention the border, and officials of the Turkish Ministry of Foreign Affairs denied that the agreement involved a definition of borders.[19] A Turkish diplomatic source said 'a certain accord' had been reached with regard to Hatay but what this accord consisted of remained unclear (Acinci 2004). The following year, Turkish media again reported that an agreement concerning a recognition of the border had in fact been signed, but that Syrian TV continued to show Hatay as Syrian territory during for instance weather forecasts (*Milliyet* 19 January 2005).

In 2006, the website of the Syrian Arab News Agency for the first time referred to Hatay as 'the Turkish province Hatay' (Syrian Arab News Agency 17 October 2006), albeit only in its English version. The following year, Syria and Turkey agreed to the renovation of the present border gates and the opening of new ones.[20] Although it remains unclear whether any new gates would be constructed on the Hatay border, an agreement to restore the two functioning ones clearly indicates that these border gates, and hence the border itself, were meant to stay.

During the following years, Syrian media occasionally reported on Syrian-Turkish cooperation and exchanges that implicitly recognised Hatay as Turkish. Although neither Hatay nor the border were mentioned, cities in, and delegations from, Hatay were understood to be Turkish (see for instance *al-Baath* 25 February 2008, *Tishreen* 14 November 2009). When Syrian press occasionally referred to Hatay as a Turkish region, its Turkish name (and not *liwa Iskandarun* as it is known in Arabic) was used (see for instance *Tishreen* 19 July 2009, 27 October 2010, *Tishreen* 11 September 2010). A formal recognition of the border was, however, still out of question. Towards the end of 2009, an agreement on the amount of water to be released from Turkey to Syria via the Euphrates and Tigris rivers was reportedly stalled due to a Syrian refusal to officially recognise Hatay as Turkish (*Today's Zaman* 24 December 2009).[21] President Bashar al-Asad still commented on the signing of a number of other agreements during the same period saying that the map of the Middle East had been redrawn and that the Turkish-Syrian border had 'been broken' (*inkasar*).[22] Among the agreements signed was one whereby compensation would be given to about half the people whose land and property had been confiscated on either side of the border (*Il Mediterraneo* 4 March 2009). Although Liel claims the issue of nationalised property on both sides of the border had been settled in 1972–1973 (2001:194), secret talks concerning this had reportedly been initiated in 2003 in order to reach a final settlement.[23] Negotiations meant to settle the question of confiscated property through compensation must also be understood as an acceptance of the fact that the border separating Syria from Hatay was meant to stay.

The Syrian insistence on the Orontes as a river outside of Turkish territory ended in 2010 when it agreed to construct a shared Turkish-Syrian Friendship dam on this river (BBC Arabic 21 June 2010). Syrian press reported on the plans without mentioning its connection to Hatay (*al-Baath* 8 October 2010). As the Syrian and Turkish governments agreed on national jurisdiction on each side of the dam (Daoudy 2013:142), the border was indirectly recognised. However, instead of being formally and openly recognised and demarcated, it was to be blurred by the construction of the dam. Only weeks prior to the outbreak of the Syrian uprising, the foundation stones were laid in Hatay and, on the Syrian side, in Idlib in February 2011. During the groundbreaking ceremony in Hatay, Turkish Prime Minister Erdoğan welcomed Syrian Prime Minister Naji al-Utri in Turkey and spoke of the construction of the dam as a history changing event that would bring Syria and Turkey closer together (TGRT Haber TV 6 February 2011). As a result of the Syrian civil war and the extremely tense Syrian-Turkish relations it brought, construction was halted in 2012 (*Gerçek Gündem* 14 October 2012).

Syrian maps after 2003

Although Syria had in practice gradually shown a recognition of Hatay as Turkish territory since 2004, most Syrian maps continued to depict the area as Syrian. There had, however, been signals that this could change. In 2003, the homepage of the Syrian Ministry of Information included a passage saying that Syria's surface stretches over '185,180 km² (not counting liwa' iskandarun, the surface of which is 5,000 km²)',[24] suggesting that Hatay was not necessarily part of Syria. Simultaneously, the English version of the homepage had a map of Syria where the region was included. Later versions of the homepage have not mentioned Hatay but the region has been included whenever there have been maps of Syria (Lundgren Jörum 2013:121). In August 2005, Syrian officials brought a map with Hatay as part of Syria to a meeting with Turkish officials. The Syrian Minister of Oil, Ibrahim Haddad, apologised saying that this had been a mistake and that the map would be immediately corrected (*Radikal* 16 August

2005). Perhaps as a way of rectifying the embarrassment caused during this meeting, Syrian newspaper *Tishreen* in September 2005 for the first time published a map of Syria without Hatay (Wieland 2006:69). In 2010, the Syrian Arab News Agency's website included a map which portrayed Hatay as part of Syria but still marked it as different: while all of Syria's provinces were green in colour, Hatay was gray. No explanation for this difference in colour was given (Lundgren Jörum 2013:121). Syrian TV showed maps of Syria with a large legend covering Hatay in order to avoid specifying whether Hatay was Turkish or Syrian (Moubayed 2013:74). At the same time, in 2008, when Samir al-Taqi, General Director of the Orient Centre for International Studies in Damascus, covered Hatay on the Syrian map that hung in his office as a friendly gesture when welcoming a Turkish delegation, he received a call from the Ministry of Information telling him to uncover it.[25] As had been the case during earlier periods, Turkish media occasionally reported on Syrian maps showing Hatay as part of Syria (*Milliyet* 19 January 2005, haberaktuel.com 21 June 2007, internethaber.com 21 March 2010). At the outbreak of the Syrian uprising in March 2011, the vast majority of official Syrian maps continued to include the area as Syrian territory. (Curiously, the one official map of Syria that did not include Hatay, was the one published at the home page of the General Authority for Palestinian Arab Refugees, in charge of administrating Palestinian refugee camps in Syria.)

The Syrian uprising: Hatay resurfaces

With the outbreak of the Syrian uprising, Syrian-Turkish relations again deteriorated. As Turkey openly sided with oppositional forces and explicitly called for Bashar al-Asad to step down, Syria in return accused Turkey of interfering in Syrian domestic affairs and arming and training terrorists (Syrian Arab News Agency 3 March 2013, Ulusal Channel 5 April 2013, *Tishreen* 8 March 2013). Although Turkey became one of the major hosts of Syrian refugees and a hub for funds and weapons for the opposition, Hatay remained a topic forgotten for the first two years. When Syrian media reported on the Syrian refugees in Hatay, it was always clear that they were in

Turkey (and not on 'occupied Syrian territory' as could have been the case had the Syrian government wanted to raise the question of the border). Likewise, rebel forces headquartered in Hatay were reported to be based in Turkey (Lundgren Jörum 2012:22). This remained the case until November 2012 when Hatay suddenly reappeared in Syrian media, now referred to exclusively by its Arabic name *Liwa Iskandarun* and with the epithet 'the stolen province'. Two important events immediately preceded this sudden reappearance. Earlier in November, a Syrian oppositional conference had been held in Doha, Qatar. Internationally widely reported on as the founding conference for the National Coalition for Syrian Revolutionary and Opposition Forces, another alleged outcome of the conference was of more interest to the Syrian media. A Kuwaiti participant to the conference claimed that the meeting had resulted in a secret agreement between representatives from Qatar, Turkey, the UAE and USA on one hand, and a number of representatives from different Syrian oppositional forces on the other. According to this secret agreement, Syria would, among other things, be forced to give up all claims to Hatay and cede a number of border villages inhabited by Turkmens to Turkey (*Tishreen* 23 November 2012). While it is not possible to confirm whether such an agreement was actually concluded, the fact that non-Syrian Arab media reported on it was probably one of the factors causing Hatay to reemerge in Syrian press. Another factor was that Turkey had, at about the same time, requested NATO anti-aircraft missiles to be positioned along its border with Syria. Following these two events, several articles in Syrian press reported on popular demands for the return of Hatay to 'the motherland Syria'. For instance, in December 2012 the Forum for the Support of the Syrian Prisoners of War was reported to demand the return of the area and in March 2013 The National Dialogue Forum did the same (*Tishreen* 5 December 2012 and 26 March 2013). Later the same month, Tishreen reported on twin demonstrations in Lataqiyah (Syria) and Antioch (Hatay) 'condemning Erdoğan's policy and stressing the Arabness of liwa iskandarun and the necessity to return it to the motherland' (*Tishreen* 23 December 2012). In early 2013, the chairman of the Arab Democratic Solidarity Party, one of the new political parties registered as a result of the 2011 new party law, stressed that the priority of the party is to keep Syria territorially intact and work for the return of the occupied territories – the Golan Heights and Hatay (*Tishreen* 5 February 2013). Likewise, the chairman of another recently registered party, the Syrian Patriotic Youth Party, stated that the return of Hatay is a national duty (*Tishreen* 3 December 2012, 26 February 2013 and 4 March 2013). The private pro-government TV channel Sama TV had several reports on Hatay, its history and geography in its news broadcasts following the Doha meeting. Describing the history and geography of Hatay, these reports made clear that the inhabitants of Hatay are Syrian and that the occupation of Hatay is on a par with the occupation of the Golan Heights (see next chapter).[26] Likewise, the Syrian Al-akhbariyyah TV channel showed a short documentary on how Hatay was lost, the turkification policies it had been subjected to and the demonstrations held by its inhabitants in support of Syria.[27] Hatay was also brought up during at least one parliamentary session where one of the deputies warned Turkish Prime Minister Erdoğan that Syria will not forget about Hatay.[28] After decades in oblivion Hatay had thereby made a forceful comeback as an explicitly mentioned occupied Syrian territory.[29] It should be noted, however, that as of May 2014, none of the references to Hatay as occupied and stolen had been made by representatives of the government. While reports and comments on Hatay would not have appeared in Syrian media without a green light from the regime, it is indicative that while Bashar al-Asad on several occasions was very clear in his dislike of Turkish policies towards Syria, he did not mention Hatay at all. For instance, in his interview with Turkish TV channel Ulusal in April 2013, he talked of Turkish support of terrorism in Syria and the Israeli occupation of the Golan but did not mention Hatay. Likewise, in the two letters the Syrian Ministry of Foreign Affairs sent to the UN Secretary General and the President of the Security Council, complaining about Turkish interference in Syrian affairs (*Tishreen* 8 March 2013), Hatay was not mentioned. The clearest possible message to Turkey that Syria did not want the question of Hatay to stir up trouble between the two had however been sent already in June 2012. When Syria accidentally downed a Turkish jet off the Syrian coast, the map shown on Syrian TV during reports on the incident left no room for doubt. While Turkish media had the previous day pointed to Syrian tourist maps including Hatay (*Sabah* 21 June 2012), the map exhibited on Syrian TV, showing the route of the plane, had the border separating Hatay from Syria clearly marked in yellow.[30] At this specific point of extremely tense relations, Syria thereby clearly signaled that Hatay was Turkish. Following this incident, Syrian TV went back to showing maps including Hatay as Syrian territory and Turkish media occasionally reported on these maps as the 'Syrian dream' to reincorporate Hatay (see for instance Karaman 2012, *Gazeteport* 19 May 2013). School children continued to be taught that Hatay was among the territories stolen from the Arab Homeland but as during earlier periods school textbooks did not demand its return or specify Syrian goals for the region.[31] (Not very surprising, when Syrian oppositional organizations in Turkey distributed textbooks to be used by Syrian refugee children there, Hatay had been removed from maps of Syria. This was only one of many changes done to the 'national narrative' taught in Syrian schools, Abdulrahim 2013).

As mentioned above, in the context of the Syrian civil war a pro-regime militia called the Popular Front for the Liberation of liwa Iskandarun – The Syrian Resistance (*al-jabhah al-shaabiyyah li-tahrir liwa iskandarun – al-muqawamah al-suriyyah*) appeared on the scene in November 2012. Reportedly consisting of Alawites only, it fought anti-regime rebel forces in the Lataqiyah area and claimed to have stopped armed rebels from crossing into Syria from Turkey on several occasions. Its professed goal was to liberate Hatay from Turkish rule and representatives of the militia claimed most members were 'Syrian Arabs' from this area (al-Sharq al-Awsat 8 May 2013). Its commander, Hatay-born Alawite Mihraç Ural (also known as Ali al-Kayali) had, according to Turkish sources, a long history of links to the Syrian regime and security services. Carrying Syrian citizenship since the 1980s, he was allegedly part of Syrian-PKK contacts prior to the 1998 expulsion of PKK leader Öcalan from Syria (Albayrak 2013). The Popular Front for the Liberation of liwa Iskandarun was accused of perpetrating the massacres of Sunni inhabitants of Bayda and Banyas in Syria in early May 2013 and the Reyhanlı bombings in Hatay later the same month. Its fighting has so far been made on Syrian territory, and it seems unlikely that it would extend armed struggle into Hatay unless serious intercommunal violence breaks out there.

Syria had reportedly also gone back to accepting students from Hatay into Syrian Universities (Abdullah 2014) although it is not clear whether students from Hatay had actually opted for this possibility or not.

Conclusions: Syrian policies towards Hatay

While the scarcity of sources is a difficulty when analysing Syrian policies towards Hatay, it also suggests that Hatay has not been a Syrian priority. Syrian policies have been ambiguous and contradictory. The dominating, over-all policy has been to not formally recognise Turkish sovereignty over Hatay while at the same time avoiding making a fuss about it. This policy originates from the 1946 agreement between Syria and Turkey whereby Hatay had in reality been traded for Turkish support of Syrian independence. With the exception of the reign of Husni al-Zaim, Syria has never openly and formally recognised the border separating it from Hatay. With the exception of the UAR period, during which Syria had ceased to exist as an independent state, nor has it ever formally demanded its return. As Syrian-Turkish relations greatly improved during the first decade of the 2000s, the border was gradually more openly recognised *in practice*. But rather than ending in an open and formal recognition of the border, Syrian policy aimed at blurring it. The establishment of a free-trade area and the decision to construct a shared Friendship Dam on the Orontes river were both steps in this direction. The outbreak of the Syrian uprising and Turkey's stand against the government of Bashar al-Asad put an effective halt to the construction of the dam and the further development of bilateral relations. Initially this did not affect Syrian policy or discourse regarding Hatay. In November 2012, after decades of domestic silence on Hatay, this suddenly changed. Syrian press began reporting on 'popular demands' for the return of Hatay (now referred to only by its Arabic name *liwa Iskandarun*) and Syrian TV channels aired short films and reports stressing that the area should return 'to the motherland'. There were no formal demands for the return of Hatay and no Syrian officials mentioned it.

Syrian decision makers have in reality long ago accepted the fact that Hatay will remain Turkish. This was most probably so even at the time of the annexation in 1939. The sudden reappearance of Hatay in Syrian media should not be interpreted as irredentist policies but rather as a consequence of the need for an issue to rally around and mobilise popular disdain for Turkey. The real question, with regard to Hatay, is therefore why the area has remained on Syrian maps for all these years and through the ups and downs of Syrian-Turkish relations. This is a topic discussed in the final chapter of the book.

CHAPTER 5

THE GOLAN HEIGHTS: FROM THE ARAB TO THE SYRIAN CAUSE

While Lebanon and Hatay were both lost due to mandatory decisions prior to Syria's independence, the Golan Heights were lost in war 21 years after independence. Details of the war have been dealt with extensively elsewhere and will not be further studied here. Suffice it to say that by the time of the ceasefire, about 1,250 km² out of the total 1,750 km² that constitute the Golan Heights had been captured by Israel (Muslih 1993:621). At the outbreak of the war, the Golan Heights had been inhabited by approximately 153,000 people out of which 130,000–140,000 lived in 249 villages in the part conquered by Israel (Abu Fakhr 2000:5, Muslih 1993:628, Mara'i & Halaby 1992:78). Out of these, about 6,400 persons remained within occupied territory (Tarabieh 1995:43) while the rest left for Syria. Today there are approximately 22,000 (ICRC 2 March 2010) Syrian citizens in five villages (four Druze and one Alawite)[1] and a similar number of Israeli citizens in 35–40 settlements.[2]

At the time of the loss of the Golan Heights, the border between Syria and Israel had already been subject to negotiations on two occasions. The first one followed immediately after the 1948–1949 Arab-Israeli war, when Syria had been the only Arab state conquering territory marked as Israeli according to the 1947 partition plan for Palestine. Syria requested that the armistice line reflect these territorial gains. Israel, on the other hand, demanded Syrian withdrawal to the border drawn between French-mandated Syria and British-mandated Palestine in 1923 (Shalev 1994:18, Rabinovich 1991:68, Seale 1965:62). The negotiations resulted in an armistice agreement, signed the 20 July 1949. As a consequence, Syria withdrew from the conquered areas and these were subsequently demilitarised. No agreement was reached on the sovereignty of the three demilitarised zones (DMZ) established; a 2–3 km wide strip on the southeastern shore of Lake Tiberias, a triangle in the northeastern corner of the Hula Valley including the springs of Banyas, and a 19 km^2 area north of Lake Tiberias at the southern tip of the Hula Valley (Rabinowitz & Khawalde 2000:514). It was nevertheless made clear that neither the armistice line nor the DMZs were to be understood as having any relation to a final territorial arrangement. The DMZs became, from the outset, the cause of tension due to differences mainly over their legal status, the progressive extension of Israeli cultivation towards the east and the Israeli drainage project in Lake Hula (Khouri 1963:16).

The second round of negotiations took place in the early 1950s following a Syrian-Israeli confrontation over Israel's above mentioned Lake Hula drainage project in May 1951. The parties were again unable to reach an agreement on the partition of the DMZ (Shalev 1994:32). The result of these two failed attempts to negotiate a solution was that between July 1949 and June 1967 no clearly defined border existed between Syria and Israel. In certain sections the armistice line corresponded with the international 1923 border while other sections reflected the gradual de facto partition of the DMZ, which left the bulk of the territory under Israeli control (Shalev 1994:33, Cobban 1999:30, Rabil 2003:9). Already before the 1967 loss of the Golan Heights there was therefore an Israeli-Syrian territorial dispute in the area. This has added to the difficulties of solving the conflict as the parties differ on what is to be defined as 'the international border' – the 1923 border or the de facto partition line as of 4 June 1967.

Syrian policy towards the Golan Heights, 1967–1990

About a week after the 1967 ceasefire, Syrian President Nur al-Din al-Atasi addressed the UN General Assembly, protesting the Israeli occupation of the Golan Heights (Moubayed 2006:617). During the months following the war, the Israeli government presented a peace proposal whereby Israel would withdraw until the 1923 border in exchange for a complete demilitarisation of the Golan Heights and a Syrian guarantee that it would not interfere with the flow of water from the Jordan River to Israel. Syria rejected the proposal demanding unconditional Israeli withdrawal (Shalev 1994:51–52, Rabil 2003:19). In September 1967 the Arab Summit in Khartoum decided on 'the three no's': no to negotiations with Israel, no to recognition of Israel and no to peace with Israel. This decreased the possibility of finding a solution by non-military means, and in the early 1970s, Syrian President Hafez Al-Asad made clear that a coming Arab military showdown with Israel was unavoidable and that occupied territory would be liberated through war.[3]

The 1973 October War and the 1974 Disengagement Agreement

In 1973 Syria and Egypt went to coordinated war in an attempt to liberate the Golan Heights and the Sinai Peninsula. This resulted in an additional loss of Syrian territory. UN Security Council resolution 338, calling for an immediate cease fire and the termination of all military activity, was adopted the 22 October 1973. An Israeli-Syrian Disengagement Treaty was signed 31 May 1974.[4] As part of this agreement the territory that Israel had conquered in 1973 and an additional 100 km² of the territory conquered in 1967 were returned to Syria. As a result, the currently occupied Golan Heights amounts to 1,150 km². Although sceptical about the usefulness of a step-by-step approach, Syria accepted this agreement under the condition that the rest of the Golan Heights be returned later (Yearbook of the United Nations 1975:238). The agreement provided for the separation of forces by the so called Area of Separation (AOS) in which the United Nations Disengagement Observer Force (UNDOF) was subsequently deployed.

The AOS was placed under Syrian administration and civilians were allowed to return. A second, more sensitive, agreement detailing military limitations imposed on both sides, was also produced. According to the Chairman of the negotiations, limitations on armaments and troops as well as Syrian guarantees to inhibit Palestinian guerrilla raids from across the disengagement line were so sensitive to the Syrian decision makers that they would not include them in a public protocol.[5] In practice, the limitations on guerrilla activity were not a problem as these had never been allowed from across the Syrian ceasefire line (Siilasvuo 1992:260), despite numerous public announcements to the contrary. Al-Asad had on occasion specifically pointed out that Syria would never make such guarantees to anyone[6] and after the conclusion of the Disengagement Agreement, he continued to claim that the Palestinian guerrillas had complete freedom of action from Syrian territory.[7]

The area returned in 1974 included the capital of the Golan Heights, Qunaytrah. Before Qunaytrah was handed over, the buildings of the town were practically all destroyed and the ruins are today used as a monument of 'Zionist cruelty', open to visitors after (routine) permission from the intelligence service. In company of special guides visitors are shown the bullet hole ridden remains of residential houses, a church, a mosque and a hospital, and told of atrocities committed by Israeli soldiers.

Syrian policy towards the Golan Heights after the 1974 Disengagement

Ever since the disengagement treaty, the disengagement line has been patrolled by the UNDOF, the mandate for which is re-approved by both sides every six months. Apart from occasional disturbances,[8] the disengagement line has remained quiet since 1974 even when tension between Syria and Israel has been high in other areas – for instance, during Israeli-Syrian fighting in Lebanon in the early 1980s. This is a fact appreciated by Israel. In April 1995, Israeli Prime Minister Yitzhak Rabin said 'I wish all the lines separating us from the Arab states were as quiet as the line between us and the Syrians on the

Golan Heights' (Cobban 1999:36). The quiet that has characterised the disengagement line compared to Syrian activities in Lebanon with time earned President Hafez al-Asad the epithet *Asad Lubnan, fa'r al-jawlan* – the Lion of Lebanon, the mouse of the Golan (see for instance Kedar 2005:182).

Although Syria had accepted partial Israeli withdrawal as a first step, it made clear that nothing short of a complete Israeli withdrawal would be acceptable as a final solution. Nothing that might be interpreted as remains of the Israeli occupation or a breach of Syrian sovereignty over its territory would be accepted. The Golan Heights could not be demilitarised unless an equally sized territory on the Israeli side be subject to the same rules.[9] In 1975, Syria complained to the UN that the Disengagement Treaty had only helped Israel buy time instead of serving as a first step to a complete withdrawal (Yearbook of the United Nations 1975:238). President al-Asad stressed that Syria had a right to the Golan Heights and that not an inch (*shibr*) or an atom (*dhura*) would be given up.[10] He also made clear that holding on to every inch of the land was the will of the Syrian people and it would be fought for, no matter how long it would take. For instance, in a 1977 speech President al-Asad stated that 'I have told the US that if one single inch remains under occupation we are ready to fight a 100 years for it'.[11] Although Hafez al-Asad talked of the Golan as occupied Syrian territory[12] that had to be returned to Syria, a reading of his speeches, interviews and press conferences during the 1967–1990 period shows that the Israeli occupation of the Golan Heights is presented as an issue subordinated to the Palestine question. In fact, while he mentions occupied Arab land on numerous occasions he mentions the Golan Heights – which he refers to as 'the Syrian Heights' – for the first time in 1971.[13] An Israeli withdrawal from the Golan Heights would not, according to the president, mean anything unless the rights of the Palestinian people were respected.[14] Al-Asad also claimed that Syria could have negotiated a solution for the Golan Heights but declined because Palestine was still under occupation.[15]

On 14 December 1981, Israel extended Israeli law, jurisdiction and administration to the Golan Heights, thereby effectively annexing the area. Following a Syrian letter of complaint, United Nations Security

Council resolution 497 declared the Israeli decision null and void. Between 1967 and 1990, Syria continuously brought the attention of the United Nations to the Israeli occupation of the Golan Heights. There were numerous protests regarding the Israeli integration of the Golan Heights, the demolition of Syrian villages, Israeli policies towards the Syrian citizens remaining on the Golan, the construction of settlements, the establishment of an Israeli settler population, plans for the extension of Israeli jurisdiction, plans for and the actual annexation of the Golan Heights and Israeli excavations on the Golan.[16]

Negotiations with Israel, 1991–2000

Negotiations as a way of regaining the Golan Heights were again tried as part of the Arab-Israeli peace process initiated in 1991. This brought ministerial delegations from Syria, Lebanon, Jordan and Israel together in order to reach a final agreement on peace in the Middle East. The conference included bilateral talks between Israel and each surrounding Arab state still officially in a state of war with Israel, with a special arrangement for the Palestinians. Syria insisted peace be built upon UN Security Council resolution 242 of 1967, which mentions occupied territory in exchange for peace and declined to take part in the multilateral talks focusing on regional security, water resources, Palestinian refugees, environment and regional economic development. The Syrian priority thus clearly lay with the territory only, which was made clear by Syrian Foreign Minister Farouq al-Shara's opening speech.[17]

Syrian-Israeli bilateral negotiations within the peace process can roughly be divided into four different phases: 1) October 1991–June 1992, which was characterised by deadlock; 2) August 1993–March 1996, when a deal seemed possible as Israeli Prime Minister Rabin was prepared to withdraw first partially and then fully from the Golan Heights and his successor Shimon Peres' expressed wish to 'fly high and fast' (Rabinovich 1998:9) to conclude an agreement; 3) May 1996–July 1999 with stalled negotiations as Israeli Prime Minister Benjamin Netanyahu insisted on negotiations with no prior conditions and Syrian president Hafez al-Asad found it unacceptable to negotiate without taking into account progress made during negotiations with the previous Israeli government. 4) September 1999–January 2000 when both Hafez al-Asad and Israeli Prime Minister Ehud Barak signaled optimism about the possibility of an agreement. The negotiations ended in failure and have not been resumed since.

The failure of the Syrian-Israeli peace negotiations has been the subject of a number of studies and several reasons have been given for their unsuccessful outcome. Our aim here is not to find out whether these explanations are plausible but rather to examine what territorial solutions were acceptable to Syria.

Syrian-Israeli bilateral negotiations, October 1991– June 1992

The fact that Syria agreed to attend the 1991 Madrid conference meant that it had abandoned one of its principal conditions: an explicit Israeli commitment that negotiations would lead to a complete withdrawal from the Golan Heights (Baker 1995:447). Syrian demands during the conference nevertheless showed that full withdrawal was still the only acceptable outcome. The head of the Syrian delegation, Foreign Minister Farouq al-Shara, opened the first round of negotiations in Madrid addressing Israel: 'We have come here for the purpose of implementing United Nations Security Council resolution 242, the essence of which is territory for peace; accordingly, we are ready to carry out our part of the equation as soon as we hear from you that Israel is ready to withdraw from all the Arab territories you conquered in the June 1967 war' (Ben-Aharon 2000:1). The question of full Israeli withdrawal from the Golan Heights was so essential to Syria that it initially decided to cancel its bilateral talks with Israel altogether unless US President Bush's opening speech, which mentioned the need for territorial compromise, was changed (Ross 2004:81). As the bilateral talks then showed that the Israeli government under Prime Minister Yitzhak Shamir did not agree that resolution 242 even applied to the Golan Heights, negotiations deadlocked immediately (Rabinovich 1998:39, Ross 2004:81). They found a new start after the Israeli 1992 election brought Yitzak Rabin to the post of Prime Minister. He recognised the applicability of resolution 242 to the Golan Heights and Syria was then prepared to speak of a framework agreement. It would not, however, specify its contents or speak of peace (Ross 2000:100, Rabinovich 1998:56) as the Syrian position was that as long as there was no Israeli commitment to a full withdrawal from the Golan Heights, there would be no point in discussing the other possible components of peace.

Syrian-Israeli bilateral negotiations, 1993–1996

In August 1993, Rabin asked the US administration to convey to Syria that Israel would withdraw fully from the Golan Heights provided Israel's needs were met and that the Syrian agreement would not be dependent on any other agreement (Ross 2004:111). Al-Asad then accepted the basic equation full peace for full withdrawal. He also told US Secretary of State Warren Christopher that he needed to know the Israeli definition of 'full withdrawal' (Ross 2004:113). When hearing that Christopher thought Rabin meant the 1923 border, the offer was rejected as this line, according to al-Asad, was a line drawn by imperialism without the participation of independent Syria (Seale 1999:4). He instead demanded withdrawal to the 4 June 1967 line. In June 1994 Rabin conveyed, again through Christopher, that Israel would withdraw to the line demanded by al-Asad: the 4 June 1967 line, provided Rabin's demands on normalisation and security were met (Seale 1999:3). This offer – full Israeli withdrawal to the 4 June 1967 line in exchange for fulfillment of the Israeli demands – became known as 'the deposit' (Schiff 1998). It was not made public and later became the object of great controversy as Syria would not continue negotiations without an Israeli recognition of the existence of this deposit and Israel, then under a new government, refused to recognise that it existed. During the second half of the 1993–1996 negotiations, the Chiefs of Staff from both states met twice and discussed security matters. Israel demanded early-warning stations on the Golan Heights, which Syria rejected as a symbol of continued occupation (Cobban 1999:97). Israel further demanded reciprocal but not symmetrical security arrangements in agreed-upon areas (Savir 1998:267). This was also rejected by al-Asad who argued that security arrangements would have to be the same on both sides of the border as 'not only Israel needs security arrangements. The Arabs also need them considering the fact that Israel was almost always the aggressor' (Cobban 1999:97). Israeli demands for limitations on the development of the Golan Heights were also rejected (Ross 2004:145). Al-Asad's comment on Israeli demands in exchange for a full withdrawal from the Golan Heights was that instead of withdrawing from the Golan Heights Rabin wanted to occupy all of Syria and deprive it of its capability to defend itself. He further added that the needs of one state must stop at the borders of another (Seale 1999:4).

Following the assassination of Rabin in November 1995, Shimon Peres became Israel's new Prime Minister. Like Rabin before him, Peres said withdrawal depended on satisfaction of Israeli needs. These needs, however, differed from those expressed by Rabin. While Rabin had focused on security, Peres was more interested in economic growth, development and water guarantees with a vision that a new regional system of cooperation and integration would eventually turn the Middle East into a stable and peaceful region (Peres & Arye 1993). Negotiations began in Wye River, USA, late December 1995. Peres asked for shared Syrian-Israeli projects on the Golan Heights and wanted the area be turned into a free economic zone. Al-Asad rejected this as something the Syrian public would consider a continuation of occupation and a risk of future Israeli hegemony (Rabinovich 1998:200–212, Savir 1998:274). Although Peres focused on economic development he did not disregard security, which remained a difficult issue to resolve due to different perceptions of the relationship between peace and security; while Israel held that security arrangements would guarantee peace, Syria held that peace would guarantee security (Savir 1998: 276–277). Syrian rejections of Israeli demands were explained by Hafez al-Asad in the following way:

> You might ask: Now that they have responded to this Syrian demand [of withdrawal to the 1967 line], why was peace not achieved? [...] Many issues that constituted the elements of peace were still pending. These issues include the elements of security and other elements, and all of them are basic. The security issues might make the regained land something that

is not worthwhile, and also might discount dignity and rights (Rabinovich 1998:12).

The mere return of the entire Golan Heights to Syria was thus not enough. The terms and conditions had to be such that they would not in any way be perceived as a limitation on Syrian sovereignty over the area.

Another point of contention brought up was water, an issue strongly connected to the exact location of the 4 June 1967 line. Israeli occupation of the larger parts of the DMZs and later the Golan Heights had denied Syria access to the water of Banyas and Lake Tiberias. The difficulty when negotiating over water was centered around the latter. Israel's closure in 1964 of the outlet of the Jordan River from Lake Tiberias had caused the high-water level of the lake to rise by four meters. This made the waterline expand outwards and increased the surface area of the lake. As a result, while the 1923 border between Syria and Palestine had run 10 meters away from the natural waterline on the northeastern shore of the lake, by 4 June 1967 this line ran through the lake (Haddadin 2002:330). Like the security issues, the water issues did not find a solution during the Wye River negotiations as Israel did not agree to give Syria access to the lake and Syria did not agree to any other line than that of 4 June 1967 (Haddadin 2002:330). Negotiations stalled during early 1996 due to events on the ground,[18] and in May Peres Labour Party lost the Israeli elections.

Syrian-Israeli bilateral negotiations, 1996–1998

New Prime Minister Netanyahu announced his willingness to negotiate with Syria but only without prior conditions. He denied that either Rabin or Peres had offered full withdrawal from the Golan Heights and negotiations would therefore have to start from scratch.[19] Al-Asad, on the other hand, refused to negotiate unless negotiations start where the previous ones had ended. Negotiations did not resume and in May 1999 Netanyahu was replaced as Prime Minister by Ehud Barak.

THE GOLAN HEIGHTS 123

Syrian-Israeli bilateral negotiations, September 1999–January 2000

Shortly after Barak's victory, optimism rose with confidence building measures in the form of an unprecedented exchange of positive statements between al-Asad and Barak (*Al-Hayat* 23 June 1999). In September 1999, the two parties met secretly in Switzerland in order to prepare for the resumption of the negotiations. Syria would not accept a resumption without an Israeli commitment to full withdrawal, and Israel had reservations about parts of the 4 June 1967 line. As this line had not been depicted on maps, Syrian and Israeli representatives met secretly again two weeks later in USA for discussions on the exact location of the Syrian and Israeli military forces when the war started in 1967. This would decide the 4 June 1967 line (Ross 2004:518–526). Syria then for the first time gave indications that it might accept a border that would not fully coincide with its own perception of the 4 June 1967 line, as it seemed willing to eventually recognise a border 50 meters off Lake Tiberias (Ross 2004:526). That would imply giving up territory that had been Syrian even according to the 1923 border. Syrian Foreign Minister al-Shara further told US President Clinton that Syria could accept an early warning station on the Golan Heights as long as it was not manned by Israelis. It could, however, be manned by Americans, preferably under a UN flag. Barak insisted that Israel would need a limited presence on the Golan Heights even after withdrawal. This was rejected by Syria and the possibility for an early warning station was subsequently withdrawn altogether by al-Asad (Ross 2004:529–530).

In mid-December the two parties met for a 48-hour-long first round of negotiations in preparation of an intensive round to begin in January 2000. Syria had agreed to these two days of negotiations without explicit prior conditions (Albright 2004:534, Ross 2004:536), which indicated a Syrian eagerness to resume negotiations. There were several other indications that Syria was interested in reaching a solution. For instance, it raised the level of the official negotiations. Instead of having Syrian ambassador to the US negotiate, it sent Foreign Minister Farouq al-Shara. Hafez al-Asad also told President

Clinton's Middle East envoy Dennis Ross that he wanted to reach an agreement quickly (Ross 2004:537). The fact that Syria had agreed to resume negotiations without explicit prior conditions did not mean that its demands concerning full withdrawal had changed. Al-Shara, in his opening statement, repeated that 'peace for Syria means the return of all its occupied land'.[20] But even though al-Shara continued to press for an Israeli commitment to the 4 June 1967 line throughout the December round, he also acknowledged that this line could not be found on any map (Ross 2004: 540–543). He thereby confirmed the possibility of discussing the exact location of the line. The round was followed by positive reports and hopes for an imminent agreement remained high.

In January 2000, an intensive round of negotiations was held in West Virginia. According to Dennis Ross, Syria demonstrated 'uncharacteristic flexibility on every issue' (Ross 2004:561). Not only did it agree to Israeli sovereignty over the entire Lake Tiberias and a 50-meter strip off the shoreline, it also implied that the entire border could be adjusted with up to 50 meters in order to meet mutual needs and concerns (Ross 2004:560–561). Early warning stations, hitherto rejected, were acceptable for five years after Israeli withdrawal provided they were not manned by Israelis (Ross 2004:555). Syria proposed security zones – areas within which the amount of arms would be limited – where the Syrian zones would be twice the size of the Israeli ones (Ross 2004:560 note *). It also accepted extensive active and passive monitoring of Syrian and Israeli ground forces, weapons depots and logistic support units. Syria further accepted a water management board to ensure the quality and the quantity of the water flowing from the Golan Heights into Lake Tiberias and proposed a series of confidence building measures as a way of gradually introducing normalisation steps (Ross 2004:561). In return, Syria wanted an Israeli acknowledgement that the basis for the discussion of the border was the 4 June 1967 line. Israel did not respond to these Syrian offers, nor did it agree to acknowledge the 4 June 1967 line directly to the Syrian delegation (although it had done so to the US envoy) (Ross 2004:561, 539–540, 565–567). A draft of the US understanding of the Syrian and Israeli positions leaked to the Israeli media, making it look as if Syria had yielded and got nothing in return. This caused criticism by the Arab Writers' Union in Damascus (Rubin 2000). In a speech to the Union, Syrian Foreign Minister al-Shara, stressed the importance of going beyond the strict land for peace equation. While Israel would still have to withdraw from all occupied territory, and no traces of Israeli presence on the Golan would ever be accepted, peace would necessarily entail more than just the absence of war. Armed struggle would be exchanged for a competition based on culture, economy and trade as a better way to stop Israel from expansion.[21]

After the leak, al-Asad would not resume negotiations without an explicit Israeli commitment to withdraw to the 4 June 1967 line. Israel responded that it would make such a commitment only if the Israeli-Lebanese talks were resumed. As such a resumption was not possible without a Syrian green light (see chapter three), al-Asad countered saying that these talks would resume only after the Syrian-Israeli border had been demarcated (Ross 2004:566–567). He nevertheless still indicated that he was prepared to be flexible on the exact location of the line (2004:570).

In February 2000, Barak made a public statement that he intended to conclude a deal with Syria based on the 4 June line (Ross 2004:577–579). Barak told Ross what he would demand in return, and at the end of March, President Clinton, Ross and US Secretary of State Madeleine Albright conveyed the Israeli demands to al-Asad. By now, the flexible Syrian attitude had grown rigid. Israel demanded to retain sovereignty over the entire Lake Tiberias and the River Jordan and therefore the borderline could not touch either one. Barak offered a borderline 400 metres off the lake shoreline and 80 metres off the Jordan river (Albright 2004:540, Ross 2004:583). As compensation Syria would receive a piece of land that was to the west of the 1923 line and had thus never belonged to Syria (Albright 2004:540, Ross 2004:585). Al-Asad was no longer prepared to settle for a line that left the entire Lake Tiberias outside of Syria as 'he wanted to be able to sit on the shore of the lake with his feet in the water' (Clinton 2004:1000). As soon as he saw the map with Israeli prime Minister Ehud Barak's proposal of a line to the east of Lake Tiberias he said, 'Then he does not want peace, it is over' (Albright 2004:540, Ross 2004:584). After this meeting with President al-Asad, the US administration referred to the differences between the two sides as 'significant' and did not believe it would be productive to resume negotiations at that time.[22] The official Syrian-Israeli negotiations ended there and have since then been frozen.

It can be concluded that from the initiation of the peace process until the end of the negotiations in 2000, Syrian rhetoric with regard to the area did not change. As during the previous period, the Syrian President maintained that Syria had a right to the Golan Heights. He further claimed that the Israeli annexation in 1981 had not changed anything with regard to the Syrianness of the Golan[23] and no matter how long it would take, it would have to return to Syria.[24] Initially, the Syrian official statements continued to claim that not a single inch of the Golan Heights could be given up, as evident for instance in a 1992 speech where Hafez al-Asad states that 'anyone who makes concessions on a piece of the homeland is a traitor to the people,'[25] and Syrian chief negotiator Walid al-Muallim's claim that 'nothing can compensate the Syrian people for losing one inch of the Golan Heights. Not even the moon. The Golan Heights is our territory. It is a sacred cause for our people' (Butler 1997:90). On the eve of the 1991 negotiations al-Asad had stressed the importance of finding a comprehensive solution to the Arab-Israeli conflict as this is '*one* problem and splitting it into several parts will not help peace'.[26] As the Arab-Israeli peace process progressed, while continuing to stress Arab land, the centrality of the *Syrian* territory became evident. For instance, in 1998 al-Asad claimed that 'the deposit' was the most important part of the entire Arab-Israeli peace process.[27] In 1999, Walid al-Muallim said that 'if the opportunity comes for Syria and Lebanon to make peace with Israel, we won't wait for a solution of the Palestinian problem' (Cobban 1999:187), thus breaking the taboo of splitting the 'Arab cause' into smaller parts. Although Syrian basic demands with regard to an Israeli withdrawal thus remained the same, during the 1991–2000 period focus shifted from a comprehensive Arab-Israeli peace involving an Israeli withdrawal from all Arab territory to the possibility of a Syrian-Israeli peace which would be based on a withdrawal from the Golan Heights only. Throughout the 1991–2000 period Syria continued to bring up the Golan Heights in the United Nations, protesting the expansion of settlements and Israeli policies towards the Syrian inhabitants (although to a lesser extent than during the previous period).[28]

Bashar al-Asad takes over

In his inauguration speech, Bashar al-Asad made clear that he intended to follow his father's approach with regard to the Golan Heights; nothing less than full withdrawal up until the 4 June 1967 line would be accepted:

> They send us envoys who ask us to agree to a modified line of 4 June and ask us to call this modified line 4 June, as if the difference is about what we call the line. Or they suggest giving us 95 per cent of our land and when we ask about the remaining 5 per cent they say it is only a problem of a few meters and this should not be an obstacle to peace. If those few meters are not a problem and should not be an obstacle to peace, then why don't they bring back the 4 June line and give us 5 per cent of the western part of the Lake?[29]

Since his take-over, Bashar al-Asad and other Syrian representatives have continued to repeat that an Israeli commitment to withdraw to the 4 June 1967 line is a condition for resuming negotiations. For instance, in 2005 Syrian Information Minister Muhsin Bilal said that Syria would like to continue negotiations over the Golan Heights based on the 'Rabin deposit' (Syrian Ministry of Information 30 November 2005) and in 2007 Bilal repeated that the 4 June 1967 line is an irrevocable demand (Kuwait News Agency 12 March 2007). This was repeated by Foreign Minister Walid al-Muallim in 2009 (*The Daily Star* 13 July 2009) and Bashar al-Asad in 2010 (Syrian Arab News Agency 8 October 2010). While Syrian officials in the post-2000 period have stressed that Middle East peace will require an Israeli withdrawal from all Arab territory (i.e. the Golan Heights, the West Bank, Gaza and the Shebaa Farms) and the establishment of an independent Palestinian state with eastern Jerusalem as its capital,[30] the Golan Heights have remained the Syrian priority. In 2003 Bashar al-Asad confirmed al-Muallim's 1996 statement saying that Syria's principal interest was the Golan Heights (Syrian Ministry of Information 11 May 2003), and in 2004, he confirmed the separation of the Golan Heights from the Palestinian cause by referring to the 'Syrian cause' and 'the Palestinian cause' separately instead of a single 'Arab cause'.[31]

Negotiations in the post-2000 period

Official negotiations have not resumed after the freezing of Syrian-Israeli talks in January 2000. Nevertheless, there have been various reports of ongoing low-level negotiations. In August 2002 there were Israeli reports that Syrian representatives to a closed-door conference announced that if necessary Syria would consider 'border corrections' in an agreement with Israel (Sadeh 2002). Between September 2004 and July 2006, a series of secret meetings were reportedly held between Syrian and Israeli representatives. This resulted in a 'non-paper', the contents of which were reported in Israeli media. As both the Israeli and the Syrian governments denied knowledge of these negotiations, it is difficult to assess the importance of the non-paper. Should it reflect reality, it points to an increased Syrian flexibility on the definition of full withdrawal and sovereignty as a 'peace park' is part of the agreement. Although under Syrian sovereignty, this park would be open to Israeli visitors without a visa requirement (for full text see Eldar 2007b).[32] The final border remained to be agreed upon but would be based upon the 4 June 1967 line. The most important issue for Syria, the exact location of the border, had thus not been solved in this non-paper and there are no signs that Syria had changed its basic demand for full withdrawal. In June 2007 Israeli Deputy Prime Minister Shaul Mofaz confirmed that Israel had been sending secret messages to Syria regarding the possibility of resuming negotiations through a third party (BBC 23 April 2008). The following month, President al-Asad repeated that he was in favour of resumed negotiations with Israel provided they were based on the land for peace principle and withdrawal until the 4 June 1967 line.[33] In April 2008, Syria announced that Israel had, through the mediation of Turkey, offered to withdraw from the Golan Heights in order to conclude a peace agreement with

Syria (BBC 23 April 2008). This was later confirmed by Israel (BBC World News 21 May 2008), but, again, an agreement satisfactory to both sides was not reached and no face-to-face bilateral negotiations were initiated. In August 2010, France took the initiative to try to re-launch Syrian-Israeli negotiations. Syria's fundamental demand for a peace agreement with Israel was, again, a complete Israeli withdrawal to the 4 June 1967 line (Syrian Arab News Agency 8 October 2010). In November the same year, the Israeli Knesset passed a new law stating that no Israeli government can withdraw from the Golan Heights (or East Jerusalem) without a referendum approving such a step (Ravid 2010). Syria's response to this was in line with previous comments on Israeli policy: 'This procedure taken by Israel is unequivocally rejected, and does not change the fact that the Golan is occupied Syrian territory, not up for negotiations, and that the full return of the Golan to the line of June 4, 1967 constitutes the basis for establishing peace.'[34] In October 2012, it was reported that Syria and Israel had been involved in secret, US-brokered discussions for several months during 2010. Again, a full Israeli withdrawal was the Syrian demand while Israeli demands focused on security and regional relations such as Syrian ties to Hizbullah and Iran. No agreement was reached and discussions were then cut short by the Syrian uprising (Kershner 2012).

Work on the ground: Beyond war and negotiations

According to Major Bo Wranckler, 2000–2003 Force Commander of the UNDOF, there has been a steady development of the Syrian-controlled part of the Golan Heights since the beginning of the 21st Century: while six roads led into the AOS in 1974, there were 24 such roads in 2001. The electrical power net has been updated and technological advances within agriculture have been made. According to a UNDOF survey, between 1974 and 2001 the number of inhabitants in the AOS increased from 6,000 to 52,000 (Interview Bo Wranckler, Damascus 18 March 2003). Following the 1974 return of territory, Syria rebuilt 10 villages and resettled 60,000 Golani refugees there. The 53,000 refugees originating from Qunaytrah had been expected to return when it was handed back to Syria,[35] but the town has remained in ruins. In 2004 there was talk of rebuilding Qunaytrah and former residents were left with a 31 October deadline to prove that they used to live there. According to Medhat Saleh, former member of the Syrian parliament and International Committee of the Red Cross (ICRC) liaison officer, the rebuilding of Qunaytrah is a good faith measure as it shows that Syria does no longer believe that its claim to the Golan Heights will be settled by war. At the same time it should, according to Saleh, be seen as a sign that Syria will not abandon one inch of the Golan Heights (MacFarquhar 2004). In 2005 the foundation stones for the reconstruction of two villages outside of Qunaytrah were laid and a hospital was inaugurated in the town (Internal Displacement Monitoring Centre 2005). By the outbreak of the Syrian uprising in 2011, the reconstruction of the town itself had not begun and the time-frame for such a reconstruction remained unclear. Meanwhile people had started to buy land around Qunaytrah in order to re-sell and make a profit after reconstruction.[36]

Approximately 130,000 Golan Heights refugees who fled the area during the 1967 war settled in camps and residential areas mainly in and around Damascus, Daraa and Homs. Sources vary between 350,000 – 500,000 (including descendants of original refugees) with regard to the number of refugees now living in Syria.[37] The official Syrian policy holds that these refugees are only temporarily settled and will return to the Golan Heights following an Israeli withdrawal (Interview Medhat Saleh, Damascus 22 March 2003). The refugees from the Golan Heights are rarely mentioned in speeches, interviews or other official discourse. Exceptions to this was Foreign Minister Farouq al-Shara's opening speeches at both the Madrid Peace Conference and the Shepardstown negotiations where he wished to remind the world that the Israeli occupation of the Golan Heights had led to the displacement of half a million Syrian citizens from their homes in the Golan Heights.[38]

Following the 2006 Hizbullah-Israel war, Bashar al-Asad talked of the possibility of armed struggle as a way of liberating the Golan Heights. He said that if the rights of the people are not returned, armed resistance is the natural choice but that this 'is the people's decision, it is not for the state to decide'.[39] The possibility of armed resistance was pointed to again in 2010. In an interview with Hizbullah TV-station al-Manar, al-Asad repeated that it would be a decision taken by the people but that popular armed struggle emerges 'naturally' when there is no state that acts for the people. This, he explained, was not the case on the Golan Heights because there Syria acts for the people.[40] He thereby made clear that popular armed struggle on the Golan is neither necessary nor desired.

With the outbreak of the Syrian uprising there were signs that continued calm along the Syrian-Israeli disengagement line on the Golan Heights could not be taken for granted. In May 2011, Palestinian and Syrian demonstrators managed to breach a fence and move into the occupied part of the Golan Heights. Several demonstrators were shot dead. This was also the case three weeks later when another attempt to breach the fence was made (Harel 2011). As the Syrian uprising turned into a full scale war there were also incidents of Syrian shells hitting Israeli posts on the Golan Heights, followed by Israeli retaliation. When Syria redeployed troops previously stationed close to the disengagement line to other areas in Syria, Israel expressed concern that the vacuum would be filled by armed groups that could eventually engage in attacks on Israel. This was particularly stressed when jihadi fighters gained ground on the Syrian controlled side of the Golan in March 2013 (Chulov & Sherwood 2013). Furthermore, UN observers were abducted by Syrian armed rebels on two occasions during spring 2013 and in response to these developments the UN sought to increase the number of UNDOF troops.

Activities across the disengagement line

Syrian authorities have since the time of occupation made an effort in keeping the Golan Heights 'part of Syria'. Since 1983 the ICRC has been involved in the facilitation of marriages across the border. The majority have involved a bride passing from Syria to marry a husband in the occupied area. Since 1988, with the ICRC and the UNDOF as intermediaries, Syrian students from the Golan Heights cross into Syria to study at Syrian universities. About 500–600 students study in Syria at any given time (about 80–90 new students begin their studies in Syria each academic year). Like all other Syrian students, they have to pass the entrance exams in order to be able to study. Once accepted, like all other Syrian students they study for free at the state-owned universities (but have to pay for their own living expenses). During summer vacation and after graduation, these students are required to return to the occupied side of the Golan Heights. Reasons given for this requirement differ.[41] Students in the final years of their studies continued to cross the Syria after the outbreak of the civil war but by autumn 2013 there were no new Golani students entering Syrian Universities (Lazareva 2013). Since 1988, passage from the Golan Heights into Syria further occurs at the time of the Druze pilgrimage to Zabadani west of Damascus in September each year (ICRC 22 September 2010) as well as during occasional special arrangements, such as during the funeral of President Hafez al-Asad in 2000 (Mualem 2000). The pilgrims are received either by the President or a Minister (Asad Safadi, interview Majdal Shams 15 November 2007), indicating the importance of these visits. The ICRC also facilitated visits by Syrians from the Golan Heights to Syria 1988–1992. These visits were stopped by Israel and ICRC efforts to resume them have failed so far. The possibility for the ICRC to bring visitors from the Golan Heights to Syria through Jordan is rejected by Syria (Asad Safadi, interview Majdal Shams 15 November 2007). Syrian individuals from the Golan Heights who wish to travel to Syria through Jordan privately are however allowed to do so since the 1994 Israeli-Jordanian peace treaty was signed (Lana Baydas, interview Damascus 18 March 2003). Syrian radio and TV further both directs programs to the inhabitants of the Golan Heights as well as reports on the lives of 'our Syrian people on the Golan Heights' (Asad Safadi, interview Majdal Shams 15 November 2007 and Fawzi Abu Jabal, interview Majdal Shams 14 November 2007).

In 2005 Syria approved the first official trade links between Syria and occupied Golan Heights when allowing the buying of apples produced by the Syrian inhabitants of the Golan Heights. Facilitated by the ICRC and UNDOF, between 5,000–12,000 tons of apples have since then been transported annually from the occupied Golan Heights into Syria (ICRC 22 April 2010). According to Syrian statements, this trade was accepted because of the difficult economic circumstances of the Syrian citizens on the Golan Heights. Syria at the same time emphasised that this did not represent a commercial tie with Israel as the apples are 'grown on Syrian land and owned by Syrians' (Fattah 2005).

Attempts to 'administrate' the inhabitants and influence their actions

Since the beginning of the occupation of the Golan Heights in 1967, births and deaths among the Syrian citizens there have been registered in Damascus (Paul Conneally, interview Tel Aviv 12 November 2007). Since 2000, Syria pays compensation salaries to Syrian teachers who have been fired by Israeli authorities.[42] According to Mr. Asad Safadi, ICRC liaison officer on the Golan Heights, the Syrian focus on the Golan has increased since its withdrawal from Lebanon. For example, Syria has increasingly emphasised the fact that a number of Golan Heights Syrians are imprisoned in Israel and in 2005 a marathon in their support was held in Damascus. Further, in 2006 al-Asad announced that all Syrian citizens who have gone to live in the Golan Heights (through marriage) will still be paid a Syrian salary (Asad Safadi, interview Majdal Shams 15 November 2007). In the second half of 2007, it was also announced that all Syrians in occupied Golan Heights would be given Syrian ID numbers (Syrian Ministry of Information 28 October 2007).

In September 2010, two residents of occupied Majdal Shams were arrested by the Israeli security service, accused of spying on Israel for Syria (Lappin 2010). There are also strong indications that there are agents within the community, reporting to Syria on what is said and done. The implication of the presence of agents is not totally clear, but since 70 per cent of the Syrian population on the Golan Heights have first degree relatives in Syria, it is likely that there is a fear that relatives may be targeted should the Golani Syrians not behave as expected.

There are examples of Syria influencing what takes place on the ground on the Golan Heights. In 2006 a planned ICRC medical centre in Majdal Shams was stopped as the Syrian authorities did not want the centre to open. The Syrian Ministry of Foreign Affairs accused the ICRC of violating international humanitarian law by providing medical assistance directly under the ICRC flag (*sic*) (ICRC 20 and 21 June 2006). The exact reason for the Syrian rejection of the project, which it had initially approved, is not known. A possible explanation is that Syria understood the fact that the Syrians in the Golan Heights would have to use their mandatory Israeli health insurance to seek assistance at the centre as a sign of normalisation of the occupation.[43] The local community was, according to the ICRC, strongly in favour of the project but asked that the ceremony for the signing of a memorandum of understanding between the ICRC and the local community be adjourned as Syria did not want it to sign (ICRC 20 June 2006). Syrian associations on the Golan Heights, registered as NGOs in Israel, are also rejected by Syria as a registration in Israel is viewed by Syria as a normalisation of the occupation (Paul Conneally, interview Tel Aviv 12 November 2007).

The inhabitants of the Golan Heights are talked about as part of the national population. Prior to the Israeli annexation this was mainly evident in protests to the UN. In speeches they were rarely mentioned by President Hafez al-Asad except during periods of international attention: following the Israeli annexation in 1981 and during the peace process 1991–2000. President Hafez al-Asad then referred to them as 'our people', 'our brothers' or 'our sons' on the Golan Heights.[44] Bashar al-Asad has continued the same way in statements such as 'I salute our resistant people [on the Golan Heights] and our prisoners of war'.[45]

Conclusions: Syrian policies towards the Golan Heights

Ever since the Israeli occupation of the Golan Heights in 1967 Syria has demanded their return. It has tried to regain the area both by war and through negotiations. During negotiations nothing short of a full Israeli withdrawal to the June 4 1967 line would be accepted in exchange for peace. Israeli willingness to commit to such a withdrawal was what decided Syrian attitudes towards the usefulness of negotiating. Even during the January 2000 negotiations, where Syria showed unprecedented flexibility on both the exact location of the 4 June 1967 line and the other components of a peace deal, this was done in anticipation of an Israeli commitment. When this commitment failed to materialise, Syria broke off negotiations. Since the take over of Bashar al-Asad in June 2000, there have been both rumours of secret low-level negotiations and confirmed indirect negotiations between Israel and Syria. The information available holds no evidence that the Syrian position on full withdrawal to the 4 June 1967 line has changed and Syrian statements have continued to stress the necessity of an Israeli commitment to withdraw to this line as a precondition for the resumption of talks.

Syria has, to any extent possible, attempted to influence events within the Syrian villages on occupied Golan. The inhabitants are treated as any other Syrian citizens, records of deaths and births are kept in Damascus and salaries are paid to some of the inhabitants.

While there are, during the period studied, no changes concerning Syrian goals with regard to the Golan Heights, a gradual transformation in the perception of the Golan Heights can nevertheless be detected in both action and speech. The Syrian focus gradually shifted from the Palestine question and occupied Arab land, where the Golan Heights is a subordinated part, to the Syrian cause and occupied Syrian land where the Golan Heights are, of course, central. The case of the Golan Heights is further indicative of a gradual change in the Syrian conception of the contents of peace. President Hafez al-Asad had, during the 1970s, clearly stated that Syria's definition of peace was the absence of acts of war,[46] and not the open borders, normalisation, diplomatic relations and joint projects that Israel was looking for (see for instance Ben-Aharon 2000:4, Peres & Arye 1995). During the years of negotiations, Syria nevertheless showed an increasing willingness to negotiate these Israeli demands as well as an increasing flexibility with regard to satisfying Israeli security and water needs.

Even though Syria showed a willingness to compromise on the exact location of a future Syrian-Israeli border – and is likely to repeat this in the future should the opportunity to strike an acceptable deal with Israel present itself – there is no doubt that the return of the entire territory of the Golan remains the Syrian goal.

CHAPTER 6

CONCLUSIONS

Lebanon, Hatay and the Golan Heights are all Syrian territories lost. They were detached from Syria in different ways and at different points in time but have all, in some way, remained within Syrian discourse on the extension of its national territory. Syrian views of and goals for them nevertheless clearly differ. Even though Syria is often accused of ambitions to annex Lebanon and has refused to remove Hatay from its maps, the only territory Syria aims at regaining and reincorporating is the Golan.

The first territory to be separated from French-mandated Syria, Greater Lebanon, was effectively renounced in the mid-1930s in exchange for a French-Syrian treaty promising Syrian independence. In the early 1940s, the Syrian government formally recognised Lebanon as a separate state. The 1943 Lebanese National Pact, which Syrian Prime Minister Jamil Mardam helped negotiate, included clear instructions on Syrian-Lebanese relations: Syria would respect the independence of Lebanon within its 1920 borders and Lebanon would, in turn, refrain from in any way becoming a threat to Syria. This equation – or some version of it – has guided Syrian policy towards Lebanon ever since. It has resulted in a clear Syrian tendency to try to control events in Lebanon and have it act in accordance with Syrian interests. Verbal affirmations of Lebanese independence were therefore coupled with non-verbal policies that blatantly overlooked Lebanese sovereignty. With the outbreak of the second Lebanese civil war, the necessity to control events in Lebanon increased and Syria's 1976 military intervention greatly facilitated this. Practically given a free hand in Lebanon following the 1989 Taif Agreement, Syria established its hegemony. No actions were taken to incorporate Lebanon into Syria, even though this could realistically have been attempted during the 1990–2004 period when Lebanon was firmly in Syrian control. Instead, even though it was clear that Syria had the upper hand, it took efforts to maintain the appearance of Lebanon and Syria as two separate states voluntarily coordinating policies. The 2005 Syrian withdrawal was carried out reluctantly and changed the rules of the game. With a Lebanese parliamentarian majority that openly defied Damascus, Syria was no longer able to exercise direct control over its neighbour. Instead, Syria worked through powerful allies in the Lebanese political arena. Foremost of these was Hizbullah, through which Syria continued to have an indirect say in Lebanese domestic and foreign affairs, albeit to a lesser degree than during the 1990–2004 period. As Hizbullah's influence increased in Lebanon following the May 2008 Doha Agreement, so did Syria's. During 2009 and 2010, most important personalities within the anti-Syrian March 14 coalition therefore found it wiser to reconcile with Damascus and turn a new page in Syrian-Lebanese relations. In an effort to prove its respect for Lebanese independence, Syria established diplomatic relations with Lebanon for the first time in 2009. This was a move appreciated by the international community. However, in the light of previous Syrian policies towards Lebanon, the establishment of diplomatic relations merely followed a familiar pattern – to uphold the image of the Syrian-Lebanese relationship as that of two equal states whose interests are so similar that they naturally act in concordance, while at the same time attempting to influence and control developments in Lebanon. Lebanon has long ceased to be perceived as part of Syria. Syrian goals are therefore not to incorporate or annex it as has often been claimed. Rather, Syria aims at extracting the political and economic advantages that come from controlling it.

Eighteen years after the creation of Greater Lebanon, another French decision led to the loss of Hatay. Unlike Greater Lebanon, which was renounced in exchange for an expected (but not materialised) independence, the loss of Hatay has never been formally recognised. It can nevertheless be concluded that Hatay, like Greater Lebanon, was eventually in practice traded for the main priority of the Syrian National Bloc: independence from France. In 1946 Syria agreed not to make any formal claims to the area provided Turkey recognised Syrian independence. Syrian policies have since been ambiguous. Despite several Turkish attempts to get a formal Syrian recognition of the border, none has been made. During times of heightened bilateral tension, such as during the 1958–1961 UAR period and the run-up to the 1998 Syrian-Turkish crisis, Hatay resurfaced as a point of conflict. Although Hatay has remained on (almost) all Syrian maps until today, the question of Hatay has never been a priority for Syrian officials. During the 2004–2011 period, when Syrian-Turkish relations boomed to an unprecedented level, Syrian officials showed a clear desire not to share their understanding of the status of the border separating Syria from Hatay. As bilateral relations developed, the solution Syria and Turkey decided upon was to blur the border. Steps towards this end were taken with decisions to establish a free trade area and a shared Friendship Dam on the Orontes river. Blurring the border was a convenient solution for both parties. The shared dam would help Syria avoid having to clearly specify to whom Hatay belonged while Turkey, on the other hand, got a clear – albeit indirect – Syrian recognition of the border when an agreement on the national jurisdiction of both sides of the dam was signed. With increasingly deteriorating bilateral relations, in November 2012 Hatay reemerged in Syrian media as a 'stolen' region, occupied by Turkey. Reports in Syrian media pointed to 'popular demands' for the return of Hatay to Syria. As during previous periods of Syrian-Turkish tension, however, no such demands were made by Syrian officials. Instead, Hatay had again turned into a rallying point for national mobilisation.

The third and final territory lost, the Golan, was occupied by Israel during the 1967 Six Day War. It is less ambiguous than Lebanon and Hatay as Syrian policies have remained consistent, and discourse and action have been coherent.

Although both the Golan Heights and Hatay remain on Syrian maps as part of the Syrian national territory and although Syria has refused to formally recognise Israeli and Turkish sovereignty over the two areas, this is where similarities between these two cases end. In the case of Hatay, a free trade area was established on the border, a shared Friendship Dam was to be constructed and the border itself was referred to as 'broken'. In the case of the Golan, Israeli ideas of joint projects were firmly rejected.[1] While Syrian claims to Hatay have been formulated verbally on rare occasions, claims to the Golan Heights have been continuously repeated since their occupation in 1967. While Syria went to war in an attempt to liberate the Golan Heights, no such attempts were made with regard to Hatay. Prior to the Turkish annexation, Syria agreed to negotiations on the partition of Hatay while, with regard to the Golan Heights, Syria has always insisted that the entire area must be returned.

As Syrian-Turkish relations improved following the 1998 crisis, Syria avoided discussing Hatay. Instead, it stressed the importance of starting with points of agreement, developing relations in other areas, before trying to solve the points of conflict. With regard to the Golan Heights, the Syrian approach was the complete opposite. Negotiations with Israel were initiated with the sole goal of regaining the Golan and no agreements within other areas could be concluded prior to an Israeli commitment to full withdrawal. While Hatay was described as an old problem that was no longer important, it was made clear that no matter how long it takes, the Golan Heights will have to return to Syria. The conflict over the Golan, unlike that of Hatay, would thus never be too old to be important. The borders decided upon and drawn by the French mandate power, separating Syria from Lebanon and Hatay, are now accepted. The 1923 border between Syria and British-mandated Palestine, drawn by the same mandate power, is however described as 'drawn by imperialism' and does therefore not qualify as a Syrian border. The future border between Syria and Israel instead has to reflect Syrian gains in the 1948–1949 Arab-Israeli war and be based on what is known as the 4 June 1967 line.

With regard to the Golan Heights, Israeli security concerns were officially rejected (but partly met during the final negotiations in 1999 and 2000), and Syria stressed that the interest of one state must stop at the border of the next. This was a principle clearly not applied in Lebanon. On the contrary, Syrian interests and – above all – security concerns, were the driving forces behind continuous Syrian interventionist policies in Lebanon.

Taken together, this study of Syrian policies towards Lebanon, Hatay and the Golan Heights has pointed to the complexity of the relationship between territory and state. In light of this, the often assumed 'givenness' of state territory becomes problematic. As we have seen, a state may treat a territory outside of its border as an extension of its own territory without raising claims to it, it may signal territorial claims but not act upon them and it may express its territorial ambitions so vaguely that they seem to be in a more or less constant flux.

Possible explanations for differences in Syrian policies towards Lebanon, Hatay and the Golan Heights

One of the obvious differences between Lebanon, Hatay and the Golan Heights is that they were lost on different occasions and in different ways. Of the three, only the Golan was included in Syrian post-independence state building. When it was lost in war in 1967, it had formed part of independent Syria for more than two decades. Lebanon and Hatay, on the other hand, were lost due to French decisions prior to Syrian independence. While Lebanon was separated from Syria just one week after the imposition of the French mandate in 1920, Syrian acceptance of this came in exchange for an anticipated independence some fifteen years later. Hatay was ceded to Turkey towards the end of the mandate period and was, like Lebanon, in practice let go of in exchange for independence. The 1946 modus vivendi reached with Turkey over the area – no official Syrian demands for the area in exchange for Turkish recognition of Syrian independence – clearly spells this out. Both Lebanon and Hatay were thereby given up as ways of securing statehood and independence for Syria. The Golan Heights, on the other hand, were taken from independent Syria with its internationally recognized borders. This, and the fact that they were occupied by the state the Syrian Baath Party had pledged to defeat, as well as the fact that Hafez al-Asad served as Minister of Defence when they were lost, have added to the importance of regaining the Golan.

Syrian policies towards Lebanon, Hatay and the Golan Heights clearly reflect the existence or lack of internationally recognised borders. Even though policies towards Lebanon have clearly ignored Lebanese *sovereignty*, Syria has continuously strove to uphold the image of Lebanon as a separate state. The *existence* of a border between them has not been questioned since the 1930s. Despite Syrian maps showing Hatay as part of Syria, prior to the Syrian civil war the border separating Syria from Hatay was functioning as an 'ordinary' border with border gates on both sides and with no indications of Syrian opposition to the existence of this border. With regard to the disengagement line between Syria and the occupied part of the Golan Heights, it has a UN crossing used by students, brides and pilgrims, but is otherwise closed.

Especially in the case of Lebanon, it is clear that Syrian policies have to a large extent been dependent on and shaped by the international context. During the period of the Lebanese civil war 1975–1990, Syrian policy in Lebanon was given tacit consent by all important actors including the USA, the USSR, the Arab League and Israel (the latter on the condition that certain 'red lines' were respected, see Fisk 2003:103–104). Neither was there international opposition during the post-war period prior to 2003. Following Syria's opposition to the 2003 invasion of Iraq, Syrian policies in Lebanon (and elsewhere) came under heavy international criticism. UN Security Council resolutions urged Syria both to withdraw its army and not to interfere in Lebanese domestic affairs. Pressure to withdraw further increased following the assassination of Lebanese Prime Minister Rafiq al-Hariri in February 2005, and Syria did so in order to 'show that Syria respects UN resolutions'. Syrian determination to, if unable to *control* events, at least block undesired developments in Lebanon was still pursued by proxy through its allies in Lebanon. As Syria's isolation cracked towards the end of the first decade of the 2000s, its influence in Lebanon again increased. While regional and international circumstances have thus clearly affected Syrian possibilities to act, and thereby its choice of policies, they have not affected the long-term Syrian goal.

The Council of the League of Nations did not discuss or question the 1939 French secession of Hatay to Turkey. The Permanent Mandates

Conclusions 143

Commission did bring it up, protesting the secession as a 'flagrant violation' of the Mandate text (Philip 1939), but did not demand the return of the area to Syria. It thereby, in practice accepted the French move. The Arab World chose to act with variance: Iraq (which had negotiated the 'no claims no recognition' deal between Syria and Turkey) and Jordan, both recognised Turkish sovereignty over Hatay in 1946. In 1961 a conference of Arab League lawyers called for the 'Syrianisation' of Hatay (Walz 1961), and in the mid-1980s, Saudi Arabia choose not to grant visas for hajj pilgrimage to Turkish nationals from Hatay (Yilmaz 2006:113, Liel 2001:193). Although the reason for this denial is not clear, the fact that this Saudi policy was introduced 40 years after the Turkish annexation of Hatay and only maintained for a short period of time suggests that a principled position on Turkish sovereignty over Hatay was not behind it. All in all, Syria has not had particularly strong international support for claiming Hatay. It should, however, be pointed out that it has never *sought* international support. Even though the French secession of Hatay was a violation of both the Mandate text and the 1923 Lausanne Treaty, Syria did not, after independence, try to take its case to the international arena. It has not complained to the United Nations nor attempted to have the Turkish annexation of Hatay tried in international court. The lack of intense Syrian verbal claims to the region and actual efforts to regain it has instead resulted in the Hatay question remaining largely unknown to the international community. It is therefore not possible to conclude that a lack of international support has discouraged Syrian claims. The opposite may also be true; a lack of active Syrian claims to Hatay may have resulted in a lack of support.

As neither the 1967 occupation nor the 1981 annexation of the Golan Heights are internationally recognised there is, in a sense, international support for the Syrian claims to the Golan Heights. Due to the fact that the disengagement line has remained calm since 1974 and the Syrian inhabitants on the Golan have chosen civil disobedience rather than violent means to protest the occupation, international attention has been paid to the case of the Golan Heights mostly during periods of Israeli-Syrian peace negotiations. The Israeli occupation has been condemned and demands for an Israeli withdrawal have been made in numerous UN resolutions, starting with Security Council resolution 242 of November 1967. Demands for the rescindment of the annexation are also numerous, starting with Security Council resolution 497 of December 1981, which declares the annexation null and void. It is, however, clear that international support for Syrian claims to the Golan Heights is support 'in theory' only. Apart from the UN resolutions and statements pointed to above, there is no, and has never been, any serious international pressure for Israel to withdraw from the Golan, and it is unclear how this lack of support beyond UN resolutions has affected Syrian policy on a more general level.

When trying to understand Syrian policies towards Lebanon, Hatay and the Golan Heights, the respective value of the three territories should also be considered. This is obviously a complicated endeavour as the perception of values may be very subjective. With regard to Lebanon, at the time the National Bloc accepted Lebanon as a separate entity in the mid-1930s, the types of values most evident were the intrinsic and economic ones. Numerous family ties extended across the border and especially the Sunni Muslims of Lebanon initially argued that Lebanon should not be separated from Syria. As we have seen, Syrian officials helped change their position and did not themselves find demography an obstacle to separation. It should, however, be noted that demographic reasons were often given by Syrian officials when trying to explain Syrian policies in Lebanon. The Syrian and Lebanese were then referred to as 'brothers' and 'family' with a shared history and culture. The slogan 'One people in two states' is based on the same argument. There were also shared economic interests as Syrian and Lebanese financial matters were intertwined through the customs union and *Intérêts Communs*. Syria expected these arrangements to remain in place after independence and economy and financial matters were therefore not seen as obstacles to separate statehood. This is not to say that Syria's post-independence policies towards Lebanon have not been guided by economic interests. On the contrary, trade possibilities and Lebanon as a labour market for Syrian guest workers are important factors. Smuggling, in Damascus known as the fourth branch of trade – the others being domestic, foreign and transit trade – (Batatu 1999:211) should also be added. The Syrian army was deeply involved in this business and a good number of officers could secure an extra flow of income thanks to the porousness of the border. A further source of income for the Syrian army has been drug-running from the Biqaa valley (Damali Stefflbauer 1999:236–237). Along the 260 kilometers constituting the border there are at least 72 crossing points, out of which only four are official (Abbas, al-Tars, Darwish, al-Arabi 2008). As became evident during the Syrian civil war, the many unsurveilled crossing points do not only open up for the smuggling of commodities into Syria but also for the entrance of arms and rebels.

The main Syrian security concern – Israel – was not created until after Syria's withdrawal of claims to Lebanon. As concluded in chapter three, the conflict with Israel is what has mainly guided Syrian policies towards Lebanon in the post-independence period. This has not affected the view of Lebanon as a separate state but has certainly demonstrated that controlling events in Lebanon is in itself a strategic value. Since the end of the Lebanese civil war, Syria's alliance with Hizbullah offers leverage in its conflict with Israel. The mostly low-intensity conflict between Hizbullah and the Israeli army provides Syria with a way of pressuring Israel without having to put its own military personnel on the line or assume responsibility. Prior to and during the Lebanese civil war, a Syrian ambition to control Palestinian guerrillas stemmed from the same thought: Lebanon would serve as a base for the struggle against Israel. The risk of retaliation affecting Syrian territory and citizens was thereby reduced. The alliance with Hizbollah also serves as leverage in the sense that Syria has been able to convey the image that a Lebanese-Israeli peace deal will be impossible without a green light from Damascus. Although such a peace agreement is highly unlikely after the transformed position of Hizbollah and the outbreak of the Syrian civil war, a calm Israeli-Lebanese border, guaranteed by Syria, was earlier one of the few things Syria could have offered in return for the entire Golan Heights.

For Syria, the loss of Hatay meant the loss of fertile land as about half of the total surface consists of agricultural land (Yilmaz 2006:110). According to Bandazian, Hatay was one of the richest and most fertile provinces in French-mandated Syria (Bandazian 1967:61). There were also other values, such as the port of Iskenderun, which at the time of the Turkish annexation of Hatay was the only modern port in French mandated Syria (as Beirut formed part of Greater Lebanon). Neither of these values stopped the Syrian government from in practice accepting the loss of Hatay in 1946. The enigma with regard to Hatay is rather to understand why the area has remained on Syrian maps. Although difficult to examine, it is possible that keeping Hatay on the map without entertaining the thought of trying to regain it, has taken on the value of a 'trading card'. A Syrian removal of Hatay from the map could then come in exchange of something Turkey could offer. Water could be one such possible trading good. However, the fact that Syria as late as 2009 refused to formally recognise Turkish sovereignty over Hatay in exchange for a water deal suggests that this is not it (or that the deal was not good enough). Another possibility is that removing Hatay from the map is domestically difficult as backing down from a long-lasting claim may cause loss of face. As Batatu (1999:135) has pointed out, a considerable amount of the Arab Alawites who chose to leave Hatay after the Turkish annexation joined the Baath party, reinforcing its pan-Arab tendency. As seen in chapter four, while Syrian officials quickly accepted the Turkish annexation, public opinion did not. By the early 2000s, however, public awareness in Syria about Hatay was low. Although Syrian schoolbooks continued to depict Hatay as a stolen region and 'generations of Syrians have been educated to feel a geopolitical injustice done to them' (Yilmaz 2006:112), according to Syrian analyst and journalist Sami Moubayed 'everyone can tell you the exact date of the occupation of the Golan but nobody would be able to specify even the year Hatay was lost' (interview, Damascus 15 March 2003). If documentary segments and news reports on Hatay keep being broadcast on Syrian TV, as they were during late 2012 and early 2013, this may very well change public awareness and complicate a future removal of the area from the map.

It is evident that the Syrian avoidance of and ambiguity with regard to Hatay is meant for both Turkish and domestic consumption. As policies immediately preceding the outbreak of the Syrian civil war aimed at blurring the border, it is conceivable that Syrian decision makers planned to remove the area from the map once joint Syrian-Turkish projects in Hatay had developed sufficiently to make the border lose its importance altogether.

No large movements demanding the return of Hatay to Syria have formed within the area itself. Potential activists may have been discouraged by separatism being a criminal act in Turkey, but the fact that inhabitants could choose to either stay and accept Turkish citizenship or move to Syria or Lebanon is probably also a reason. Inhabitants vehemently opposed to Turkish rule thereby left the area. In the 1990s, there were reports of at least one secret Arab movement in Hatay, The Popular Front for the Liberation of liwa Iskandarun, demanding the return of the area to Syria. The more immediate goals of the organization, as expressed in pamphlets distributed in the towns of Hatay, were of another nature; to work for the cultural and linguistic rights of Arabs in Turkey (Khalifah 1999). Since the outbreak of the civil war in Syria, Hatay, with its large Arab Alawite minority – constituting more than one third of Hatay's total of 1.5 million inhabitants (International Crisis Group 30 April 2013:i) – has seen large demonstrations in support of Bashar al-Asad. This, in combination with the great influx of Syrian, mostly Sunni, refugees and rebels, has caused fears of possible spillover effects from the Syrian civil war into Hatay. Demonstrators have, however, not formulated clear demands for the return of Hatay to Syria.

Good relations with Turkey were certainly of strategic value. Not only did Turkey in the post-2003 period continue to develop relations with Syria despite US pressure not to (Altunışık & Tür 2006:230), it also acted as a go-between and mediator in order to get Syria and Israel back to the negotiation table. Prior to the Syrian 2011 uprising, Turkey stood by Syria in times of trouble and the careful increasing official signs of recognition of Turkish sovereignty over Hatay were probably the result of this.

The Golan Heights are often pointed to as possessing strategic values. Because of their height and location they are considered a natural barrier (Muslih 1993:626). However, as Hafez al-Asad pointed out on occasion, both Syria and Israel have experienced the fact that this barrier does not provide sufficient protection to avoid an attack.[2] Israel occupied them in 1967 and Syria initially regained most of them in 1973. Further, with the technological advancement within the arms industry, the strategic value increasingly loses its strength. Still, it continues to constitute a psychologically important territory to hold. The Israeli army is today stationed 35 km from Damascus with no natural barriers to delay a possible attack. Further, the Israeli monitoring station at the top of Mount Hermon allows sight into Syria and as far as western Iraq (Muslih 1993:627). This is clearly psychologically stressful and in the Syrian capital it is not uncommon to hear people say that the Israelis on Mount Hermon are able to see the registration numbers of cars driving around in the city. The Golan Heights are also valuable as a point for national mobilisation.

As for natural resources, the Golan contains the Banyas spring and, with Syria's original definition of the 4 June 1967 line, gives access to the lake of Tiberias and the Jordan River. Two points indicate that Syria does not insist on regaining the Golan because of the water. First, during the 1993–1996 negotiations, Syria claimed that if the US and Israel would help Syria solve its water conflicts with Turkey there would be no water problem between Israel and Syria (Rabinovich 1998:219) and in 2000 Syria accepted a border off Lake Tiberias so that Israel could retain control over the water of the lake. As the lake depends on sources on the Golan for two-thirds of its water (Savir 1998:279), Syria agreed to a control mechanism to ensure that the quantity and quality of the water flowing from the Golan to Tiberias would not be changed, provided a similar guarantee was produced by Turkey (Ross 2004:554). Had Syria claimed the Golan or insisted on the 4 June 1967 line because of the water resources only, it would not have agreed to any of this. This is not to say that water is of no importance in the Syrian view of the Golan Heights. However, the fact that the Golan is internationally recognised as Syrian territory and occupied by the arch enemy Israel outweighs water in terms of explaining Syrian insistence on its return.

Prospects for the future?

If the past is a predictor of the future, Syria will continue to strive to increase its influence over Lebanon. Efforts will be made to block

Lebanese developments perceived as a threat to Syria, all the while stressing Lebanon's existence as a separate state. The Syrian ambition to control Lebanon will remain based on security concerns and not on a perception of Lebanon as part of its national territory. As a result of the Syrian civil war, relations with especially Hizbullah will grow ever stronger.

It is highly unlikely that Syria will raise claims to Hatay. As the planned blurring of the border is not an option under current circumstances, Syria will most probably keep Hatay on the map and continue to use the area as a national issue to rally around. In view of Turkey's support for the Syrian opposition, it is not likely that official Syrian views of Hatay will change should the civil war eventually result in the downfall of Bashar al-Asad's regime. For instance, Muhammad Riad al-Shaqfa of the Syrian Muslim Brotherhood, in a 2012 interview, stated that while the Golan Heights must be liberated by any means possible, Hatay is not occupied territory[3] and, as mentioned in chapter four, textbooks used in Syrian refugee schools in Turkey have already omitted Hatay from the Syrian map.

A future peace with Israel requires a full Israeli withdrawal from the Golan. At the time of writing in May 2014, such a peace agreement is distant. Syria's self-image as the last remaining frontline state makes large scale concessions on the Golan unlikely. A change of regimes in Syria can not be expected to change this.

NOTES

Chapter 1. Introduction

1. Hafez al-Asad, served as Prime Minister 1970–1971 and President 1971–2000. Prior to his 1970 coup he served as Defense Minister.

Chapter 2. The consolidation of the territorial state and the political development of the Syrian Arab Republic

1. Faysal reappeared as king the following year, this time on the throne of British-mandated Iraq. From there he strove for unification with Syria. His acceptance of the French ultimatum and his negotiations with Britain and France on Palestine and Lebanon had by then largely lost him his appeal to Arab nationalists within French-mandated Syria (Seale 2010:147).
2. *Vilayeh* was an Ottoman administrative division, usually translated as 'province'. In Syria the vilayehs ceased to exist after the establishment of the French mandate (Balanche 2006:38).
3. The Ottoman subdivision of a *vilayeh* was a *sanjak*. After independence the term sanjak was changed to *muhafazah*. The Ottoman subdivision of a sanjak was a *qadha*. While this term is still in use in Lebanon, the Syrian post-independence subdivision of a muhafazah is *mantiqah*, the subdivision of which is a *nahiyah* (Balanche 2006:38–39).
4. The Common Interests Department managed customs, postal services, antiquities and supervised concessionary companies. The income generated was at the disposal of the French High Commissioner (Chaitani 2007:18).

5. Khoury points to several reasons why the National Bloc needed to avoid getting entangled in Palestinian politics. Support for the rebels in Palestine risked robbing the Bloc of valuable British diplomatic support, needed as leverage against the French mandate authorities. Further, as Palestine was at the time mandated Syria's most valuable export market, upheaval there damaged the Syrian economy generally (1987a:331) as well as the economic interests of the Syrian political élite (which also constituted its economic élite) personally (1987b:33).
6. See for instance *Hadith al-sayyid al-rais ila bathat majallat 'Time' al-amrikiyyah 1989/3/27* (President Hafez al-Asad interviewed by the delegation of the American Time Magazine 27 March 1989), *Hadith al-sayyid al-rais Hafez al-Asad li-majallat 'Der Spiegel' al-almaniyyah al-gharbiyyah khilal ziyaratihi ila Bon 1978/6/9* (Interview with President Hafez al-Asad in the West German magazine Der Spegel during his visit to Bonn 9 June 1978) and *Hadith al-sayyid al-rais Hafez al-Asad ila jaridat 'New York Times' 1977/8/24* (Interview with President Hafez al-Asad in New York Times 24 August 1977).
7. In 1963 officers affiliated with the Baath Party overthrew the secessionist regime and embarked upon unification talks with Egypt and Iraq and later only Iraq. Both attempts failed. Al-Asad in 1971 formed the largely fictional State of the Federation of Arab Republics with Egypt and Libya. In 1978 there were unification talks with Iraq and in 1980 Libya declared its intention to unite with Syria (Kienle 1995:55).
8. For a different view, see Kelidar 1993.
9. Winder's study of Syrian deputies shows that throughout 1919–1959 Syria was governed by no more than 100 families (Winder 1963:42), and Van Dusen argues that at independence, Syria was ruled by a 'club' of 50 families (Van Dusen 1972:126).
10. The term 'civil war' is in reality a gross simplification. While all civil wars have some degree of external interference, in the Syrian case this is especially so. There are arms shipments to both the regime and the rebel groups and non-Syrians are directly involved in the fighting on both sides.
11. The *tarbush* is a traditional male hat, often used to symbolise the Ottoman Empire and/or Turkey.
12. The *kafiyeh* is a traditional Arab and Kurdish male headdress.
13. For details on this class during the Baath era, see Perthes 1991.
14. For instance, the Jabal Druz (the Druze Mountain) is known as Jabal al-Arab (the Mountain of the Arabs), the Jibal al-Alawiyin (Alawite Mountains) are known as Jibal al-sahiliyyah (the Coastal Mountains) and Wadi al-nasarah

(the valley of the Christians) is known as Wadi al-nadara (the blooming valley) (van Dam 1997:6–7, Schaebler 1998:360, Valter 2002:70 note 59).
15. The original draft had not mentioned Islam at all as the earlier constitution's declaration of Islam as the religion of the state had been omitted. Faced with massive public protests, the final version declared that Islamic jurisprudence is a major source of Syrian legislation and that the religion of the president of the republic must be Islam (thereby again confirming that the Alawite president was Muslim). This remains unchanged in the 2012 constitution.
16. These predictions were (quite naively) based on the fact that Bashar al-Asad had trained as an ophthalmologist in London for 18 months and had thereby been exposed to 'Western values'. Analysts nurturing hope that this would somehow affect Syrian foreign policy in a 'pro-Western' direction have had to join ranks with Winder who in 1963 concluded that although a majority of Syrian Members of Parliament 1919–1959 had been 'extensively exposed to the West' through studies and travelling, there was 'a lack of positive results in foreign policy' (Winder 1963:43).

Chapter 3. 'We are not strangers here': Syrian policy towards Lebanon

1. The article, 'The Legacy of Equivocation', written in September 1939, is reproduced as Prologue to Salma Mardam Bey's *Syria's Quest for Independence 1939–1945* (1994).
2. *Shukri al-Quwatli yukhatib ummatahu: mukhtarat min khutabihi wa-bayanat* (Skukri al-Quwatli speaks to his nation: selected speeches and announcements), p 91.
3. Ibid. p 98.
4. These included a Joint Customs Directorate which made it necessary for Syria and Lebanon to try to reconcile their fundamentally different economic interests and seek agreements for tariffs and quotas. As Syria favoured protectionism while Lebanon preferred a free import, these agreements were hard to reach (see Chaitani 2007).
5. See for instance President Husni al-Zaim's note of protest to the Lebanese government 4 April 1949, available in *Middle East Journal*'s chronology (vol 3, no 3, p 323) and *Al-alaqat al-lubnaniyyah as-suriyyah 1943–1985: waqai bibliyughrafiyyah, wathaiq* (Lebanese-Syrian Relations 1943–1985: Bibliographical Proceedings, Documents), vol 1, p 220 for President Nazim al-Qudsi's protest in January 1962 to criticism directed against him in Lebanese press and his proposal that both governments should forbid their press to 'attack the presidents of states with friendly intentions'.

6. See for instance the *Middle East Journal*'s Chronology for 1953, vol 7, no 1, p 81.
7. See *Middle East Journal*'s Chronology for October 1957, vol 11, no 1, p 74.
8. The US envoy to mediate in the crisis however claimed that the tapping of telephone lines between Beirut and Damascus had proved that Lebanese rebels were receiving outside support (Murphy 1964:490).
9. See 1–2 August 1962 in *Al-alaqat al-lubnaniyyah as-suriyyah 1943–1985: waqai bibliyughrafiyyah, wathaiq* (Lebanese-Syrian Relations 1943–1985: Bibliographical Proceedings, Documents), vol 2.
10. The second step was partly taken care of in the Lebanese constitution where the border is specified in writing, albeit not in great detail. See paragraph 1 of the Lebanese Constitution.
11. Excerpts of interview with Kuwaiti newspaper *Al-ray al-am* 7 January 1976, available in *Al-alaqat* vol 1 1986:254. The official reason given as to why a partition along sectarian lines could not be permitted was later given by President al-Asad who said that small states based on religion would be in Israel's interest only as Israel would be strongest among them. This would also weaken the argument that the 'Zionist state' was racist (see *Khitab al-sayyid al-rais Hafez al-Asad khilal liqaihi ma adaa majlis al-muhafazat li-l-idarah al-mahaliyyah 76/7/20*, Hafez al-Asad's speech during his meeting with members of the Council of the Provinces for Local Administration 20 July 1976).
12. 'Protocol from the Aramoun summit', 30 January 1976 (p 256), available in *Al-alaqat* vol 1 1986:255–260. 'Erroneous Palestinian behaviour' is not specified but would probably equal Palestinian guerillas focusing on issues not related to Israel. As al-Asad put it: 'They have forgotten or pretend to have forgotten [...] that Lebanon is not Palestine. Beirut is the capital of Lebanon, not the capital of Palestine' and 'I can not imagine the link between fighting in the mountains of Lebanon and the liberation of Palestine' (speech 20 July 1976, see note 11).
13. *Kalimat al-sayyid al-rais Hafez al-Asad fi al-mutamar al-am al-thani li-ittihad shbibat al-thawrah 76/4/12* (Speech by Hafez al-Asad at the Second General Congress of the Youth of the Revolution, 12 April 1976).
14. 'Protocol from the Aramoun summit', 30 January 1976 (p 256), available in *Al-alaqat* vol 1 1986:255–260.
15. Hafez al-Asad's speech 20 July 1976, see note 11.
16. Full text of the speech available in *Al-alaqat* vol. 1 1986:260–263.
17. Hafez al-Asad's speech 20 July 1976, see note 11.
18. Whenever asked about reasons for the intervention, this is the answer delivered by Hafez al-Asad throughout the period 1976–2000, see for instance

NOTES 155

Hadith al-sayyid al-rais Hafez al-Asad ila-sahifat 'Washington Post' al-amrikiyyah 1976/11/29 (Interview with President Hafez al-Asad in the American paper Washington Post 29 November 1976) and *Hadith al-sayyid al-rais Hafez al-Asad ila sahifat 'Washington Post' wa-majallat 'Newsweek' al-amrikiyyatayn 1991/7/28* (interview with President Hafez al-Asad in the American paper Washington Post and the journal Newsweek 28 July 1991). This is confirmed by Bashar al-Asad, see for instance *Muqabalat al-sayyid al-rais Bashar al-Asad ma sahifat 'Corriere della Sera' al-italiyyah bi-tarikh 16 shubat 2002* (Interview of President Bashar al-Asad with the Italian newspaper *Corriere della Sera*, 16 February 2002).

19. This is repeated by al-Asad Sr throughout the 1976–2000 period and al-Asad Jr until today, see for instance speech delivered by Hafez al-Asad 20 July 1976 (see note 11), *Kalimat al-sayyid al-rais Hafez al-Asad fi madubah al-asha alati aqamah ala sharafihi al-qadah al-sufiyit fi-l-Kremlin 1977/4/18* (President Hafez al-Asad's speech at the dinner party given in his honour by the Soviet leaders in Kremlin 18 April 1977), interview for the *Washington Post* and *Newsweek Magazine* 28 July 1991 (see note 81), *Hadith al-sayyid al-rais Hafez al-Asad fi al-mutamar al-sahafi aladhi aqadahu maa al-rais al-faransi Jacques Chirac 1996/10/21* (President Hafez al-Asad during the press conference he held together with French president Jacques Chirac 21 October 1996) For Bashar al-Asad, see for instance *Muqabalat al-sayyid al-rais Bashar al-Asad ma sahifat al-watan al-qatariyyah* (President Bashar al-Asad's interview with the Qatari newspaper al-Watan), 27 April 2008.

20. Speech 20 July 1976 (see note 11), *Hadith al-sayyid al-rais ila al-katib wa-l-sahafi al-sayyid Patrick Seale li-sahifat 'The Observer' 1982/3/2* (President Hafez al-Asad interviewed by British writer and journalist Patrick Seale for The Observer 2 March 1982).

21. See for instance *Kalimat al-sayyid al-rais Hafez al-Asad fi dhikra al-thalitha ashara li-thawrat al-thamin min adhar 1976/3/8* (Speech by President Hafez al-Asad's on the 13th anniversary of the 8th of March revolution 8 March 1976, speech 20 July 1976 (see note 11), *Kalimat al-sayyid al-rais Hafez al-Asad fi al-jalsah al-thalitha alati aqadaha al-mutamar al-arabi al-ifriqi al-awwal 1977/3/8* (Speech by President Hafez al-Asad during the third session convened by the first Arab-African Congress 8 March 1977).

22. See for instance speech 20 July 1976 (see note 11).

23. See for instance *Hadith al-sayyid al-rais Hafez al-Asad li-l-sahafah al-iraniyyah 1975/12/24* (Interview with Hafez al-Asad by Iranian press 24 December 1975), speech 20 July 1976 (see note 11), *Kalimat al-sayyid al-rais Hafez al-Asad bi-maduba asha aqamaha ala sharaf al-rais Mengistu Haile Mariam 1988/10/11* (Speech by President Hafez al-Asad during the dinner

party he held in honour of Ethiopian President Mengistu Haile Mariam 11 October 1988).

24. *Hadith al-sayyid al-rais Hafez al-Asad ila shabkat al-televizyon al-amriki 'ABC' 1984/4/22* (Interview with President Hafez al-Asad with the American TV network ABC 22 April 1984).
25. For instance, in 1978 he claimed that had it been possible to conduct a survey in Lebanon, it would show that 90 per cent of the Lebanese wanted Syrian forces in Lebanon (*Hadith al-sayyid al-rais Hafez al-Asad ila al-televizyon al-faransi 'al-qanah al-thania' 1978/10/28* Interview with President Hafez al-Asad for French TV Channel Two 28 October 1978) and in 1989 he said that 80 per cent of the Lebanese were in favour of Syrian policies in Lebanon (*Hadith al-sayyid al-rais Hafez al-Asad ila baathat majallat 'Time' al-amrikiyya 1989/3/27* (Interview) with President Hafez al-Asad in Time Magazine 27 March 1989).
26. *Khitab al-sayyid al-rais Hafez al-Asad fi al-dhikra al-rabia wa-l-ishrin li-thawrah al-thamin min adhar 1987/3/8* (Speech by President Hafez al-Asad at the 24th anniversary of the 8th of March revolution 8 March 1987).
27. *Kalimat as-sayyid al-rais Hafez al-Asads fi iftitah al-dawrah al-riyadiyyah al-arabiyyah al-khamisah 1976/10/6* (Speech at the opening of the fifth Arab Sports Round 6 October 1976), *Hadith al-sayyid al-rais Hafez al-Asad li-l-wafd al-ilami al-murafiq li-wazir al-kharijiyyah almanya al-ittihadiyyah al-sayyid Hans-Dietrich Genscher 1977/02/09* (President Hafez al-Asad interviewed by the press delegation accompanying the West German Foreign Minister Hans-Dietrich Genscher 9 February 1977), *Hadith al-sayyid al-rais Hafez al-Asad ila al-majallah al-faransiyyah 'Le Point' 1983/12/20* (President Hafez al-Asad interviewed by the French magazine Le Point 20 December 1983), *Hadith al-sayyid al-rais Hafez al-Asad ila al-sahafi wa-l-mualliq al-britani Patrick Seale 1984/5/16* (President Hafez al-Asad interviewed by British journalist and analyst Patrick Seale 16 May 1984), interview in *Time Magazine* 27 March 1989 (see note 7) and *Hadith al-sayyid al-rais Hafez al-Asad ila mumaththili al-ilam al-suri wa-l-lubnani fi khitam mubahathatihi maa al-rais al-lubnani Elias Hrawi bi-dimashq 1990/01/23* (President Hafez al-Asad interviewed by representatives of the Syrian and Lebanese media after his discussions with Lebanese Presdient Elias Hrawi 23 January 1990).
28. *Hadith al-sayyid al-rais Hafez al-Asad li-l-wafd al-amriki al-murafiq li-l-sayyid Cyrus Vans wazir al-kharijiyyah al-amriki 1977/2/21* (President Hafez al-Asad interviewed by the press delegation accompanying the American Foreign Minister Cyrus Vance 21 February 1977 and interview in Le Point 20 December 1983, see note 27.
29. Originally a Symbolic Arab Security Force consisting of 2,500 troops, it was created through an Arab League resolution in June 1976. In October

1976 the symbolic force was transformed into the Arab Deterrent Force and expanded with 30,000 troops, supposedly operating under the personal command of the Lebanese president. Syria demanded that its troops should constitute at least half of this force. The Arab League could not agree on the exact number of troops each state should contribute and left the decision up to the Lebanese President. Elias Sarkis, who had been elected President with Syrian help, decided that Syria should contribute up to 25,000 men. In 1976–1979, all non-Syrian units of the ADF withdrew from Lebanon, leaving only Syrian troops to constitute the ADF (Pogany 1987:108–110).

30. On 19 June 1976, Lebanese Prime Minister Rashid Karami asked Syria to withdraw its forces from Lebanon ('Statement by Lebanese Prime Minister Rashid Karami asking Syria to withdraw its forces from Lebanon, Beirut, June 19, 1976', *Journal of Palestine Studies*, vol 6, no 1, pp 171–172). Following the entry of Israeli forces into Beirut in 1982, Lebanese president Elias Sarkis demanded that Syrian troops withdraw from Beirut, which Syria refused. President al-Asad later gave the following explanation: '... it is illogical to demand a withdrawal of the Syrian forces as long as there are Israeli forces in Beirut. Come, let us first cooperate against the Israelis and then we can discuss matters that concern [the two of] us.' (*Kalimat al-sayyid al-rais Hafez al-Asad fi hafl al-iftar aladhi aqamahu li-saadah al-ulama wa-arbab al-shaair al-diniyyah 1982/7/18* (Speech by Hafez al-Asad during iftar dinner with Islamic scholars and leaders of religious communities 18 July 1982) and 'We did not accept that anyone would discuss the withdrawal of these forces with us and we did not accept that the withdrawal of these forces be linked to any treaty between the different parties negotiating on the Lebanese scene' *Kalimat al-sayyid al-rais Hafez al-Asad ila al-maktab al-am wa al-majlis al-tanfidhi bi-munasabat intiha aamal al-muthamar al-ishrin l-l-ittihad al-am li-naqabat al-ummal 1982/11/20* (Speech by President Hafez al-Asad to the General Assembly and the Executive Council at the closing of the twentieth conference of the General Federation of Workers' Union 20 November 1982). In September 1982, Amin Gemayel was elected president. He repeated the demand that all foreign troops be withdrawn from Lebanon (UN Yearbook 1982, p 471). Al-Asad later commented his refusal to comply: 'I do not think that President Gemayel equals the Syrian and the Israeli forces [...] The Israeli forces are the foreign ones, but with regard to the Syrian forces all Syrians and all Lebanese say 'We are brothers'. So how can we be brothers and foreigners at the same time?' (*Hadith al-sayyid al-rais Hafez al-Asad ila majallat 'al-Nahar' 1982/10/28* President Hafez al-Asad interviewed in al-Nahar Magazine 27 October 1982).

31. *Mutamar al-qimmati al-arabiyyah al-thani ashar, Fez 1981/11/25 al-dawrah al-ula 1982/9/6–9 (al-dawrah al-mustanifah)* (The 12th Arab Summit Conference Fez 1981/11/25 first round 1982/9/6–9 (resumption round)).
32. Amin Gemayel at press conference with Qatari media, transcript available in *Al-alaqat al-lubnaniyyah as-suriyyah 1943–1985: waqai bibliyughrafiyyah, wathaiq* (Lebanese-Syrian Relations 1943–1985: Bibliographical Proceedings, Documents), vol 1, pp 321–322.
33. 'Memorandum from Syrian Foreign Ministry to Arab League Secretary General, Damascus, September 5 1983', available in *Journal of Palestine Studies*, vol 13, no 2 (1984), pp 206–207. The Arab homeland (*al-watan al-arabi*) should not be understood as an euphemism for Syria but refers to the Arab World.
34. Resolution 314 states that a member state that concludes a separate agreement with Israel, whether a peace agreement or any political, military or economic agreement shall be immediately expelled from the League. Political and consular relations with the state in question shall be severed, the common frontiers shall be closed, financial and commercial relations shall be halted and all financial contacts with the subjects of the state in question shall be prohibited.
35. 'Memorandum from Syrian Foreign Ministry to Arab League Secretary General, Damascus, September 5 1983', available in *Journal of Palestine Studies*, vol 13, no 2 (1984), pp 206–207.
36. See for instance *Hadith al-sayyid al-rais Hafez al-Asad ila sahifatay 'Los Angelses Times' wa-'Washington Post' 1983/08/09* (President Hafez al-Asad interviewed by the papers Los Angeles Times and Washington Post 9 August 1983.
37. *Kalimat al-sayyid al-rais Hafez al-Asad fi madubah al-asha aqamahu ala sharafihi al-rais Gustav Husak 1985/10/7* (Speech by Hafez al-Asad delivered at the dinner party [Chekoslovak] President Gustáv Husák held in his honour 7 October 1985).
38. *Hadith al-sayyid al-rais Hafez al-Asad li-l-sahafiyin al-lubnaniyin aqb ijtimaaihi maa al-sayyid Fuad Boutrus naib rais al-wuzara wazir al-kharijiyyah wa-l-difaa al-lubnani 1978/8/28* (President Hafez al-Asad interviewed by Lebanese journalists after his meeting with Mr Fuad Boutrus, Deputy Prime Minister and Minister of Foreign Affairs and 28 August 1978, interview in Washington Post 29 November 1976 (see note 81).
39. See for instance *Hadith al-sayyid al-rais Hafez al-Asad ila bathah majallat 'Time' al-amrikiyyah 1984/3/23* (President Hafez al-Asad interviewed by the delegation of the American Time Magazine 23 March 1984, *Hadith al-sayyid al-rais Hafez al-Asad ila-l-wafd al-ilami al-murafiq li-l-sayyid Hans-*

NOTES 159

Dietrich Genscher wazir al-kharijiyyah almanya 1985/9/2 (President Hafez al-Asad interviewed by the media delegation accompanying Hans-Dietrich Genscher, Foreign Minister of Germany 2 September 1985), *Hadith al-sayyid al-rais Hafez al-Asad ila sahifat 'Al-Qabas' al-kuwaytiyyah 1987/1/24* (President Hafez al-Asad interviewed in the Kuwaiti paper Al-Qabas 24 January 1987) and *Hadith al-sayyid al-rais Hafez al-Asad ila sahifat 'Washington Post' wa-majallat 'Newsweek' 1987/9/19* (President Hafez al-Asad interviewed by the paper Washington Post and the magazine Newsweek 19 September 1987).

40. For full text of the agreement see *Al-alaqat al-lubnaniyyah as-suriyyah 1943–1985: waqai bibliyughrafiyyah, wathaiq* (Lebanese-Syrian Relations 1943–1985: Bibliographical Proceedings, Documents), vol 1, pp 342–355.
41. 'Program of the National Union Front, (Lebanon), 6 August 1985' available in *Journal of Palestine Studies*, vol 15, no 1 (1985), pp 205–209.
42. 'Au Nom de Dieu Clément et Miséricordieux, Rapport du Haut Comité Tripartite Arabe, relatif à la crise libanais adressé aux dirigeants arabes (31 juillet 1989)' in *Les Cahiers de l'Orient*, no 15 (1989), p 63.
43. Ibid. p 67.
44. Ibid. pp 81–82.
45. Full text available at the homepage of the Lebanese Parliament.
46. *Hadith al-sayyid al-rais Hafez al-Asad li-l-sahafiyin al-lubnaniyin wa-l-suriyin wa-murasili al-wikalat al-akhbariyyah 1990/1/23* (President Hafez al-Asad interviewed by Lebanese and Syrian journalists and correspondents for news agencies 23 January 1990).
47. *Muahadat al-ikhwah wa-l-taawun wa-l-tansiq bayn al-jumhuriyyah al-arabiyyah al-suriyyah wa-l-jumhuriyyah al-lubnaniyyah* (Treaty of Brotherhood, Cooperation and Coordination between The Syrian Arab Republic and the Lebanese Republic).
48. See *Man nahnu?* (About us) at the homepage of the Syrian–Lebanese Higher Council.
49. For full list of agreements and their full texts, see *Al-ittifaqiyat wa-l-ittifaqat al-munthabiqah an muahadat al-ikhwah wa-l-taawun wa-l-tansiq* (Agreements and Accords emanating from the Treaty of Brotherhood, Cooperation and Coordination).
50. *Ittifaqiyyat al-difaa wa-l-amn bayn al-jumhuriyyah al-lubnaniyyah wa-l-jumhuriyyah al-arabiyyah al-suriyyah* (The Defence and Security Agreement between the Lebanese Republic and the Syrian Arab Republic), 1 September 1991.
51. After the Syrian withdrawal, Samir Geagea was released from prison in July 2005.

52. *Hadith al-sayyid al-rais Hafez al-Asad li-sahafiyin al-suriyin wa-l-masriyin wa-mumaththili wikalat al-anba fi khitam muhadathatihi maa al-rais al-masri Muhammad Hosni Mubarak bi-l-qahirah 1994/10/18* (President Hafez al-Asad interviewed by Syrian and Egyptian journalists and representatives for new agencies after his talks with Egyptian President Muhammad Hosni Mubarak in Cairo 18 October 1994).
53. Kalimat al-sayyid al-rais fi majlis al-shaab bi-tarikh 17 tammuz 2000 (The speech of the President in Parliament 17 July 2000).
54. *Al-sayyid al-rais Bashar al-Asad fi hadith shamil li-sahifat al-safir al-lubnaniyyah* (President Bashar al-Asad in a complete talk with the Lebanese newspaper al-Safir) 27 March 2003, *Tishreen,* 28 March 2003.
55. See for instance Marlowe 2000 and the open letter 'Kitab maftuh ila Bashar al-Asad ... al-rais' (Open letter to Bashar al-Asad ... the President) published 26 July 2001 by Jibran Tweini. At the time editor and publisher of *Al-Nahar* newspaper, which published it, Tweini argues that the Syrian-Lebanese relations benefit Syria more than Lebanon, speaks of the 'old Syrian dream to include or take back the four *qadhas* on the basis of not having recognised its [Lebanon's] presence as a an entity and independent state' and points to Syria always having the last word in Lebanese politics. Tweini was among the Syria-critics killed during the wave of political assassinations following the Syrian withdrawal from Lebanon.
56. *Al-sayyid al-rais Bashar al-Asad fi hadith shamil li-sahifat al-safir al-lubnaniyyah hawla al-tatawwurat al-rahina* (The President in a complete talk with the Lebanese newspaper al-Safir about the current developments), Tishreen 24 March 2002.
57. See *Kalimat al-rais Bashar al-Asad fi mutamar al-mughtaribin al-suriyin bi-tarikh 9 tishreen al-awwal 2004* (The Speech of President Bashar al-Asad at the Conference of Syrian Emigrants, 9 October 2004).
58. *Hadith al-sayyid al-rais Hafez al-Asad ila sahifat 'al-anwar' al-lubnaniyyah 1976/7/1* (President Hafez al-Asad interviewed by Lebanese paper Al-Anwar 1 July 1976).
59. *Hadith al-sayyid al-rais Hafez al-Asad ila al-televizyon al-suisri 1983/10/7*(President Hafez al-Asad interviewed on Swiss TV [channel unspecified] 7 October 1983.
60. In early May 2000 the Lebanese government informed the UN that the area of the Shebaa Farms would be claimed by Lebanon based on resolution 425 (A/54/870/Add.1 and S/2000/443/Add.1). Syrian Foreign Minister Farouq al-Shara confirmed to the UN Secretary General that the area was indeed Lebanese and not Syrian, see *Report of the Secretary-General on the implementation of Security Council resolutions 425 (1978) and 426 (1978),* 22 May 2000, S/2000/460, p 3.

NOTES

61. The sanctions were imposed as a result of 'the Syrian government's support for terrorist groups, the continued military presence in Lebanon, its pursuit to weapons of mass destruction and its actions to undermine US and international efforts with respect to the stabilisation and reconstruction of Iraq', see *Fact Sheet: Implementing the Syria Accountability and Lebanese Sovereignty Restoration Act of 2003*.
62. *Kalimat al-rais Bashar al-Asad fi mutamar al-mughtaribin al-suriyin bi-tarikh 9 tishreen al-awwal 2004* (The Speech of President Bashar al-Asad at the Conference of Syrian Emigrants, 9 October 2004).
63. *Al-sayyid al-rais yulqi kalima shamila amam majlis al-shaab* (The President gives a complete speech to the Parliament) 5 March 2005.
64. According to article 65 of the Lebanese constitution a two third majority is needed to make decisions on 'basic national issues'.
65. Asked about the absence of diplomatic relations between Syria and Lebanon and whether such relations would be established, Hafez al-Asad answered that at independence the leadership in both states had concluded that no diplomatic relations could embody the strong relationship between the two states. Hafez al-Asad stated that this assessment of the bilateral ties was still valid and that embassies 'would only weaken the relationship' (*Hadith al-sayyid al-rais Hafez al-Asad ila majallat Der Spiegel al-almaniyyah 1979/8/22* Hafez al-Asad interviewed in the German magazine Der Spiegel 22 August 1979) and 'Why do you want to reduce our [Syrian-Lebanese] relations to an office where we would put a few officials?' (interview in *Le Monde* 27 July 1984).
66. In September 2006 Syria had agreed to increase border security with Lebanon and take measures to stop the passage of arms from Syria into Lebanon. This had been one of the demands in resolution 1701 following the 2006 Hizbullah-Israel war, see for instance: 'Syria to enforce arms embargo', BBC World News 1 September 2006 and 'Syria agrees to Lebanon Arms Embargo', *New York Times* 2 September 2006.
67. *Al-sayyid al-rais al-Asad yudli bi-hadith ila al-qana al-thaniya wa-l-khamisah fi al-televizyon al-faransi 12 adhar 2007* (President Al-Asad talks to channel 2 and channel 5 of the French Television 12 March 2007).
68. See for example *Al-rais al-Asad yulqi kalimah siyasiyyah shamilah fi iftitah amal al-mutamar al-thani wa-l-ishrin li-ittihad al-muhamiyin al-arab* (President al-Asad gives a complete political speech at the opening of the 22nd conference of the Arab Lawyers' Union) 21 November 2006 and *Al-rais al-Asad fi hadith li-qana al-manar: suriyyah lam wa lan taqbal an takun juzan min mashruu khariji, al-tayyar al-shaabi fi-l-mintaqah tallam al-dars bi-anna hall al-mshakil yakun bi-tamassuk bi-l-huquq* (President al-Asad talking to

al-Manar Channel: Syria has not and will not accept to be part of a foreign plan. The popular forces in the region have learned the lesson that the solution to the problems lies in holding on to its rights), 25 March 2010.
69. See for example speech given 21 November 2006 (see note 68).
70. *Al-rais al-Asad yudli bi-hadith shamil li-qanat Dubai al-fidaiyyah* (President al-Asad gives complete talk to the Dubai Satellite Channel) (23 August 2006).
71. Interview with al-Manar TV 25 March 2010 (see note 68).
72. *Muqabalat al-sayyid al-rais Bashar al-Asad ma al-televizyon al-rusi bi-tarikh 16 ayar 2012* (Interview with President Bashar al-Asad by Russian TV 16 May 2012.
73. Speech given 21 November 2006 (see note 68).
74. *Al-sayyid al-rais Bashar al-Asad yulqi kalimah siyasiyyah shamilah ala mudarraj jamiat Dismashq* (President Bashar al-Asad delivers a speech at the amphitheatre of Damascus University) (10 November 2005).
75. Interview with al-Manar TV 25 March 2010 (see note 68).

Chapter 4. From forgotten to stolen territory: Syrian policies towards Hatay

1. According to Guilquin all Armenians left (2000:142). Picard, however, holds that a few dozen Armenians remained as farmers in isolated villages. Today, these are difficult to identify because of the enforced turkification of place and personal names (Picard 1983:51).
2. See the website produced by descendants of these families *The History of Anjar*, http://www.mousaler.com.
3. Syria was declared formally independent in 1943, but France did not withdraw until 17 April 1946. Syria then became fully independent.
4. In fact, *all* political parties had been dissolved (Seale 1964:59).
5. See 'Developments of the Quarter: Comment and Chronology', *The Middle East Journal*, vol 14, no 4 (1960), pp 433–455.
6. Yilmaz merely refers to Guilquin, who states that during the UAR the Hatay question 'reappeared' in the Syrian press (2000:157).
7. No traces of these demonstrations were found in the sources available.
8. *Kalimat al-sayyid al-rais Hafez al-Asad fi hafl asha aqamahu takriman li-l-rais al-qubrusi Makarios 1975/6/19* (Speech by President Hafez al-Asad at a dinner party held in honor of the Cypriot President Makarios 19 June 1975).
9. *Kalimat al-sayyid al-rais Hafez al-Asad fi hafl takhrij dawrah min al-fursan al-shabibah 1980/11/7* (Speech by President Hafez al-Asad at the graduation ceremony of the youth cavalry 7 November 1980).

10. Informal talk with Şuhnaz Yılmaz, Associate Professor of International Relations, Koç University, Istanbul (Athens 21 April 2008). According to Daoudy, Turkey's insistence on including the Orontes in the negotiations was a strategy of trying to provoke a Syrian recognition of the border (2013:137).
11. Professor at Damascus University, interviewed on condition of anonymity (Damascus 12 March 2003).
12. According to TESEV (Turkish Economic and Social Studies Foundation) in Istanbul, this decision was taken to prevent these students from studying in Syria. Telephone interview with Semin Suvarierol, Project Manager for TESEV's Turkish-Syrian project, 30 May 2002. Students from Hatay with Syrian diplomas went to court in Turkey to have their diplomas recognised and were told 'This is a political issue' (Professor at Damascus University, interviewed on condition of anonymity (Damascus 12 March 2003).
13. According to Pipes (1990:141), Syria had in 1987 agreed to remove Hatay from the maps on the Pamphlets of the Mediterranean Games held in Lattakiyah in 1987 after Turkish protests. Pipes has no reference to a source and it has not been possible to verify this information.
14. See for instance *Al-tarikh al-arabi al-hadith wa-l-muasir, marhalat al-talim al-asasi, al-saf al-tasi* (Modern and contemporary history of the Arabs, Lower Secondary Education, 9th grade), Dar al-Baath 2003–2004.
15. See for instance, *Al-tarbiyyah al-qawmiyyah al-ishtirakiyyah li-l-saff al-thalith al-thanawi* (Nationalist Socialist Education for the third grade, Upper Secondary Education 2002–2003), pp 57, 197.
16. See also Sabriibrahimoğlu 2001.
17. Possible reasons suggested were that Syria decided to stop accepting these students as they were a clear irritant to Turkey. It had, for instance been suggested that these students would be used as Syrian spies. Another possible suggested reason is that Syria simply decided that all students at Syrian universities must pass the entrance exams. As the students from Hatay who choose to study in Syria were largely students who had failed the university entrance exam in Turkey, this might have discouraged newcomers (Professor at Damascus University, interviewed on condition of anonymity, Damascus 8 July 2003).
18. Professor at Damascus University, interviewed on condition of anonymity, Damascus 8 July 2003.
19. Telephone interview with two high-level officials, who do not wish to be identified, at the Turkish Ministry of Foreign Affairs, 8 and 9 April 2008.
20. 'Turkey's Political Relations with Syria', Turkish Ministry of Foreign Affairs.

21. 'Hatay row complicates water talks', *Zaman,* 24 December 2009.
22. *Mutamar sahafi li-l-sayyid al-rais Bashar al-Asad wa-l-sayyid Erdoğan rais wuzara turkiya dimashq bi-tarikh 23 kanun al-awwal 2009* (Press conference with President Bashar al-Asad and Mr Erdoğan, Prime Minister of Turkey, Damascus 23 December 2009).
23. Professor at Damascus University, interviewed on condition of anonymity (Damascus 8 July 2003).
24. *Al-mawqi al-yughrafi li-l-jumhuriyyah al-arabiyyah al-suriyyah* (The Geographical Position of the Syrian Arab Republic), Homepage of the Syrian Ministry of Information (accessed 25 Augusti 2003).
25. The incident was relayed by Samir al-Taqi during the conference on Syrian-Turkish relations held at the University of St. Andrews 7–9 July 2011.
26. See for instance 'Liwa iskandarun al-mughtasab haqq suriy lan yunsa istirdadihi' (The violated region of Hatay is a Syrian right the recovery of which will not be forgotten) Sama TV uploaded 28 November 2012, 'liwa iskandarun al-salib fi dhakirah wa-qalb kul suriy ala amal an yarja ma kul ard suriyyah muhtallah' (The stolen region Hatay is in the mind and heart of every Syrian with the hope that it will return together with all occupied Syrian land), Sama TV uploaded 27 November 2012 and liqa ham maa Ali al-Qasim hawl urubat liwa iskandarun' (Important meeting with Ali al-Qasim about the Arabness of Hatay) uploaded 2 Decemebr 2012.
27. 'Film wathaiqi mufassal an liwa iskandarun al-salib' (Detailed documentary on the stolen region Hatay), Al-Akhbariyyah uploaded 9 March 2013.
28. 'Ya Erdoğan samahnakum bi-liwa iskandarun wa alan sanutalibukum bihi' (Erdoğan, we let you have Hatay and now we will demand it from you), video clip from the Syrian satellite channel uploaded on Youtube 29 March 2013.
29. The fact that one of the presidential candidates in the June 2014 elections, Hasan al-Nuri, explicitly mentioned Hatay as an occupied territory that needed to be regained shows the extent of this comeback.
30. 'Suriye televizyonu, Türk uçağının rotasına dair harita yayınladı' (Syrian television broadcast a map of the Turkish plane's route), Youtube uploaded 23 June 2012.
31. This is in sharp contrast to how the same school books deal with the Golan; 'Syria works with all its might for [...] the liberation of the Golan', see for instance *Al-tarbiyya al-wataniyyah, kitab al-talib, al-saff al-tasi al-asasi 2012–2013* (Homeland education, the student's book, ninth class elementary level) (Damascus 2012), pp 49–53.

Chapter 5. The Golan Heights: From the Arab to the Syrian Cause

1. Originally six villages, the village of Shitah was razed to the ground by Israel 1969–1970 (Mara'i & Halabi 1992:79) and 'Appendix: Testimonies from the Occupied Golan Heights', *Journal of Palestine Studies*, vol 8, issue 3 (1979). The remaining ones are Ein Qiniyyeh, Mas'ade, Buqata, Ghajar and Majdal Shams. It has been argued that the Israeli army allowed only Druze to remain on the Golan Heights as they were expected to become loyal to the state of Israel the same way their co-religionists in Israel are (Mara'i & Halabi 1992:80, Hajjar 1996:5). Hajjar argues that the fact that the residents of one of the villages, Ghajar, were Alawites was not realized by the Israeli military until 'after the expulsion campaign had ended' (Hajjar 1996:10 note 17). It has also been argued that it was not originally occupied but left in a 'no man's land' between the Israeli army and the Lebanese border, that it was not welcome in Lebanon and therefore leaders from the village asked the Israeli army to extend its occupation to include it, interview with Mr Asad Safadi, ICRC liasion officer on the Golan Heights, Majdal Shams 15 November 2007.
2. Sources differ on the number of inhabitants as well as Israeli settlements. According to the document *Al-jawlan muhafazat Qunaytrah* (Golan: The Province of Qunaytrah), handed to me at the Baath Regional Command Headquarters in Damascus 18 July 2003, there are 18,000 Israeli settlers in 40 settlements. According to the UN General Assembly Economic and Social Council's report of June 2003 there are 37 Israeli settlements. According to the Golan Heights Information Server there are 18,000 Israelis in 33 settlements, see www.english.Golan Heights.org.il.
3. *Kalimat al-sayyid al-fariq Hafez al-Asad rais majlis al-wuzara wazir al-difaa fi mutamar al-shaabi al-kabir fi tarabulus 'libya'* (Speech by Prime Minister and Minister of Defense General Hafez al-Asad at the Great Popular Conference in Tripoli Libya 1970/12/9) and *Kalimat al-sayyid al-fariq Hafez al-Asad rais majlis al-wuzara wazir al-difaa fi dhikra al-thaminah li-thawrat al-thamin min adhar 1971/3/8* (Speech by Prime Minister and Minister of Defense General Hafez al-Asad on the eighth anniversary of the revolution of 8th of March 8 March 1971).
4. Full text of the agreement available in *S/11302/Add.1 Report of the Secretary–General concerning the Agreement on Disengagement between Israeli and Syrian Forces*.

5. These points were instead registered in a separate document called the Statement of the Chairman, which was read in the presence of and agreed to by both parties.
6. *Hadith al-sayyid al-rais Hafez al-Asad ila jaridat al-Nahar al-lubnaniyyah 17/3/71* (Interview with President Hafez al-Asad in the Lebanese newspaper Al-Nahar 17 March 1971) and *Hadith al-sayyid al-rais Hafez al-Asad li-majallat al-Musawwer al-Qahiriyyah 22/8/71* (Interview with President Hafez al-Asad in the Cairo-based magazine al-Majallah 22 August 1971).
7. *Hadith al-sayyid al-rais Hafez al-Asad ila majallat Newsweek al-amrikiyyah 14/9/1975* (Interview with the American magazine Newsweek 14 September 1975).
8. Throughout the years there have been complaints of minor violations of the agreement from both sides, see for instance *Yearbook of the United Nations* 1975:21, and the UNDOF reports. In January 2002 an infiltration point through which weapons were smuggled into the Golan Heights was discovered. This discovery was the first – and hitherto only of its kind along the Syrian-Israeli disengagement line, see 'ISA uncovers Golan Heights weapons infiltration'. In January 2003 a member of the Syrian security forces was killed and another one taken to custody by the Israeli Defense Forces, see 'Syrian shot dead in Golan Heights', BBC 9 January 2003. In 2011 mainly Palestinian demonstrators managed to break through the security fence between Syria and the occupied part of the Golan.
9. *Hadith al-sayyid al-rais Hafez al-Asad ila sahifat 'Washington Post' 1975/3/1* (President Hafez al-Asad interviewed by the paper Washington Post 1 March 1975), *Hadith al-sayyid al-rais Hafez al-Asad li-l-wafd al-ilami al-danmarki al-murafiq li-l-sayyid Andersson wazir al-kharijiyyah al-danmark 1977/6/14* (President Hafez al-Asad interviewed by the Danish media delegation accompanying Mr Anderson, Denmark's Minister of Foreign Affairs 14 June 1977).
10. For instance, see *Tasrih al-sayyid al-rais Hafez al-Asad bi-munasabat raf al-alam al-arabi al-suri fawq madinat al-Qunaytrah al-muharrarah* (Statement by President Hafez al-Asad at the ceremony raising the Arab Syrian flag over the liberated city of Qunaytrah 24 June 1974), *Liqa al-sayyid al-rais Hafez al-Asad maa majallat al-Hawadith al-lubnaniyyah 1975/6/22* The meeting of President Hafez al-Asad with the Lebanese magazine al-Hawadith 22 June 1975) and *Hadith al-sayyid al-rais Hafez al-Asad li-l-wafd al-ilami al-murafiq li-l-sayyid Vance Cyrus wazir al-kharijiyyah al-amriki 1977/2/21*(President Hafez al-Asad interviewed by the press delegation accompanying US Foreign Minister Cyrus Vance press conference with American journalists 21 February 1977).

NOTES   167

11. *Kalimat al-sayyid al-rais Hafez al-Asad aqb al-tawqi ala ilan insha qiyadah siyasiyyah muwahhada tadumm suriya-al-sudan-misr 1977/2/28* (The speech by President Hafez al-Asad following the signing of the creation of a unified political leadership including Syria, Sudan and Egypt 28 February 1977).
12. *Kalimat al-sayyid al-fariq Hafez al-Asad rais majlis al-wuzara wazir al-difa fi iftitah al-maktab al-daim li-ittihad al-muhamiyin al-arab fi dimashq 1971/2/20* (Speech by Prime Minister and Minister of Defense General Hafez al-Asad during the inauguration of the permanent office of the Arab Lawyers' Union in Damascus 20 February 1971) and *Kalimat al-sayyid al-rais Hafez al-Asad bi iftitah mutamar al-tadamun al-afru al-asiawi fi dimashq 1971/6/23* (Speech by President Hafez al-Asad at the opening of the Afro-Asian solidarity conference in Damascus 23 June 1971).
13. Speech 20 February 1971, see note 134.
14. See for instance *Hadith al-sayyid al-rais Hafez al-Asad ila majallat Novel Observateur al-faransiyyah 1971/3/22* (President Hafez al-Asad interviewed by the French magazine Novel Observateur 22 March 1971), *Hadith al-sayyid al-rais Hafez al-Asad ila jaridat al-Nahar al-lubnaniyyah 1971/3/17* (President Hafez al-Asad interviewed in the Lebanese paper al-Nahar 17 March 1971), *Hadith al-sayyid al-rais Hafez al-Asad li-l-sahafiyin al-lubnaniyin 1975/8/2* (President Hafez al-Asad interviewed by Lebanese journalists 2 August 1975), *Khitab al-sayyid al-rais Hafez al-Asad fi hafl iftitah al-mutamar al-am al-sadis li-l-ittihad al-watani l-talabat suriya 1975/2/26* (Speech by President Hafez al-Asad at the opening of the sixth general conference of the National Union of Syrian Students 26 February 1975, *Hadith al-sayyid al-rais Hafez al-Asad ila al-televizyon al-britani 1975/9/7* (President Hafez Al-Asad interviewed by British TV 7 September 1975) and *Kalimat al-sayyid al-rais Hafez al-Asad fi madabat al-asha allati aqamaha ala sharafihi al-rais shautsheshku fi bukharest 1977/2/15* (Speech by President Hafez al-Asad at the dinner party given in his honor by President Ceausescu in Bucharest 15 February 1977).
15. Hafez al-Asad's speech 20 July 1976, see note 11.
16. See for instance S/8742 (9 August 1968) and S/8749 (16 August 1968), S/8857 (15 Oct 1968), S/8893 (7 November 1968), S/8904 (21 November 1968, S/8971 (16 January 1969), S/9042 (4 March 1969), S/9131 (4 April 1969), S/9139 (8 April 1969), S/9150 (11 April 1969), S/10213 (28 May 1971), S/11533 9 October 1974, S/14411 (19 March 1981), E/CN.4/1982/22 (25 February 1982), E/CN.4/1982/25 (3 March 1982), E/CN.4/1982/28 (12 March 1982). S/9643 (9 February 1970), S/11283 (6 May 1974), A731/251 (25 February 1976), S/14383 (24 February 1981), S/14876 (18 February 1982),

S/14893 (3 March 1982) S/14411 (17 Mars 1981), S/14569 (22 June 1981), A/41/184 (3 March 1986), S/17889 (30 March 1986), E/CN.4/1987/59 (13 March 1987), A/42/173 (10 March 1987), S/18782 (3 April 1987), A/44/515 (11 September 1989). S/8928 (12 Dec 1968), S/8971 (16 January 1969), S/9823 (5 June 1970), S/11220 (14 February 1974), S/11238 (20 March 1974), S/11219 (12 February 1974), S/11220 (14 February 1974) , S/11234 (14 March 1974) S/11330 (9 July 1974), S/14239 (27 October 1980), S/14383 (24 February 1981), S/14411 (17 March 1981), S/11219 (12 February 1974), S/11220 (14 February 1974), S/14239 (27 October 1980), A/43/985 (19 December 1988), A/45/333 (28 June 1990), S/9220 (23 May 1969) and (S/9299) 1 July 1969.

17. See Syrian Foreign Minister Farouq al-Shara's opening address at the Madrid Peace Conference, 'The Madrid Peace Conference', *Journal of Palestinian Studies*, vol 21, no 2 (winter 1992), pp 139–141, see also Ross 2004:79.

18. On 5 January 1996, Israel assassinated the Palestinian militant Yahya Ayash ('the Engineer') in Gaza, in late February and early March there were suicide bombings in Askelon, Jerusalem and Tel Aviv and on the 11 March Peres ordered the commencement Grapes of Wrath campaign in Lebanon.

19. A government statement, however, confirmed that there had been an agreement between Rabin and the US, but said that the agreement was not binding and that it did not constitute an agreement with the Syrians, see al-Majli 1999, Schiff (1998:156–157).

20. Remarks by President Clinton, Prime Minister Barak of Israel and Foreign Minister Al-Shara of Syria, 15 December 1999.

21. *Kalimat al-sayyid Faruq al-Sharaa wazir al-kharijiyyah amam al-mutamar al-sanawi li-ittihad al-kutab al-arab* (The speech by Foreign Minister Farouq al-Shara at the yearly conference of the Arab Writers' Union, *al-Fikr al-Siyasi*, vol 3, no 8.

22. Lockhart, Joe, White House Press Secretary, Press Briefing Following President Clinton and President Assad Meeting, President Wilson Hotel, Geneva, Switzerland, 26 March 2000.

23. See for instance *Hadith al-sayyid al-rais Hafez al-Asad fi al-mutamar al.sahafi fi khitam liqaihi maa al-rais Hosni Mubarak* (President hafez al-Asad at the press conference held after his meeting with President Hosni Mubarak 30 July 1997) and *Hadith al-sayyid al-rais ithna istiqbal wafd al-jawlan al-muhtall 1992/2/8* (Speech given by President Hafez al-Asad during the reception of a delegation from the occupied Golan speech held during a visit by a delegation from occupied Golan 8 February 1992).

24. See for instance *Kalimat al-sayyid al-rais Hafez al-Asad fi iftitah al-mutamar al-thani wa-l-ishrin li-l-ittihad al-am li-naqabat al-ummal 1992/12/14* (Speech delivered at the opening of the 22nd conference of the Workers' Union in

Damascus 14 December 1992), *Kalimat al-sayyid al-rais Hafez al-Asad ila al-muwatinin bi-munasabat al-istifta alladhi jara ala tarshih siyadatihi li-wilaya dusturiyyah khamisa 1999/2/13* (Speech by President Hafez al-Asad to the citizens at the occasion of the referendum held on his nomination for a fifth round constitutional rule 13 February 1999), *Kalimat al-sayyid al-rais Hafez al-Asad ila quwwatna al-musallahah fi dhikra tasis al-jaysh al-arabi al-suri 1996/8/1* (Speech by President Hafez al-Asad at the anniversary of the creation of the Syrian Arab army 1 August 1996) and *Kalimat al-Sayyid al-Rais Hafez al-Asad ila qjuwwatna al-musallahah fi dhikra al-54 li-tasis jayshna al-basil 1999/8/1* (Speech by President Hafez al-Asad delivered to our armed forces on the 54th anniversary of the creation of our brave army Syrian army 1 August 1999).

25. *Hadith al-sayyid al-rais Hafez al-Asad ila bathat majallah 'Time' al-amrikiyyah 1992/11/13* (President Hafez al-Asad interviewed by the delegation from the American Time magazine 13 November 1992).
26. *Hadith al-sayyid al-rais Hafez al-Asad ila mahattat al-televizyon al-amrikiyyah – ai bi si 1991/9/16* (President Hafez al-Asad interviewed for the American TV station ABC 16 September 1991) and *Hadith al-sayyid al-rais Hafez al-Asad fi al-mutamar al-sahafi alladhi aqadahu wa-al-rais Hosni Mubarak li-ruasa tahrir al-suhuf al-suriyyah wal-misriyya fi khitam mubahathatihima 1991/7/17* (President Hafez al-Asad during the press conference he convened with President Hosni Mubarak for the editors in chief of the Syrian and Egyptian newspapers following their talks 17 July 1991).
27. *Hadith al-sayyid al-rais Hafez al-Asad ila mumathili al-qanah al-ula li-l-televizyon al-faransi 1998/7/16* (President Hafez al-Asad interviewed by representatives for Channel 1 of the French TV 16 July 1998).
28. See for instance A/47/255 (3 June 1992) and A/53/876 (24 March 1999), A/46/475 (16 September 1991), S/22654 (3 June 1991), A/46/284 (5 July 1991), A/47/255 (3 June 1992), A/52/202 (23 June 1997), A/AC.145/R.51 (1998) and A/53/876 (6 April 1999).
29. *Kalimatu al-sayyid al-rais fi majlis al-shaab bitarikh 17 tammuz 2000* (The speech of his the President in the Parliament 17 July 2000).
30. *Kalimat al-sayyid al-rais fi qimmati al-duwwal al-islamiyyah fi al-doha 13 November 2000* (The speech of the President at the summit of the Islamic States in Doha 13 November 2000), *Al-sayyid al-rais fi al-qimmati al-arabiyyah ghayr al-adiyah* (The Speech of the President at the Emergency Arab Summit, 21 October 2000 and *Al-salam al-adil wa-l-shamil fi-l-mintaqah yatatallab insihab Israil hata khatt huzayran aam 1976* (A just and comprehensive peace in the region requires that Israel withdraws to the line of June 4th 1967), 25 November 2007.

31. *Hadith al-sayyid al-rais Bashar al-Asad ila qanah al-jazirah al-qatariyyah* (Interview with the President on the Qatari al-Jazeerah channel), 26 April 2004.
32. The idea of a peace park had originally been floated by Israeli security Uri Saguy, who headed the Israeli negotiation team during Ehud Barak's term as Prime Minister Al-Shara then seemed to embrace the idea but Barak did not accept it, see Ross 2004:529.
33. *Al-nass al-kamil li-kalimat al-rais Bashar al-Asad fi majlis al-shaab bad ada al-qasam al-dusturi* (Full text of the speech of President Bashar al-Asad in the Parliament after swearing the Constitutional Oath), 19 July 2007.
34. Statement by the Syrian Embassy in Washington, cited at *Syria Comment* 12 December 2010, cited 13 December 2010.
35. World Refugee Survey 2002 Country Report, 28 December 2002.
36. As relayed by informant who wishes to remain anonymous, 12 October 2010.
37. According to Abu Fakhr (2000:5), the number amounts to 350,000. In his opening speech at the 1991 Madrid Conference Syrian Foreign Minister Farouq al-Shara stated that the Israeli occupation of the Golan Heights had led to the displacement of approximately half a million Syrian citizens ('The Madrid Peace Conference', *Journal of Palestine Studies*, vol 21, no 2 (1992), p 140). President Asad confirms this number in an interview with *Time Magazine* 13 November 1992.
38. 'The Madrid Peace Conference', *Journal of Palestine Studies*, vol 21, no 2 (Winter 1992), p 140 and 'Remarks by President Clinton, Prime Minister Barak of Israel and Foreign Minister Al-Shara of Syria', 15 December 1999.
39. *Al-rais al-Asad yudli bi-hadith shamil li-qanah Dubai al-fidaiyyah* (President al-Asad gives complete talk to the Dubai Satellite Channel) (23 August 2006).
40. Interview with al-Manar TV channel, see note 85.
41. According to Ms. Lana Baydas, Legal Advisor, ICRC Damascus, this is a Syrian policy in order to not leave the Golan Heights empty, interview Damascus 18 March 2003. According to Mr Medhat Saleh, ICRC Syrian liasion officer, this is an Israeli restriction, interview Damascus 22 March 2003.
42. This money does not reach the Golan Heights. It is collected by relatives in Syria or students going to Syria to study, interview Mr Asad Safadi, ICRC liasion officer on the Golan Heights (Majdal Shams 15 November 2007).
43. This was suggested by Mr Paul Conneally, Deputy Head of the ICRC Delegation in Tel Aviv, interview (Tel Aviv 12 November 2007).

44. *Kalimat al-sayyid al-rais Hafez al-Asad ila al-quwwat al-musallahah fi dhikra al-thamini wa-l-arbain li-tasis al-jaysh al-arabiy al-suri 1993/8/1* (Speech by President Hafez al-Asad at the 48th anniversary of the creation of the Syrian Arab Army 1 August 1993) and *Hadith al-sayyid al-rais Hafez al-Asad ila bathat majallah 'Time' al-amrikiyyah 1992/11/13* (President Hafez al-Asad interviewed by the delegation from the American Time magazine 13 November 1992).
45. *Al-nass li-kalimati al-rais Bashar al-Asad fi majlis al-shaab bad ada al-qasam al-dusturi* (Full text of the speech of President Bashar al-Asad in the Parliament after swearing the Constitutional Oath), 17 July 2007.
46. See for instance *Hadith al-sayyid al-rais Hafez al-Asad ila al-televizyon al-britani 1975/9/7* (President Hafez Al-Asad interviewed by British TV 7 September 1975), *Hadith al-sayyid al-rais Hafez al-Asad ila majallat 'Newsweek' al-amrikiyyah 1977/7/20* (President Hafez al-Asad interviewed by the American magazine Newsweek 20 July 1977). Among other things, he made clear that Israeli demands for trade and diplomatic relations were not only not necessary for peace but in fact obstacles to peace (see Hadith al-sayyid al-rais Hafez al-Asad ila sahifat 'Washington Post' al-amrikiyyah 1976/11/29 President Hafez al-Asad interviewed in the American paper Washington Post), an acceptance of open borders and trade with Israel would imply accepting imperialism (interview Newsweek 20 July 1977) and a recognition of the existence of Israel would not follow from a peace agreement; 'We will end the state of war [in case of a complete Israeli withdrawal from occupied Arab territory], thereby there will be peace. There is no law saying that one state must recognise another, but there is a law saying that a state that occupies territory must withdraw' (Interview with Danish journalists 14 June 1977, see note 9).

Chapter 6. Conclusions

1. As seen in chapter 6, there were reports of a non–paper where a 'peace park' had been accepted during secret negotiations in 2004–2006. As the Syrian government denied any knowledge of this non–paper it is difficult to assess whether this indicates a possible change in policy with regard to joint projects.
2. See for instance *Hadith al-sayyid al-rais Hafez al-Asad li-l-wafd al-ilami al-faransi al-murafiq li-l-sayyid Louis de Guiringaud wazirkharijiyyah faransa*

(President Hafez al-Asad interviewed by the French media delegation accompanying Mr. Louis de Guiringaud, Foreign Minister of France) and *Hadith al-sayyid al-rais Hafez al-Asad ila bathat majallah 'Time' al-mrikiyyah 1992/11/13* (President Hafez al-Asad interviewed by the delegation from the American Time magazine 13 November 1992).

3. Interview on the *Al-Sharia al-arabi* (The Arab Street) show, Dubai Media Corporation 10 June 2012.

REFERENCES

All speeches by and interviews with Hafez al-Asad have been retrieved from the CD-rom *Khutab wa-kalimat wa-tasrihat al-sayyid al-rais Hafez al-Asad 1966–2000* (Speeches, announcemnet and statements by President Hafez al-Asad 1966–2000) compiled by the National Information Centre in Damascus. Unless otherwise specified, all speeches by and interviews with Bashar al-Asad have been retrieved from www.presidentassad.net.

Printed sources

Abu Fakhr, Sakr, 'Voices from the Golan', *Journal of Palestine Studies*, vol 29, no 4 (2000), pp 5–36.

Al-alaqat al-lubnaniyyah al-suriyyah 1943–1985: waqai bibliyughrafiyyah, wathaiq (Lebanese-Syrian Relations 1943–1985: Bibliographical Proceedings, Documents) vols 1 and 2, Markaz at-tawthiq wa-l-buhuth al-lubnaniyyah (Beirut, 1986).

Albright, Madeleine, *Madam Secretary: A Memoir* (New York, 2004).

al-Majli, Nazir, 'Interview with Israeli prime Minister Benjamin Netanyahu, published in *al-Sharq al-Awsat*, 18 January 1999', *Journal of Palestine Studies*, vol 28, no 3 (1999), pp 156–157.

Al-Muallim, Walid, *Suriyah 1916–1946: al-tariq ila-l-huriyah* (Syria 1916–1943: The Road to Freedom) (Damascus, 1998).

'Al-rais al-Asad yabda wa-l-sayyida aqilatuhu al-yawm ziyarat dawlah ila turkiyyah wa-yuakkid fi hadith li-mahattat televizyon CNN alaqatna tarikhiyya' (President al-Asad begins state visit to Turkey with his wife today and assures in interview with TV station CNN: 'Our relations are historic') *Tishreen*, 6 January 2004.

Al-tarbiyyah al-qawmiyyah al-ishtirakiyyah li-l-saff al-thalith al-thanawi (National Socialist Education for the Third grade, Upper Secondary Education, 2002–2003) (Damascus, 2002).

Al-tarbiyya al-wataniyyah, kitab al-talib, al-saff al-tasi al-asasi 2012–2013 (National education, the student's book, ninth class elementary level) (Damascus 2012).

Al-tarikh al-arabi al-hadith wa-l-muasir, marhalat al-talim al-asasi, al-saf al-tasi (Modern and contemporary history of the Arabs, Lower Secondary Education, 9th grade) (Damascus, 2002).

Altunışık Benli, Meliha & Tür, Özlem, 'From Distant Neighbors to Partners? Changing Syrian-Turkish Relations', *Security Dialogue*, vol 37, no 2 (2006), pp 229–248.

Anderson, James & O'Dowd, Liam, 'Borders, Border Regions and Territoriality: Contradictory Meanings, Changing Significance', *Regional Studies*, vol 33, no 7 (1999), pp 593–694.

'Ankara met en garde Damas: Aucun centimètre ne pourra être dissocié de la Turquie, affirme Yilmaz à propos d'Iskandaroun', *L'Orient le Jour*, 24 July 1998.

Antonius, George, *The Arab Awakening: The Story of the Arab National Movement* (London, 1938).

'Au Nom de Dieu Clément et Miséricordieux, Rapport du Haut Comité Tripartite Arabe, relatif à la crise libanaise adressé aux dirigeants arabes (31 juillet 1989)' in *Les Cahiers de l'Orient*, no 15 (1989), pp 61–82.

Avi-Ran, Reuven, *The Syrian Involvement in Lebanon since 1975* (Boulder 1991).

Baker, James A. III, *The Politics of Diplomacy, War and Peace 1989–1992* (New York,1995).

Balanche, Fabrice, 'Transports et espace', *Annales Géographie*, vol 112, no 630 (2003), pp 146–166.

Balanche Fabrice, La région alaouite et le pouvoir syrien, (Paris, 2006).

Barnett, Michael N., *Dialogues in Arab Politics: Negotiations in Regional Order* (New York, 1998).

'Bashar expects invitation from Turkey', *Turkish Daily News*, 6 July 2000.

Batatu, Hanna, *Syria's Peasantry: The Descendants of its Lesser Rural Notables and Their Politics* (Princeton, 1999).

Bitterlin, Lucien, *Alexandrette: Le Munich de l'Orient ou quand la France capitulait* (Paris, 1999).

Blurring the Borders: Syrian Spillover Risks for Turkey, International Crisis Group Europe Report no 225, 30 April 2013.

Boghossian, Roupen, *La Haute Djezireh* (Aleppo, 1952).

Bokova, Lenka, 'Le traité du 4 mars 1921 et la formation de l'état du Djebel Druze sous le Mandat français', *Revue de l'Occident Musulman et de la Méditerranée*, no 48/49 (1938), pp 213–222.

Bou-Nacklie, N. E., 'Les Troupes Speciales: Religious and Ethnic Recruitment, 1916–46', *International Journal of Middle East Studies*, vol 25, no 4 (1993), pp 645–660.

Boykin, John, *Cursed is the Peacemaker: The American Diplomat Versus the Israeli General, Beirut 1982* (Belmont, 2002).

References

Butler, Linda, 'Fresh Light on the Syrian-Israeli Peace Negotiations: An Interview with Ambassador Walid al-Moualem', *Journal of Palestine Studies*, vol 26, issue 2 (1997), pp 81–94.

Buzan, Barry, People, *States and Fear: An Agenda for International Security Studies in the Post-Cold War Era* (London, 1991).

Cederman, Lars-Erik, *Emergent Actors in World Politics: How States and Nations Develop and Dissolve* (Princeton, 1997).

Chaitani, Youssef, *The Decline of Arab Nationalism and the Triumph of the State: Post-Colonial Syria and Lebanon* (London, 2007).

Chatty, Dawn, 'The Bedouin in Contemporary Syria: The Persistence of Tribal Authority and Control', *The Middle East Journal*, vol 64, no 1 (2010), pp 29–49.

Clinton, Bill, *My Life* (London, 2004).

Cobban, Helena, *The Israeli-Syrian Peace Talks: 1991–96 and Beyond* (Washington D.C., 1999).

Çarkoğlu, Ali & Eder, Mine, 'Water Conflict: The Euphrates-Tiger Basin' in Rubin, Barry & Kirişci, Kemal, *Turkey in World Politics: An Emerging Multiregional Power* (London, 2001a), pp 235–250.

Çarkoğlu, Ali & Eder, Mine, 'Domestic Concerns and the Water Conflict over the Euphrates-Tigris Basin', *Middle Eastern Studies*, vol 37, no 1 (2001b), pp 41–71.

Crowfoot, J. W., 'Syria and Lebanon: The Prospect', *Geographical Journal*, vol 99, no 3 (1942), pp 130–141.

Daoudy, Marwa, 'Back to Conflict? The Securitization of Water in Syrian-Turkish Relations', Hinnebusch, Raymond & Tür, Özlem, *Turkey-Syria Relations: Between Enmity and Amity* (Farnham, 2013), pp 133–143.

'Developments of the Quarter: Comment and Chronology', *The Middle East Journal*, vol 14, no 4 (1960), pp 433–455.

Drysdale, Alastair, 'The Syrian Political Elite 1966–1976: A Spatial and Social Analysis', *Middle Eastern Studies*, vol 17, no 1 (1981), pp 3–30.

Drysdale, Alastair, 'Syria and Iraq: The Geopathology of a Relationship' in *GeoJournal*, vol 28, no 3 (1992), pp 347–355.

Drysdale, Alastair & Hinnebusch, Raymond A., *Syria and the Middle East Peace Process*, (New York, 1999).

Duygy, Güvenç, 'Hatay sorunu'nu Esad bitiriyor' (al-Asad ends the Hatay question), *Yeni Şafak*, 6 January 2004.

el-Khazen, Farid, 'Political Parties in Postwar Lebanon: Parties in Search of Partisans', *Middle East Journal*, vol 57, no 4 (2003), pp 605–624.

Engaging Syria? US Constraints and Opportunities, International Crisis Group Report no 83, 11 February 2009.

Firro, Kais S., *Inventing Lebanon: Nationalism and the State under the Mandate* (London, 2003).

Fisk, Robert, *Pity the Nation: The Abduction of Lebanon* (New York, 2003).

Freedman, Robert O., 'The Soviet Union and Syria: A Case Study of Soviet Policy' in Efrat, Moshe & Bercovitch, Jacob (eds.), *Superpowers and Client states in the Middle East* (London, 1991).
Fromkin, David, *A Peace to End All Peace: The Fall of the Ottoman Empire and the Creation of the Modern Middle East* (New York, 1989).
Fuccaro, Nelida, 'Minorities and Ethnic Mobilization: The Kurds in Northern Iraq and Syria' in Méouchy, Nadine & Sluglett, Peter (eds.), *The British and French Mandates in Comparative Perspectives* (Leiden, 2004), pp 579–595.
Galip Över, Kivanç, 'Second Spring with Damascus', *Turkish Daily News*, 25 February 2003.
Garzouzi, Eva, 'Land Reform in Syria', *Middle East Journal*, vol 17, no 1–2 (1963), pp 83–90.
Gelvin, James L., *Divided Loyalties: Nationalism and Mass Politics in Syria at the End of Empire* (Berkely, 1998).
Guilquin, Michel, *D'Antioche à Hatay: L'histoire oubliée du sandjak d'Alexandrette. Nationalisme turc contre nationalisme arabe* (Paris, 2000).
Güçlü, Yücel, *The Alexandretta Question 1936–1939*, PhD thesis, Department of Political History, University of Helsinki, (Helsinki, 1994).
Güçlü, Yücel, *The Question of the Sanjak of Alexandretta: A Study in Turkish-French-Syrian Relations* (Ankara, 2001).
Haddad, Bassam, *Business Networks in Syria: The Political Economy of Authoritarian Resilience* (Stanford, 2012).
Haddadin, Munther J., 'Water in the Middle East Peace Process', *The Geographical Journal*, vol 168, no 4 (2002), pp 324–340.
Halliday, Fred, 'The Middle East, the Great Powers and the Cold War' in Sayigh, Yezid & Shlaim, Avi, *The Cold War and the Middle East* (Clarendon, 1997), pp 6–26.
Hanf, Theodor, *Co-Existence in Wartime Lebanon: Decline of a State and Rise of a Nation* (London, 1993).
Hanna, Abdallah, 'The Attitude of the French Mandatory Authorities towards Land Ownership in Syria' in Méouchy Nadine & Sluglett, Peter, *The British and French Mandates in Comparative Perspectives* (Leiden, 2004), pp 457–475.
'Harb al-tarashshuh li-riasat al-jumhuriyyah: al-qarar la yazal fi yad al-suriyin' (The war for the nomination for the Presidency of the Republic: the decision is still in the hands of the Syrians), *al-Nahar*, 17 June 2004.
Helbaoui, Youssef, 'La Population et la Population Active en Syrie', *Population*, no 4 (1963), pp 697–714.
Heydemann, Steven, *Authoritarianism in Syria: Institutions and Social Conflict 1946–1970* (Ithaca,1999).
Hinnebusch, Raymond A., 'Revisionist Dreams, Realist Strategies: The Foreign Policy of Syria' in Korany, Bahgat & Hillal Dessouki, Ali E., *The Foreign Policies of Arab States: The Challenge of Change* (Boulder, 1991).

Hinnebusch, Raymond A., 'The Foreign Policy of Syria' in Hinnebusch & Ehtesami, Anoushiravan (eds.), *The Foreign Policies of Middle East States* (Manchester, 2002a).
Hinnebusch, Raymond A., *Syria: Revolution from Above* (New York, 2002b).
Hinnebusch, Raymond A., 'Syria under Bashar: Between Economic Reform and Nationalist Realpolitik' in Hinnebusch, Raymond A., Kabalan, Marwan J., Kodmani, Bassma and Lesch, David, *Syrian Foreign Policy and the United States: From Bush to Obama*, St Andrews Papers on Contemporary Syria (Boulder, 2010), pp 3–26.
Honvault, Juliette, 'La coopération nationaliste avec le pouvoir mandataire: ambiguïtés et éthique politique chez l'émir 'Adil Arslân lors des négociations d'Ankara sur le Sandjak d'Alexandrette' in Méouchy, Nadine (ed.), *France, Syrie et Liban 1918–1946: les ambiguïtés et les dynamiques de la relation mandataire* (Damascus, 2002), pp 211–228.
Hourani, Albert, *Syria and Lebanon: A Political Essay* (London, 1946).
Inbar, Efraim, 'The Strategic Glue in the Israeli-Turkish Alignment' in Rubin, Barry & Kirişci, Kemal (eds.), *Turkey in World Politics: An Emerging Multiregional Power* (Boulder, 2001), pp 115–127.
Jackson, Robert A., 'Boundaries and International Society' in Roberson, B. A. (ed.) *International Society and the Development of International Relations Theory* (London, 2002), pp 156–172.
Jörum, Emma, 'The October 1998 Turkish-Syrian Crisis in Arab Media' in Brandell, Inga (ed.) *State Frontiers: Borders and Boundaries in the Middle East* (London, 2006), pp 159–183.
Kabalan, Marwan J, 'Syrian Foreign Policy between Domestic Needs and the External Environment' in Hinnebusch, Raymond A., Kabalan, Marwan J., Kodmani, Bassma and Lesch, David, *Syrian Foreign Policy and the United States: From Bush to Obama*, St Andrews Papers on Contemporary Syria (Boulder, 2010), pp 27–42.
Kandil, Hazem, 'The Challenge of Restructuring: Syrian Foreign Policy' in Korany, Bahgat & Dessouki Hillal, Ali E. (eds.), *The Foreign Policies of Arab States: The Challenge of Globalization* (New York, 2008), pp 421–456.
Kaufman, Asher, 'Who owns the Shebaa farms? Chronicle of a territorial dispute', *The Middle East Journal*, vol 56, no 4 (2002), pp 576–595.
Kaylani, Nabil M., 'The Rise of the Syrian Bath 1940–1958: Political Success, Party Failure', *International Journal of Middle East Studies*, vol 3, no 1 (1972), pp 3–23.
Kedar, Mordechai, *Asad in Search of Legitimacy: Messages and Rhetoric in the Syrian Press under Hafiz and Bashar* (Brighton and Portland, 2005).
Kelidar, Abbas, 'States without Foundations: The Political Evolution of State and Society in the Arab East', *Journal of Contemporary History*, vol 28, no 2 (1993), pp 315–339.
Khadduri, Majid, 'The Alexandretta Dispute', *American Journal of International Law*, vol 39, no 3 (1945), pp 406–425.

Khadduri, Majid, 'Constitutional Development in Syria: With Emphasis on the Constitution of 1950', *Middle East Journal*, vol 5, no 2 (1951), pp 137–160.

Khalidi, Walid, 'Lebanon yesterday and tomorrow', *Middle East Journal*, vol 43, no 3 (1989), pp 375–387.

Khouri, Fred John, 'Friction and Conflict on the Israeli-Syrian Front', *Middle East Journal*, vol 17, no 1–2 (1963), pp 14–34.

Khoury, Philip S., *Syria and the French Mandate: The Politics of Arab Nationalism 1920–1945* (London, 1987a).

Khoury, Philip S., 'The Syrian Independence Movement and the Growth of Economic Nationalism in Damascus', *Bulletin (British Society for Middle Eastern Studies)*, vol 14, no 1 (1987b), pp 25–36.

'Khutut siyahiyyah nawiyyah bayn suriyah-turkiyyah' (Specific touristic links between Syria and Turkey) *Tishreen* 19 July 2009.

Kienle, Eberhard, 'Arab Unity Schemes Revisited: Interests, Identity and Policy in Syria and Egypt', *International Journal of Middle East Studies*, vol 27, no 1 (1995), pp 53–71.

Kirkbride, Alec Seath, *A Crackle of Thorns: Experiences in the Middle East* (London, 1956).

Kurian, Alt, Chamber, Garett, Levi & McClaim, *Encyclopedia of Political Science* (Washington D.C., 2011).

Kushner, David, 'Turkish-Syrian Relations: An Update' in Ma'oz, Moshe, Joseph, Ginat & Onn, Winckler (eds.), *Modern Syria: From Ottoman Rule to Pivotal Role in the Middle East* (Brighton, 1999), pp 228–241.

Lalonde, Suzanne, *Determining Boundaries in a Conflicted World: The Use of Usi Possidetis* (Montreal, 2002).

Landis, Joshua M., 'Shishakli and the Druzes: Integration and Intransigence' in Philipp Thomas & Schäbler, Birgit (eds.), *The Syrian Land: Processes of Integration and Fragmentation* (Stuttgart, 1998), pp 369–396.

Landis, Joshua M., 'Syria and the Palestine War: Fighting King Abdullah's "Greater Syria Plan"' in Rogan, Eugene L. & Shlaim, Avi, *The War for Palestine: Rewriting the History of 1948* (Cambridge, 2001), pp 176–203.

'La Syrie ne renoncera jamais à Alexandrette, souligne Damas', *L'Orient le Jour*, 20 October 1998.

Lawson, Fred H. (ed.), *Demystifying Syria* (London, 2009).

Lerner, David, *The Passing of Traditional Society: Modernizing the Middle East* (New York, 1958).

Liel, Alon, *Turkey in the Middle East: Oil, Islam and Politics* (London, 2001).

Longrigg, Stephen H., *Syria and Lebanon under French Mandate* (London, 1958).

Lundgren Jörum, Emma, 'Discourses of a Revolution: Framing the Syrian Uprising', *Ortadoğu Etütleri* (Middle Eastern Studies), vol 3 no 2 (2012), pp 11–39.

Lundgren Jörum, Emma, 'The Importance of the Unimportant: Understanding Syrian Policies towards Hatay 1939–2012', Hinnebusch, Raymond A. & Tür, Özlem (eds.), *Turkey-Syria Relations: Between Enmity and Amity* (Farnham, 2013), pp 112–123.

Lustick, Ian S., *Unsettled States, Disputed Lands: Britain and Ireland, France and Algeria, Israel and the West Bank* (Ithaca, 1993).

Ma'oz, Moshe, 'Attempts at Creating a Political Community in Modern Syria', *Middle East Journal*, vol 26, no 4 (1972), pp 389–404.

Mara'i, Tayseer & Halabi, Usama R., 'Life under Occupation in the Golan Heights', *Journal of Palestine Studies*, vol 22, no 1 (1992), pp 78–93.

Mardam Bey, Jamil, 'The Legacy of Equivocation (1939)' in Mardam Bey, Salma, *Syria's Quest for Independence 1939–1945* (London, 1994).

Marlowe, Lara, 'Most Lebanese See Syrian Presence as Necessary Evil', *The Irish Times*, 21 June 2000.

Massigli, René, *La Turquie devant la Guerre: Mission à Ankara 1939–1940* (Paris, 1964).

'Memorandum from Syrian Foreign Ministry to Arab League Secretary General, Damascus, September 5 1983', *Journal of Palestine Studies*, vol 13, no 2 (1984), pp 206–207.

Micallef, Roberta, 'Hatay joins the Motherland' in Brandell, Inga (ed.), *State Frontiers: Borders and Boundaries in the Middle East* (London, 2006), pp 141–158.

Migliorino, Nicola, '"Kulna Suriyyin"? The Armenian Community and the State in contemporary Syria', *Revue des mondes musulmans et Méditerranée*, no 115–116 (2006), pp 97–115.

Moubayed, Sami, *Damascus between Democracy and Dictatorship* (Lanham, 2000).

Moubayed, Sami, 'Aftershocks of Assad's passing hit Lebanon', *Gulf News*, 24 August 2001.

Moubayed, Sami, *Steel & Silk: Men and Women Who Shaped Syria 1900–2000* (Washington, 2006).

Moubayed, Sami, '"Milking the male goat" and Syrian-Turkish relations' in Hinnebusch, Raymond A. & Tür, Özlem (eds.), *Turkey-Syria Relations: Between Enmity and Amity* (Farnham, 2013).

Mualem, Mazal, 'Druze to cross into Syria for Tuesday service', *Ha'aretz*, 12 June 2000.

'*Mubahathat suriyyah-turkiyyah li-taqil al-taawun al-bahri*' (Syrian-Turkish discussions in order to effectuate maritime cooperation), *al-Baath*, 25 February 2008.

Mufti, Malik, *Sovereign Creations: Pan-Arabism and Political Order in Syria and Iraq* (New York, 1996).

Murphy, Robert, *Diplomat among Warriors* (New York, 1964).

Muslih, Muhammad, 'The Golan: Israel, Syria and Strategic Calculations', *The Middle East Journal*, vol 47, no 4 (1993), pp 611–632.

Nasrallah, Fida, 'Syria after Taif: Lebanon and the Lebanese in Syrian Politics' in Kienle, Eberhard (ed.), *Contemporary Syria: Liberalization between Cold War and Cold Peace* (London, 1994).

Neep, Daniel, *Occupying Syria under the French Mandate: Insurgency, Space and State Formation* (Cambridge, 2012).

Neff, Donald, 'Israel-Syria: Conflict at the Jordan River, 1949–1967', *Journal of Palestine Studies*, vol 23, no 4 (1984), pp 26–40.
Norton, Augustus Richard, 'Lebanon after Taif: Is the Civil War Over?', *Middle East Journal*, vol 45, no 3 (1991), pp 457–473.
Oktar, Zeynep Ö., 'Turkish-Syrian Relations at the Crossroads', *Turkish Review of Middle East Studies*, vol 11 (2000).
Oruc, Saadet, 'From the Middle East to Cyprus, Turkish Foreign Policy debated at OIC summit', *Turkish Daily News*, 13 November 2000.
Paasi, Anssi & Newman, David, 'Fences and neighbors in the postmodern world: boundary narratives in political geography', *Progress in Human Geography*, vol 22, April (1998), pp 186–207.
Pace, Joe & Landis, Joshua, 'The Syrian Opposition: The Struggle for Unity and Relevance 2003–2008' in Lawson, Fred H. (ed.), *Demystifying Syria*, (London, 2009), pp 120–143.
Painter, Joe, 'Stateness in Action', *Geoforum*, vol 38, no 4 (2007), pp 605–607.
Peres, Shimon & Naor, Aryeh, *The New Middle East* (New York, 1993).
Perlmutter, Amos, 'From Obscurity to Rule: The Syrian Army and the Ba'th Party', *The Western Political Quarterly*, vol 22, no 4 (1969), pp 827–845.
Perthes, Volker, 'A Look at Syria's Upper Class: The Bourgeiosie and the Baath', *Middle East Report* no 170 (1991), pp 31–37.
Perthes, Volker, 'The Syrian Industrial and Commercial Sectors and the State', *International Journal of Middle East Studies*, vol 24, no 2 (1992), pp 207–230.
Perthes, Volker, *The Political Economy of Syria under Asad* (London, 1995).
Perthes, Volker, 'Syrian Predominance in Lebanon: Not Immutable' in Hollis, Rosemary & Shehadi, Nadim (eds.), *Lebanon on Hold: Implications for Middle East Peace* (London,1996).
Perthes, Volker, 'Politics and Élite Change in the Arab World' in Perthes, Volker (ed.), *Arab Élites: Negotiating the Politics of Change* (Boulder, 2004a), pp 1–33.
Perthes, Volker, 'Syria: Difficult Inheritance' in Perthes, Volker (ed.) *Arab Élites: Negotiating the Politics of Change* (Boulder, 2004b), pp 87–115.
Philip, P. J., 'France signs pact giving Turks Hatay', *New York Times* 24 June 1939.
Picard, Elizabeth, 'Retour au Sandjak', *Maghreb-Mashrek*, no 99 (1983), pp 47–64.
Picard, Elizabeth, *Lebanon: A Shattered Country: Myths and Realities of the Wars in Lebanon* (London, 2002).
Pipes, Daniel, *Greater Syria: The History of an Ambition* (New York, 1990).
Podeh, Elie, *The Decline of Arab Unity* (Brighton, 1999).
Pogany, Istvan, *The Arab League and Peacekeeping in the Lebanon* (Aldershot, 1987).
'Proposed ICRC hospital for Occupied Golan Heights', *Daily Bulletin*, issue 2, 21 June (2006).
Rabil, Robert G., *Embattled Neighbors: Syria, Israel and Lebanon* (Boulder, 2003).

Rabinovich, Itamar, *Syria under the Ba'th 1963–66: The Army-Party Symbiosis* (Jerusalem, 1972).
Rabinovich, Itamar, *The Road not Taken: Early Arab-Israeli Negotiations* (New York, 1991).
Rabinovich, Itamar, *The Brink of Peace: The Israeli-Syrian Negotiations* (Princeton, 1998).
Rabinowitz, Dan & Khawalde, Sliman, 'Demilitarized then dispossessed: the Kirad Bedouins of the Hula Valley', *International Journal of Middle East Studies*, vol 32, no 4 (2000), pp 511–530.
Ross, Dennis, *The Missing Peace: The Inside Story of the Fight for Middle East Peace* (New York, 2004).
Rubin, Barry, *The Truth About Syria* (New York, 2007).
Russel, Malcolm B., *The First Modern Arab State: Syria and Faysal 1918–1920* (Minneapolis, 1985).
Salih, Shakeeb, 'The British-Druze Connection and the Druze Rising of 1896 in the Hawran', *Middle Eastern Studies*, vol 13, no 2 (1977), pp 251–257.
Salloukh, Bassel F., 'Syria and Lebanon: A Brotherhood Transformed', *Middle East Report*, no 236 (2005), pp 14–21.
Salloukh, Bassel F., 'Demystifying Syrian Foreign Policy under Bashar al-Asad' in Lawson, Fred H. (ed.), *Demystifying Syria* (London, 2009), pp 159–179.
Sanjian, Avedis, 'The Sanjak of Alexandretta (Hatay): Its Impact on Turkish-Syrian Relations (1939–1956)', *Middle East Journal*, vol 10, no 4 (1956), pp 379–394.
Savir, Uri, The Process: 1,100 Days that Changed the Middle East (New York, 1998).
Schiff, Ze'ev, 'What Did Rabin Promise the Syrians?', *Ha'aretz* 29 August 1997, reproduced in *Journal of Palestine Studies*, vol 27, no 2 (1998), pp 156–157.
Seale, Patrick, *The Struggle for Syria: A Study of Post War Arab Politics 1945–1958* (London, 1965).
Seale, Patrick, *Asad of Syria: The Struggle for the Middle East* (London, 1988).
Seale, Patrick, 'Syria' in Sayigh, Y. & Shlaim, A. (eds.), *The Cold War and the Middle East* (Oxford, 1997), pp 48–76.
Seale, Patrick, *The Struggle for Arab Independence: Riad al-Solh and the Makers of the Modern Middle East* (New York, 2010).
Shalev, Aryeh, *Israel and Syria: Peace and Security on the Golan* (Tel Aviv, 1994).
Shields, Sarah D., *Fezzes in the River: Identity Politics and European Diplomacy in the Middle East on the Eve of World War II* (New York, 2011).
Shlaim, Avi, 'Husni Za'im and the Plan to Resettle Palestinian Refugees in Syria', *Journal of Palestine Studies*, vol 15, no 4 (1986), pp 68–80.
Shukri al-Quwatli yukhatib ummatahu (Shukri al-Quwatli speeks to his nation) (Beirut, 2001).

Siilasvuo, Ensio, *In the Service of Peace in the Middle East* (London, 1992).
Sluglett, Peter, 'Will the Real Nationalists Stand Up? The Political Activities of the Notables of Aleppo, 1918–1946' in Méouchy, Nadine (ed.), *France, Syrie et Liban 1918–1946: Les ambiguïtés et les dynamiques de la relation mandataire* (Damascus, 2002), pp 273–290.
Soysal, İsmail, 'The Middle East Peace Process and Turkey', *Turkish Review of Middle East Studies*, vol 8 (1994/95), pp 69–96.
Soysal, İsmail, 'Turkish-Syrian Relations (1946–1996)', *Turkish Review of Middle Eastern Studies*, vol 10 (1998/99), pp 25–37.
'Statement by Lebanese Prime Minister Rashid Karami asking Syria to withdraw its forces from Lebanon, Beirut, June 19, 1976', *Journal of Palestine Studies*, vol 6, no 1 (1976), pp 171–172.
Syria Unmasked: The Suppression of Human Rights by the Asad Regime (New Haven and London, 1991).
Syria 2000: Geographical and Economic Yearbook (Damascus, 2001).
Syria's Kurds: A Struggle Within a Struggle, International Crisis Group Middle East report no 136, 22 January 2013.
Tarabieh, Bashar, 'Education, Control and Resistance in the Golan Heights', *Middle East Report*, no 194/195 (1995), pp 43–47.
Tauber, Eliezer, 'The Struggle for Dayr al-Zur: The Determination of Borders between Syria and Iraq', *International Journal of Middle East Studies*, vol 23, no 3 (1991), pp 361–385.
Tauber, Eliezer, *The Formation of Modern Syria and Iraq* (New York, 1995).
Tejel Gorgas, Jordi 'Les Kurdes de Syrie, de la "dissimulation" à la "visibilité"', *Revue des mondes musulmans et Méditerranée*, no 115–116 (2006), pp 117–133.
Tejel Gorgas, Jordi, *Syria's Kurds: History, Politics and Society* (London, 2008).
'The Madrid Peace Conference', *Journal of Palestine Studies*, vol 21, no 2 (1992), pp 125–141.
Thompson, Eric V., 'Will Syria Have to Withdraw from Lebanon?', *Middle East Journal*, vol 56, no 1 (2002), pp 72–93.
Thomas, Martin, 'Bedouin Tribes and the Imperial Intelligence Services in Syria, Iraq and Transjordan in the 1920s', *Journal of Contemporary History*, vol 38, no 4 (2003), pp 539–561.
Too Close for Comfort: Syrians in Lebanon, International Crisis Group Middle East Report no 141, 13 May 2013.
Torrey, Gordon H., *Syrian Politics and the Military 1945–1958* (Columbus, 1964).
Tweini, Jibran, 'Kitab maftuh ila Bashar al-Asad ... al-rais' (Open letter to Bashar al-Asad ... the President), *al-Nahar* 26 July 2001.
'Utri Turkmani Araoğlu, tatwir al-taawun al-thunai, suriyyah wa-turkiyyah tataffiqan ala al-shurut al-faniyyah li-insha sadd al-sadaqah' (Utri, Turkmani and Araoğlu, development of bilateral cooperation, Syria and Turkey agree

on the strategic conditions for launching the Friendship Dam), *al-Baath* 8 October 2010.

Valter, Stéphane, *La construction nationale syrienne: Légitimation de la nature communautaire du pouvoir par le discours historique* (Paris, 2002).

Walz, Jay, 'Arabs Eye Hatay Province as Turks Glare Back', *New York Times* 26 February 1961.

Van Dam, Nikolaos, *The Struggle for Power in Syria: Politics and Society under Asad and the Ba'th Party* (London, 1997).

Van Dusen, Michael H., 'Political Integration and Regionalism in Syria', *The Middle East Journal*, vol 26, no 2 (1972), pp 123–136.

Vassiliev, Alexei, *Russian Policy in the Middle East: From Messianism to Pragmatism* (Reading, 1993).

'Wazir al-ilam al-suri: la yumkin al-tafrit fi al-iskandarunah' (The Syrian Minister of Information: It is impossible to forsake Iskandarunah), *al-Bayan*, 20 October 1998.

Wedeen, Lisa, *Ambiguities of Domination: Politics, Rhetoric and Symbols in Contemporary Syria* (Chicago, 1999).

Weinberger, Naomi Joy, *Syrian Intervention in Lebanon: The 1975–76 Civil War* (New York, 1986).

Wendt, Alexander, *Social Theory of International Politics* (Cambridge, 1999).

White, George W., *Nationalism and Territory: Constructing Group Identity in Southeastern Europe* (Oxford, 2000).

Wieland, Carsten, *Syria – Ballots or Bullets? Democracy, Islamism, and Secularism in the Levant* (Seattle, 2006).

Winder, Bayly R. 'Syrian Deputies and Cabinet Ministers 1919–1959, Part II', *Middle East Journal*, vol 17, no 1–2 (1963), pp 35–54.

Yearbook of the United Nations (1946–2010).

'Yet another dispute with Syria', *Turkish Daily News* 17 June 1996.

Yilmaz, Richard, 'Le Sandjak d'Alexandrette, barometer des relations entre la Turquie et la Syrie', *Outre-terre*, vol 1, no 14 (2004), pp 109–116.

Young, Michael, *The Ghosts of Martyrs Square: An Eyewitness Account of Lebanon's Life Struggle* (New York, 2010).

Zamir, Meir, 'Faisal and the Lebanese Question', *Middle Eastern Studies*, vol 27, no 3 (1991), pp 404–426.

Zamir, Meir, 'The Franco-Syrian Treaty Negotiations and the Question of Lebanon 1936–1939' in Ma'oz, Moshe, Joseph, Ginat & Onn, Winckler (eds.), *Modern Syria: From Ottoman Rule to Pivotal Role in the Middle East* (Brighton, 1999), pp 191–208.

Zamir, Meir, *Lebanon's Quest: The Road to Statehood 1926–1939* (London, 2000).

Zisser, Eyal, *Asad's Legacy: Syria in Transition* (London, 2001).

Zorob, Anja, 'Partnership with the European Union: Hopes, risks and challenges for the Syrian economy' in Lawson, Fred H. (ed.), *Demystifying Syria* (London, 2009), pp 144–158.

Internet sources

Abbas, al-Tars, Darwish, al-Arabi, 'Smuggling Across the Syrian–Lebanese Border', *al-Sharq al-Awsat*, 27 April 2008, http://www.asharq-e.com/news.asp?section=3&id=12560 [accessed 25 February 2011].

Abdullah, Yasar, 'Al-iskandarun wa-l-azmatu-s-suriyyah': hal takfi al-tazahurat? (Iskandarun and the Syrian Crisis: are demonstrations enough?), al-hayah al-ama l-l-idhaah wa-t-televizion, 10 April 2014, http://www.rtv.gov.sy/index.php?d=21&id=149411

Abdulrahim, Raja, 'Al-muaradah tuid kitabat al-tarikh al-suri' (The opposition rewrites Syrian history), *Al-Hayat*, 8 May 2013, http://daharchives.alhayat.com/issue_archive/Hayat%20INT/2008%20to%202013/Alhayat_2013/05-May-2013/05-General/2013–05–08/08p17–01.xml.html [accessed 26 August 2013].

Acinci, Burak, 'Newly found friendship between Turkey and Syria', *Middle East Online*, 23 December 2004, http://www.middle-east-online.comenglish/?id=12236 [accessed 17 October 2007].

'Al-Asad: barak qawwi wa-yurid al-salam', (Al-Asad: Barak is strong and sincere and wants peace), *Al-Hayat*, 23 June 1999, http://www.library.cornell.edu/colldev/mideast/seale.htm [accessed 22 October 2004].

'Al-duktur Hasan al-Nuri yulan barnamijahu al-intkhabi' (Doctor Hasan al-Nuri announces his election program), al-hayah al-ama l-l-idhaah wa-t-televizion, 14 May 2014, http://www.rtv.gov.sy/index.php?d=100244&id=146903

Al-dustur al-lubnani (The Lebanese Constitution), http://www.lp.gov.lb/SecondaryAr.Aspx?id=12 [accessed 16 March 2011].

'*Al ikhwan al-muslimun: iskandarun laysa suriyyah wa-laysa muhtallan* (The Muslim Brotherhood: Iskandarun is not Syria and it is not occupied), Interview on the *Al-Sharia al-arabi* (The Arab Street) show, Dubai Media Corporation, 10 June 2012, at http://www.youtube.com/watch?v=y85uy1C8738 [accessed 28 April 2013].

Al-ittifaqiyat wa-l-ittifaqat al-munthabiqah an muahadat al-ikhwah wa-l-taawun wa-l-tansiq (Agreements and Accords emanating from the Treaty of Brotherhood, Cooperation and Coordination), http://www.syrleb.org/conference.asp?conftype=1&page=2 [accessed 20 May 2008].

'Al-kharijiyyah fi risalatayn mutatabiqatayn ila rais majlis al-amn wa-amin am al-umam al-mutahidah: turkiyyah mustamirrah fi al-tadakhul fi al-shuun al-suriyyah wa iywa wa-tadrib wa-l-taslih wa-l-tamwil al-majmuat al-irhabiyyah' (The Ministry of Foreign Affairs in two identical letters to the President of the Security Council and the Secretary General of the United Nations: Turkey keeps interfering in Syrian affairs and persists in harbouring, training, arming and funding terrorist groups), *Tishreen*, 8 March 2013, http://tishreen.news.sy/tishreen/public/read/282033 [accessed 13 April 2013].

Al-mabadi al-asasiyyah (The Basic Principles), http://www.baath-party.org/constitution_detail.asp?id=1 [accessed 21 December 2010].

Al-mawqi al-yughrafi li-l-jumhuriyyah al-arabiyyah al-suriyyah (The Geographical Position of the Syrian Arab Republic), www.moi-syria.com [accessed 25 August 2003].

Al-nass al-kamil li-kalimat al-rais Bashar al-Asad fi majlis al-shaab had ada al-qasam al-dusturi (Full text of the speech of President Bashar al-Asad in the Parliament after swearing the Constitutional Oath), Syrian Arab News Agency, 17 July 2007, http://www.sana.sy/ara/2/2007/07/19/pr-129403.htm [accessed 15 October 2010].

'Al-rais al-Asad fi hadith li-qana al-manar: suriyyah lam wa lan taqbal an takun juzan min mashruu khariji, al-tayyar al-shaabi fi-l-mintaqah tallam al-dars bi-anna hall al-mashakil yakun bi-tamassuk bi-l-huquq' (President Al-Asad to al-Manar Channel: Syria has not and will not accept to be part of a foreign plan. The popular forces in the region have learned the lesson that the solution to the problems lies in holding on to their rights), Syrian Arab News Agency, 25 March 2010, http://www.sana.sy/ara/3/2010/03/25/pr-279708.htm [accessed 10 July 2010].

'Al-rais al-Asad li-qanah TRT: suriyyah wa-turkiyyah tamalan bi-ajinda shaa-biyyah tarbut masalih al-baladayn: suriyyah ala al-tawasul ma jami al-quwa al-iraqiyyah' (President al-Asad talking to the Turkish TRT channel: Syria and Turkey work with a popular agenda that connects the interests of both states. Syria is in contact with all Iraqi forces), Syrian Arab News Agency, 8 October 2010, http://www.sana.sy/ara/3/2010/10/08/pr-311744.htm [accessed 12 December 2010].

'Al-rais al-Asad yudli bi-hadith shamil li-qanah Dubai al-fidaiyyah' (President al-Asad gives complete talk to the Dubai Satellite Channel), Syrian Arab News Agency, 23 August 2006, http://www.sana.sy/ara/2/2006/08/23/pr-60158.htm [accessed 7 December 2007].

'Al-rais al-Asad yulqi kalimah siyasiyyah shamilah fi iftitah amal al-mutamar al-thani wa-l-ishrin li-ittihad al-muhamiyin al-arab' (President al-Asad gives complete political speech at the opening of the 22nd conference of the Arab Lawyers' Union), Syrian Arab News Agency, 21 November 2006, http://www.sana.sy/ara/2/2006/01/21/pr-13155.htm [accessed 17 October 2007].

'Al-rais al-Asad yusdir al-qanun 18 al-khass bi-tamin al-iradat al-lazimah li-l-majalis al-mahaliyyah wa-yuwajjihu bi-manh abna al-jawlan al-raqam al-watani wa-al-hawwiyyah al-suriyyah' (President al-Asad issues law no 18 concerning ensuring the necessary decrees to the local councils, starts to give the people on the Golan a national [ID–] number and Syrian ID [cards]), Syrian Ministry of Information, 28 October 2007, http://www.moi.gov.sy/_allnews.php?filename=2007102808415211, [accessed 24 April 2008].

'Al-rais al-suri wa-l-awdaa al-arabiyyah al-rahinah' (The Syrian President and current Arab circumstances), Al-Jazeerah, 1 May 2004, http://www.

aljazeera.net/NR/exeres/782698E9-85EF-4F2E-ADB9-5A1EC2BF287B. htm, [accessed 5 May 2004].

'Assad voices concern over Lebanon's security situation', *The Daily Star* 8 October 2010, http://www.dailystar.com.lb/News/Middle-East/Oct/08/Assad-voices-concern-over-Lebanons-security-situation.ashx#axzz1KXdP9Ayh [accessed 8 October 2010].

'Al-salam al-adil wa-l-shamil fi-l-mintaqah yatatallab insihab Israil hata khatt huzayran am 1976' (Just and comprehensive peace in the region requires that Israel withdraws to the line of June 4th 1967), Syrian Ministry of Information, 25 November 2007, http://www.moi.gov.sy/-declarationministry.php?filename=2007112509130426 [accessed 24 April 2008].

'Al-sayyid al-rais Bashar al-Asad fi hadith shamil li-sahifat al-safir al-lubnaniyyah' (President Bashar al-Asad in a complete talk with the Lebanese newspaper al-Safir) Syrian Arab News Agency, 27 March 2003, http://sana.sy/ara/2/2009/03/27/pr-218679.htm [accessed 28 March 2003].

'Al-sayyid al-rais Bashar al-Asad fi hadith shamil li-sahifat al-safir al-lubnaniyyah hawla al-tatawwurat al-rahina' (President Bashar al-Asad in a complete talk with the Lebanese newspaper al-Safir about the current developments), *Tishreen*, 24 March 2002, www.tishreen.info/president [accessed 10 March 2005].

'Al-sayyid al-rais al-Asad yudli bi-hadith ila al-qana al-thaniya wa-l-khamisah fi al-televizyon al-faransi 12 adhar 2007' (President al-Asad talks to channel 2 and channel 5 of the French Television), Syrian Arab News Agency, 12 March 2007, http://www.sana.sy/ara/2/2007/03/21/pr-109095.htma [accessed 17 October 2007].

'Al-sayyid al-rais yulqi kalimah shamilah amam majlis al-shaab' (The President gives a complete speech before the Parliament), Syrian Arab News Agency, 5 March 2005, http://www.sana.sy/ara/2/2005/03/05/pr-866.htm [accessed 10 October 2010].

'Al-sayyid al-rais, hadith li-mahattat CNN al-turkiyyah, Dimashq 5/1' (The President, interview with CNN Turk, Damascus 5 January), Syrian Arab News Agency, 5 January 2004, www.sana.org/The%20Arabic/Bashar/Prisedent1.htm [accessed 10 February 2004].

'Al-shabab al-watani al-suriy: liwa iskandarun ard arabiyyah suriyya sata'ud ila al-watan al-um mahma tal al-zaman', *Tishreen*, 3 December 2012, http://tishreen.news.sy/tishreen/public/read/274126 [accessed 11 April 2013].

'Al-Siniora yuakkid al-khilaf ma al-Asad hawl tarsim mazari Shebaa' (Siniora confirms the conflict with al-Asad over the delineation of the Shebaa Farms), al-Arabiyyah, 23 January 2006, [accessed 20 September 2007].

'Amin am al-shabab al-watani al-suri: darurat taawun al-jami' li-bina al-watan wa-nabdh al-unf wa-l-tatarruf' (The Secretary General of the Syrian Patriotic Youth Party: it is necessary for all to cooperate in order to build the homeland and reject violence and extremism), *Tishreen*, 4 March 2013, http://tishreen.news.sy/tishreen/public/read/281555 [accessed 11 April 2013].

'Assad's Turkish spy caught' in Press Scanner, *Turkish Daily News*, 16 October 1998, http://www.turkishdailynews.com.tr/archives.php?id=9332tesev [accessed 27 July 2007].

Bashar al-Asad interviewed on the Turkish Ulusal Channel 5 April 2013, YouTube 5 April, 2013, http://www.youtube.com/watch?v=wSEokTbFd2g [accessed 15 April 2013].

Başbakan Erdoğan, Hatay'da Dostluk Baraji temel atma törenine katildi (Prime Minister Erdoğan attended the groundbreaking ceremony of the Friendship Dam in Hatay)', TGRT Haber, 6 February 2011, uploaded on YouTube 6 February 2011, http://www.youtube.com/watch?v=PVHiRTzuFpQ [accessed 28 April 2013].

Bathish, Hani M., 'Jumblatt cries out for world leaders to "protect us"', *The Daily Star*, 1 October 2007, http://www.dailystar.com.lb/News/Politics/Oct/01/Jumblatt-cries-out-for-world-leaders-to-protect-us.ashx#axzz1KXdP9Ayh [accessed 1 October 2007].

'Baykal urges Turkey to stay calm towards "southern neighbor"', *Turkish Daily News*, 17 June 1996, http://www.turkishdailynews.com.tr/archives.php?id=2418 [accessed 27 July 2007].

Ben-Aharon, Yossi, 'Negotiating with Syria: A First Hand Account', *Middle East Review of International Affairs*, vol 4, no 2 (2000), http://meria.idc.ac.il/journal/2000/issue2/jv4n2a1.html [accessed 24 August 2005].

Chulov, Martin & Sherwood, Harriet, 'Syrian troop redeployments raises concern over Golan Heights security', *The Guardian*, 7 April 2013, http://www.guardian.co.uk/world/2013/apr/07/syria-golan-heights-security [accessed 16 April 2013].

Communication dated 20 July 1949 from the United Nations Acting mediator on Palestine to the Acting Secretary-General transmitting the text of an armistice agreement between Israel and Syria, http://dominoun.org/unispal.nsf/3822b5e39951876a85256b6e0058a478/e845ca0b92be4e3485256442007901cc!OpenDocument [accessed 10 October 2003].

Dakhlallah: Zuhur al-shahid al-muqni asqata saba bunud fi taqrir Milis (Dakhlallah: The appearance of the convincing witness invalidated seven basic points in the Milis report), Syrian Ministry of Information, 30 November 2005, http://www.moi.gov.sy/_declarationministry.php?filename=20051130204826 [accessed 30 November 2005].

'Dostluk barajı ortada kaldı' (The Friendship Dam caught in the middle), *Gerçek Gündem*, 14 October 2012, http://www.gercekgundem.com/?p=496251 [accessed 28 April 2013].

Dustur al-jumhuriyyah al-arabiyyah al-suriyyah (Constitution of the Syrian Arab Republic), http://parliament.sy/forms/new_laws/viewNew_laws.php?law_id=37 [accessed 10 April 2013].

Eldar, Akiva, 'EXCLUSIVE: Full text of document drafted during secret talks', *Ha'aretz*, 16 January 2007a, http://www.haaretz.com/news/exclusive-full-text-of-document-drafted-during-secret-talks-1.210053 [accessed 5 June 2007].

El Hassan, Jana, 'March 14 Memo urges end to Hizbollah role in Syria', *The Daily Star*, 18 June 2013, http://www.dailystar.com.lb/News/Politics/2013/Jun-18/220766-march-14-hands-sleiman-memo-over-syria-crisis.ashx#axzz2dLoHFqkc.

Fact Sheet: Implementing the Syria Accountability and Lebanese Sovereignty Restoration Act of 2003, www.whitehouse.gov/news/releases/2004/05/print/20040511–7.html [accessed 12 December 2010].

'Farouk al-Shara: Hatay is not a priority', *Turkish Daily News*, 6 February 2000, http://www.hurriyetdailynews.com/sitemap8.xml [accessed 15 October 2004].

Fattah, Hassan M., 'Syria to buy apples from Israel-occupied Golan Heights while trying to ignore Israel herself', *New York Times*, 8 February 2005, http://www.nytimes.com/2005/02/08/international/middleeast/08syria.html [accessed 1 May 2008].

Film wathaiqi mufassal an liwa iskandarun al-salib (Detailed documentary on the stolen region Hatay), Al-Akhbariyyah, uploaded on YouTube 9 March 2013, http://www.youtube.com/watch?v=VgzhxQcFi5s [accessed 13 April 2013].

Follath, Erich, 'Breakthrough in Tribunal investigation: New evidence points to Hizbullah in Hariri murder', *Spiegel Online*, published 23 May 2009, http://www.spiegel.de/international/world/0,1518,626412,00.html [accessed 29 September 2010].

Free Speech Punished in Lebanon, Human Rights Watch, 26 April 2000, http://www.hrw.org/en/news/2000/04/26/free-speech-punished-lebanon [accessed 5 May 2003].

Hadith al-sayyid al-rais Bashar al-Asad ila qanah al-jazirah al-qatariyyah (Interview with President Bashar al-Asad on the Qatari al-Jazeerah channel), 26 April 2004, http://www.presidentassad.org/Bashar_Al_Assad/Bashar_Hafez_Al_Assad_Al_Jazeera_2004.htm [accessed 10 December 2010].

Hammargren, Bitte, 'Syrien öppnar för fred' (Syria opens up for peace), *Svenska Dagbladet*, 4 March 2010, http://www.svd.se/nyheter/utrikes/syrien-oppnar-for-fred_4369737.svd [accessed 4 March 2010].

Harel, Amos, 'IDF on high alert in Golan Heights in anticipation of further protests', *Ha'aretz*, 7 June 2011, http://www.haaretz.com/blogs/2.244/idf-on-high-alert-in-golan-heights-in-anticipation-of-further-protests-1.366373 [accessed 16 April 2013].

'Hatay row complicates water talks', *Today's Zaman*, 24 December 2009, http://www.todayszaman.com/news-196473-102-pm-vows-to-build-model-partnership-with-syria.html [accessed 25 December 2010].

Hatoum, Majdoline, 'Franjieh: Syrian meddling can't continue', *The Daily Star*, 3 July 2004, http://www.dailystar.com.lb/News/Politics/Jul/03/Franjieh-Syrian-meddling-cant-continue.ashx#axzz1KXdP9Ayh [accessed 26 June 2004].

Hiwar maftuh: Jumblat wa-mustaqbal lubnan (Open Dialogue: Junblat and the future of Lebanon), Al-Jazeerah, 13 March 2010, http://www.aljazeera.net/NR/exeres/0E347BFB-5A8C-4105-A6E3-245958B4C6A8.htm [accessed 26 September 2010].

Hiwar maftuh: Suriya wa-l-milaff al-lubnani (Open Dialogue: Syria and the Lebanese portfolio), Al-Jazeerah, 23 October 2004, http://www.aljazeera.net/programs/pages/82109d2a-e2f3-4b0b-b1b4-a9175206f403 [accessed 26 September 2010].

'Hizb al-shabab al-watani al-suriy: al-hiwar al-watani al-shamil huwa al-wasilah al-wahidah li-l-khuruj min al-azmah" (The Patriotic Syrian Youth Party: Comprehensive national dialogue is the only way out of the crisis), *Tishreen*, 26 February 2013, http://tishreen.news.sy/tishreen/public/read/281056 [accessed 11 April 2013].

'Hizbullah yunfi tawaruttahu bi-ightiyal al-Hariri' (Hizbullah denies its involvement in the assassination of al-Hariri), Al-Jazeerah, 24 May 2009, http://www.aljazeera.net/NR/exeres/770549F5-1FFD-48B6-BC6F-F88213FBEBDE.htm [accessed 26 September 2010].

Ibrahim, Alia, 'Lebanon's Blended Border: Demarcation of Syrian Line will Disrupt Lives, Villagers Say', *The Washington Post*, 17 August 2008, http://www.highbeam.com/doc/1P2-17036898.html [accessed 26 September 2010].

International Committee of the Red Cross in Syria, Facts & Figures January-June 2013, ICRC, http://www.icrc.org/eng/assets/files/2013/130731-eng-syria-newsletter-ver1.1.pdf [accessed 20 April 2014].

'ISA uncovers Golan weapons infiltration', Israeli Ministry of Foreign Affairs, 9 January 2002, http://www.mfa.gov.il/MFA/Government/Communiques/2002/ISA+uncovers+Golan+weapons+infiltration+-+Jan+9-+2.htm [accessed 10 May 2006].

'Israel ready to return Golan Heights', BBC, 23 April 2008b, http://news.bbc.co.uk/2/hi/middle_east/7362937.stm [accessed 23 April 2008].

'Israel-Syria confirm Peace Talks', BBC World News, 21 May 2008, http://news.bbc.co.uk/2/hi/middle_east/7412247.stm [accessed 28 May 2008].

'Ittifaqat suriyyah lubnaniyyah bila tarsim li-l-hudud' (Syrian-Lebanese Agreements without delineation of the border), Al-Jazeerah, 19 July 2010 [accessed 26 September 2010].

Al-ittifaqiyat 1943-1974 (The Agreements 1943-1974), http://www.syrleb.org/conference_ar.asp?conftype=3 [accessed 26 September 2010].

Ittifaqiyyat al-difaa wa-l-amn bayn al-jumhuriyyah al-lubnaniyyah wa-l-jumhuriyyah al-arabiyyah al-suriyyah (The Defense and Security Agreement between the Lebanese Republic and the Syrian Arab Republic), 1 September 1991, http://www.syrleb.org/docs/agreements/02%20DEFENSE%20SECURITY.pdf [accessed 26 September 2010].

Kalimat al-rais Bashar al-Asad fi mutamar al-mughtaribin al-suriyin bi-tarikh 9 tishreen al-awwal 2004 (The Speech of President Bashar al-Asad at the Conference of Syrian Emigrants, 9 October 2004), http://www.presidentassad.

org/Bashar_Al_Assad/Bashar_Hafez_Al_Assad_Syrian_Migrants_2004. htm [accessed 12 December 2010].

'Kalimat al-sayyid Faruq al-Sharaa wazir al-kharijiyyah amam al-mutamar al-sanawi li-ittihad al-kutab al-arab' (The speech by Foreign Minister Farouq al-Shara at the yearly conference of the Arab Writers' Union), *al-Fikr al-Siyasi*, vol 3, no 8 (2000), http://www.awu-dam.org/politic/08/fkr8-001.htm [accessed 30 January 2011].

Kalimat al-sayyid al-rais fi majlis al-shaab bi-tarikh 17 tammuz 2000 (The President's speech in Parliament 17 July 2000), the Inauguration Speech of Bashar al-Asad, http://www.presidentassad.org/Bashar_Al_Assad/Bashar_Hafez_Al_Assad_Parliament_2000.htm [accessed 5 July 2001].

Karaman, Nazif, 'Suriye'ye göre Hatay kendi sınırları içinde' (According to Syria, Hatay is within its own borders', *Sabah*, 21 June 2012, http://www.sabah.com.tr/Gundem/2012/06/21/suriyeye-gore-hatay-kendi-sinirlari-icinde [accessed 18 April 2013].

Kaufman, Asher, 'Understanding the Shebaa Farms Dispute: Roots of the Anomaly and Prospects for Resolution', *Palestine-Israel Journal of Politics, Economics and Culture*, vol 11, no 1, http://www.pij.org/details.php?id=9 [accessed 15 January 2007].

Kershner, Isabel, 'Secret Israel-Syria Peace Talks involved Golan Height Exit', *The New York Times*, 12 October 2012, http://www.nytimes.com/2012/10/13/world/middleeast/secret-israel-syria-peace-talks-invol.ved-golan-heights-exit.html [accessed 12 April 2013].

'Khafaya ittifaq "al-muarada al-suriyyah" al-kharijiyyah: Istislam li-shurut al-adu al-isra'ili wa-bay al-ard' (The secrets of the 'Syrian oppostition' abroad: Surrendering to the demands of the Israeli enemy, selling the land), *Tishreen*, 23 November 2012, http://tishreen.news.sy/tishreen/public/read/273474 [accessed 20 April 2013].

Lappin, Yaakov: 'Shin Bet: 2 Druze accused of spying for Syria', *The Jerusalem Post*, 29 September 2010, http://www.jpost.com/home/article.aspx?id=189581 [accessed 10 October 2010].

Lazareva, Inna (2013) "Golan Heights students return to Syria despite war", *Almonitor*, 8 October 2013, http://www.al-monitor.com/pulse/ar/originals/2013/10/golan-heights-students-syria-war.html [accessed 20 April 2014].

'Lebanese Embassy opens in Damascus', Reuters, 16 March 2009, http://www.reuters.com/article/2009/03/16/us-syria-lebanon-idUSTRE52F44L20090316, [accessed 27 September 2010].

Lebanese prisoners detained in Syria: A priority question to raise before the Syrian authorities, SOLIDA, 8 July 2010, http://www.fidh.org/IMG/pdf/Rapport_lternatif_Solida_Syrie_2005_ENG_.pdf, [accessed 3 May 2010].

'Lebanon PM Hariri meets Syrian leader Assad', BBC, 20 December 2009, http://news.bbc.co.uk/2/hi/8422746.stm [accessed 18 October 2010].

REFERENCES

'Lebanon PM: It was wrong to accuse Syria of assassinating Rafiq al-Hariri', *The Guardian*, 6 September 2010, http://www.guardian.co.uk/world/2010/sep/06/lebanon-syria-hariri-assassination [accessed 27 December 2010].

'Lebanon president urged to resign', BBC World News, 2 June 2005, http://news.bbc.co.uk/2/hi/middle_east/4605027.stm [accessed 29 May 2008].

'Lebanon signs media cooperation agreement with Syria', *The Daily Star*, 8 October 2010, http://www.dailystar.com.lb/News/Politics/Oct/08/Lebanon-signs-media-cooperation-agreement-with-Syria.ashx#axzz1KXdP9Ayh [accessed 8 October 2010].

Lebanon: Restrictions on Broadcasting, Human Rights Watch, 1 April 1997, http://www.hrw.org/reports/1997/lebanon/ [accessed 10 July 2010].

Levy, Gideon, 'Welcoming the Bride', *Ha'aretz*, 23 July 2001, http://www.bintjbeil.com/E/occupation/levy/010723.html [accessed 10 March 2011].

Liqa ham maa Ali al-Qasim hawl urubat liwa iskandarun (Important meeting with Ali al-Qasim about the Arabness of Hatay), uploaded on YouTube 2 December 2012, http://www.youtube.com/watch?v=eZOmKXLzA9o [accessed 29 April 2013].

Liqa maa Washington Post, (Interview with Washington Post), SyrianMinistry of Information, 11 May 2003, http://www.moi.gov.sy/_recieptions.php?filename=200505121211022 [accessed 17 April 2008].

Liwa iskandarun al-mughtasab haqq suri lan yunsa istirdadihi (The violated region of Hatay is a Syrian right the recovery of which will not be forgotten) Sama TV, uploaded on YouTube 28 November 2012, http://www.youtube.com/watch?v=5BPu_yXNicQ [accessed 13 April 2013].

Liwa iskandarun al-salib fi dhakirah wa-qalb kul suriy ala amal an yarja ma kul ard suriyyah muhtallah (The stolen region Hatay is in the mind and heart of every Syrian with the hope that it will return together with all occupied Syrian land), Sama TV, uploaded on YouTube 27 November 2013, http://www.youtube.com/watch?v=bPsG42Qgf1U [accessed 13 April 2013].

Lockhart, Joe, *White House Press Secretary, Press Briefing Following President Clinton and President Assad Meeting, President Wilson Hotel, Geneva, Switzerland*, 26 March 2000, http://www.state.gov/www/regions/nea/000326_lockhart_mepp.html [accessed 9 April 2008].

'Lubnan yuhaddid bi-qam ihtijajat ala al-wujud al-suri', Al-Jazeerah, 13 March 2001 (Lebanon threatens to suppress protests against the Syrian presence), www.aljazeera.net/news/arabic/2001/3/3–13–3.htm [accessed 5 May 2003].

'Maher Karam, al-amin al-am li-hizb al-tadamun al-arabi al-dimuqrati: al-thawabit al-wataniyyah shurutna al-musbaqah li al-dukhul fi ayy hiwar' (Maher Karam, Secretary General of the Arab Democratic Solidarity Party: The national principles are our conditions for enering dialogue), *Tishreen*, 5 February 2013, http://tishreen.news.sy/tishreen/public/read/279339 [accessed 11 April 2013].

'Majdal Shams Hospital project, occupied Golan Heights: ICRC statement', 20 June 2006, www.icrc.org [accessed 7 November 2007].

Man nahnu? (About us), Syrian Lebanese Higher Council, http://www.syrleb.org/about_ar.asp [accessed 26 September 2010].

MacFarquhar, Neil, 'Syria talks of rebuilding city crushed by war', *International Herald Tribune*, 23 October 2004, www.iht.com/bin/print_ipub.php?file=/articles/2004/10/22/news/syria.html [accessed 23 October 2004].

'Maktvakum i presidentlöst Libanon' (Power vacuum in Lebanon without president), *Svenska Dagbladet*, 23 November 2007, http://www.svd.se/nyheter/utrikes/maktvakuum-i-presidentlost-libanon_621965.svd?listbox=toplists&listboxcat=mostread [accessed 5 October 2010].

Mallat, Chibli, 'The Special Tribunal for Lebanon, the staring abyss and what must be done about it', *The Daily Star*, 7 October 2010, http://www.dailystar.com.lb/Law/Oct/07/The-Special-Tribunal-for-Lebanon-the-staring-abyss-and-what-must-be-done-about-it.ashx#axzz1KXdP9Ayh [accessed 8 October 2010].

Lebanon's Lively Press Faces worst Crack-down since 1976, Middle East Watch (HRW) report, vol 5, no 2 (1993), available at http://www.hrw.org/en/reports/1993/07/01/lebanon-s-lively-press-faces-worst-crackdown-1976 [accessed 26 September 2010].

'Moallem: Damascus demands full Israeli pullout from the Golan Heights', *The Daily Star*, 13 July 2009, http://www.dailystar.com.lb/News/Politics/Jul/13/Moallem-Damascus-demands-full-Israeli-pullout-from-Golan.ashx#axzz1Jl0KRBzp [accessed 10 October 2010].

Muahadat al-ikhwah wa-l-taawun wa-l-tansiq bayn al-jumhuriyyah al-arabiyyah al-suriyyah wa-l-jumhuriyyah al-lubnaniyyah (Treaty of Brotherhood, Cooperation and Coordination between the Syrian Arab Republic and the Lebanese Republic), http://www.syrleb.org/docs/agreements/01%20TREATY.pdf [accessed 5 October 2007].

'Multaqa al-asra al-suriyyah: rafd al-unf wa al-irhab...wa-hal al-azmah hiwar' (The Forum in support of Syrian prisoners of war: Rejection of violence and terrorism...and dialogue the solution to the crisis), *Tishreen*, 5 December 2012, http://tishreen.news.sy/tishreen/public/read/274301[accessed 10 April 2013].

'Multaqa al-hiwar al-watani: al-hiwar huwa al-makhraj al-wahid li-l-azmah fi suriyah wa la shurut musbaqah alayhi' (The National Dialogue Forum: Dialogue is the only way out of the crisis in Syria and there are no preconditions), *Tishreen*, 26 March 2013, http://tishreen.news.sy/tishreen/public/read/283416 [accessed 10 April 2013].

Muqabalat al-sayyid al-rais Bashar al-Asad ma sahifat 'Corriere della Sera' al-italiyyah bi-tarikh (Interview of President Bashar al-Asad with the Italian newspaper Corriere della Sera, 16 February 2002), http://www.presidentassad.org/Bashar_Al_Assad/Bashar_Hafez_Al_Assad_Corriere_della_Serra_2002.htm [accessed 10 December 2010].

Mutamar al-qimmati al-arabiyyah al-thani ashar, Fez 1981/11/25 al-dawrah al-ula 1982/9/6–9 (al-dawrah al-mustanifah) (The 12th Arab Summit Conference

Fez 1981/11/25 (first round) 1982/9/6–9 (resumption round), http://www.arableagueonline.org/las/arabic/details_ar.jsp?art_id=416&level_id=202# [accessed 16 March 2010].

Mutamar sahafi li-l-sayyid al-rais Bashar al-Asad wa-l-sayyid Erdoğan rais wuzara turkiya dimashq bi-tarikh 23 kanun al-awwal 2009 (Press conference with President Bashar al-Asad and Mr Erdoğan, Prime Minister of Turkey, Damascus, 23 December 2009), http://www.presidentassad.org/Bashar_Al_Assad/Bashar_Al_Assad_Erdogan_23_12_2009.htm [accessed 12 December 2010].

'Nasrallah vows not to hand in accused by tribunal: UN Hariri Tribunal to accuse Hizbullah', Al-Arabiyyah, 22 July 2010, www.alarabiya.net [accessed 5 October 2010].

'National Investment Increases in Area bordering occupied Golan to encourage return', Internal Displacement Monitoring Centre, 2005, at http://www.internal-displacement.org/idmc/website/countries.nsf/(httpEnvelopes)/9DEC278FE1E6BCBF802570B8005AAE8A?OpenDocument [accessed 11 October 2010].

Nurturing Instability: Lebanon's Palestinian Refugee Camps, International Crisis Group Middle East Report no 84, International Crisis Group, 19 February 2009, p 6, http://www.crisisgroup.org/en/regions/middle-east-north-africa/iraq-syria-lebanon/lebanon.aspx [accessed 15 April 2010].

Occupied Golan: Apple Transfer Operation coming to an End, ICRC, 22 April 2010, http://www.icrc.org/eng/resources/documents/feature/2010/golan-feature-220410.htm [accessed 11 October 2010].

Occupied Golan Heights: ICRC mitigates some effects of occupation, ICRC, 2 March 2010, http://www.icrc.org/eng/resources/documents/update/israel-golan-update-020310.htm [accessed 8 October 2010].

Occupied Golan: 700 Druze Pilgrims Cross into Syria Proper with the help of ICRC, ICRC, 22 September 2010, http://www.icrc.org/eng/resources/documents/photo-gallery/golan-photos-200910.htm [accessed 8 October 2010].

'On al-Assad's visit to Turkey', arabicnews.com 19 July 2001, www.arabicnews.com/ansub/Daily/Day/010719/2001071903.html [accessed 30 July 2001].

'Over 14,000 Syrians to congratulate relatives in Turkey in Eid al-Fitr, Turkish official says', Syrian Arab News Agency, 17 October 2006, www.sana.org/eng/22/2006/10/17/76748.htm [accessed 17 October 2006].

'President Asad's interview with the Sunday Times', Syrian Arab News Agency, 3 March 2013, http://sana.sy/eng/21/2013/03/03/470326.htm [accessed 15 April 2013].

'Rafik Hariri inquiry: Syria issues 33 arrest warrants', BBC, 4 October 2010, http://www.bbc.co.uk/news/world-middle-east-11470051 [accessed 8 October 2010].

Ravid, Barak (2010) 'Barak says withdrawal referendum law could boost Israel's enemies', *Ha'aretz*, 24 November 2010, http://www.haaretz.com/print-edition/news/barak-says-withdrawal-referendum-law-could-boost-israel-s-enemies-1.326463 [accessed 24 November 2010].

Remarks by President Clinton, Prime Minister Barak of Israel and Foreign Minister Al-Shara of Syria, 15 December 1999, http://clinton6.nara.gov/1999/12/1999-12-15-remarks-by-president-pm-barak-and-foreign-minister-al-shara.html [accessed 9 April 2008].

Rubin, Barry 'Understanding Syrian Policy: An Analysis of Faruq al-Shara's Explanation', *Middle East Review of International Affairs*, vol 4, no 2 (2000), http://meria.idc.ac.il/journal/2000/issue2/jv4n2a2.html [accessed 3 January 2003].

Sabriibrahimoğlu, Laleh, 'Sidelining contentious issues, Turkey and Syria seal security ties with an agreement', *Turkish Daily News*, 12 September 2001, http://www.hurriyetdailynews.com/h.php?news=sidelining-contentious-issues-turkey-and-syria-seal-security-ties-with-an-agreement-2001-09-12 [accessed 18 August 2002].

Sadeh, Sharon, 'Syrians tell Mideast forum gov't would consider border changes', *Ha'aretz*, 23 August 2003, http://www.haaretz.com/news/syrians-tell-mideast-forum-gov-t-would-consider-border-changes-1.36067 [accessed 10 October 2003].

'Safir suriya bi-lubnan yabda mahamahu' (The Syrian Ambassador to Lebanon starts his mission), Al-Jazeerah, 29 May 2009, http://aljazeera.net/NR/exeres/FDD59FD8-E59A-4947-A4E2-B098FC59D9C7.htm?wbc_purpose=%2F%2F [accessed 26 September 2010].

Security Council report July 2007 Lebanon, 26 June 2007, http://www.securitycouncilreport.org/site/c.glKWLeMTIsG/b.2876597/k.B98E/July_2007brLebanon.htm [accessed 22 May 2008].

Lebanese prisoners detained in Syria: A priority question to raise before the Syrian authorities, Soutine aux Libanais Détanus Arbitrairement, 8 July 2010, http://www.fidh.org/IMG/pdf/Rapport_alternatif_Solida_Syrie_2005_ENG_.pdf [accessed 3 May 2010].

Stern, Yoav, 'Turkey singing a new tune', *Ha'aretz*, 9 January 2005, http://www.haaretz.com/print-edition/features/turkey-singing-a-new-tune-1.146587 [accessed 9 January 2005].

'Suriye Hatay'ı yine "yanlışlıkla" haritasına aldı' (Syria again included Hatay on its map 'by mistake'), *Radikal*, 16 August 2005, http://www.radikal.com.tr/haber.php?haberno=161541 [accessed 18 April 2013].

Suriye televizyonu, Türk uçağının rotasına dair harita yayınladı (Syrian television shows a map of the Turkish plane's route), http://www.youtube.com/watch?v=YMrBdevlouI, uploaded on YouTube 23 June 2012 [accessed 18 April 2013].

'Suriye'de Hatay hayali var', *Gazeteport*, 19 May 2013, http://www.gazeteport.com/haber/134293/suriyede-hatay-hayali-var [accessed 23 August 2013].

'Suriye'den harita krizi: Hatay Türkiye'de değil haberi' (A map crisis from Syria: Hatay is not in Turkey), haberaktuel.com, 21 June 2007, http://www.haberaktuel.com/suriyeden-harita-krizi-hatay-turkiyede-degil-haberi-77830.html [accessed 18 April 2013].

REFERENCES

'Suriye'nin harita inadı bitmedi' (Syrian insistance on the map is not over), *Milliyet*, 19 January 2005, http://www.milliyet.com.tr/2005/01/19/son/sonsiy01.html [accessed 18 April 2013].

'Suriye'nin harita skandalı' (Syria's map scandal), internethaber.com, 21 March 2010, http://www.internethaber.com/suriyenin-harita-skandali-238630h.htm [accessed 18 April 2013].

'Syria agrees to Lebanon Arms Embargo', *The New York Times*, 2 September 2006, http://www.nytimes.com/2006/09/02/world/middleeast/02nations.html [accessed 22 May 2008].

'Syria dismisses new Al-Hariri-plot', BBC World News, 31 October 2007, http://news.bbc.co.uk/2/hi/middle_east/7071107.stm [accessed 29 May 2008].

'Syria: Interview with President Bashar al-Assad (Full Version)', Ulusal TV, 5 April 2013, uploaded on YouTube 6 April 2013, available at http://www.youtube.com/watch?v=IGaSbbyYVU8 [accessed 7 April 2013].

Sherry, Virginia N., *Syria/Lebanon: An Alliance beyond the Law: Enforced Disappearances in Lebanon*, Human Rights Watch, 1997, http://www.hrw.org/en/node/24483/section/1 [accessed 16 Mars 2010].

'Syria, Lebanon presidents push for border demarcation', *Hürriyet Daily News*, 16 June 2010, http://www.hurriyetdailynews.com/n.php?n=syria-lebanon-presidents-want-borders-demarcated-quickly-2010-06-16 [accessed 27 September 2010].

'Syria seeks peace talks with Israel', Al-Jazeera English, 10 January 2004, http://english.aljazeera.net/English/archive/archive?ArchiveId=642 [accessed 18 April 2008].

'Syria's Assad grants nationality to Hasaka Kurds', BBC, 7 April 2011, http://www.bbc.co.uk/news/world-middle-east-12995174 [accessed 8 April 2011].

'Syria to enforce arms embargo', BBC World News, 1 September 2006, http://news.bbc.co.uk/2/hi/middle_east/5304682.stm [accessed 22 May 2008].

'Syrian "redeployment" raises questions: Forces start pullout of some bases in Lebanon', *The Daily Star*, 22 September 2004, http://www.dailystar.com.lb/News/Middle-East/Sep/22/Syrian-redeployment-raises-questions.ashx#axzz1JhGieUzh [accessed 10 September 2008].

'Syrian shot dead in Golan Heights', BBC, 9 January 2003, http://news.bbc.co.uk/2/hi/middle_east/2640887.stm [accessed 10 May 2006].

'Tandidan bi-siyasat Erdoğan wa-ta'kidan li-urubat liwa iskandarun wa-darurat iadathi li al-watan al-um' (Condemning Erdoğan's policy and stressing the Arabness of Hatay and the necessity of its return to the motherland), *Tishreen*, 23 December 2012, http://tishreen.news.sy/tishreen/public/read/275726 [accessed 10 April 2013].

'The final harm Assad did Turkey', *Turkish Daily News*, 15 June 2000, www.hurriyetdailynews.com [accessed 27 July 2007].

'The first post-Öcalan messages from Damascus – Hafez Assad's spokesman talks to Milliyet', *Turkish Daily News*, 11 March 1999, http://www.hurriyetdailynews.com/h.php?news=from-the-papers-1999-03-11[accessed 28 July 2007].

The Hatay Question ORE 15, 28 February 1947, www.foia.cia.gov [accessed 26 December 2010].

The History of Anjar, http://www.mousaler.com/anjar/data/history.html [accessed 29 July 2007].

The King-Crane Commission Report, 28 August 1919, http://www.hri.org/docs/king-crane/ [accessed 15 April 2011].

'Thousands of Syrians cross Turkish borders to visit relatives on Eid al-Fitr', Syrian Arab News Agency, 13 September 2010, http://sana.sy/eng/21/2010/09/12/306970.htm [accessed 13 Aug 2013].

Tlas, Mustapha, 'Al-taawun al-turki al-israili' (The Turkish-Israeli cooperation), *Al-fikr al-siyasi*, vol 1, no 1 (1997), http://www.awu-dam.org/politic/01/fkr1-003.htm [accessed 11 December 2010].

'Turkey and Syria settle decades-old dispute', *Il Mediterraneo*, 4 March 2009, http://www.ilmediterraneo.it/it/rassegna-stampa/rassegna-stampa/turkey-and-syria-settle-decades-old-property-dispute-0000875 [accessed 3 July 2010].

Turkey's Political Relations with Syria, Turkish Ministry of Foreign Affairs, http://www.mfa.gov.tr/turkey_s-political-relations-with-syria.en.mfa [accessed 19 March 2008].

'Turkey, Syria agree on cooperation on GAP project', *Turkish Daily News*, 26 August 2001, http://www.hurriyetdailynews.com [accessed 28 July 2007].

'Turkey, Syria agree to lift visa requirements', *Hürriyet Daily News*, 17 September 2009, http://www.hurriyetdailynews.com/n.php?n=turkey-syria-agree-to-lift-visa-requirements-2009–09–17 [accessed 6 October 2010].

'Turkey tells Syria's Asad: Step down!', Reuters, 22 November 2011, http://www.reuters.com/article/2011/11/22/us-syria-idUSL5E7MD0GZ20111122 [accessed 23 August 2013].

'Turkish daily and the Syrian-Turkish relations', Arabicnews.com, 9 January 2009, www.arabicnews.com/ansub/Daily/Day/010109/2001010906.html [accessed 27 July 2001].

'Turkish daily Highlights Syrian-Turkish relations', Arabicnews.com, 18 January 2001, www.arabicnews.com/ansub/Daily/Day/010118/2001011806.html [accessed 27 July 2001].

'Turkish MPs blast Syrian remarks over Hatay', *Hürriyet Daily News*, 5 August 1998, http://www.hurriyetdailynews.com/default.aspx?pageid=438&n=turkish-mps-blast-syrian-remarks-over-hatay-1998–05–08 [accessed 27 August 2013].

'Türkiye'yle ilişkimizde artık kuşkuya yer yok' (There is no longer room for doubts in our relationship with Turkey), *Milliyet*, 5 January 2004, http://www.milliyet.com.tr/2004/01/05/siyaset/asiy.html [accessed 5 January 2004].

United Nations Documents on UNDOF, http://www.un.org/en/peacekeeping/missions/undof/reports.shtml [accessed 10 December 2010].

'Wafd tijari min Iskandarun fi ghurfat tijarat Dimashq' (A business delegation from Iskenderun at the Damascus Chamber of Commerce), *Tishreen*, 14 November 2009, http://tishreen.news.sy/tishreen/public/read/195479 [accessed 14 April 2013].

'Water, borders file obstruct concluding a Syrian-Turkish statement', Arabicnews.com, 3 October 2000, www.arabicnews.com [accessed 12 October 2002].

'Wazir al-ilam al-suri: awdat al-jawlan ila al-siyadah al-suriyyah amrun hatmi' (The Syrian Information Minister: The return of the Golan to Syrian sovereignty is an irrevocable necessity), Kuwait News Agency, 12 March 2007, http://www.kuna.net.kw/ArticleDetails.aspx?language=ar&id=1717638 [accessed 12 April 2008].

'Wazir turkiy: sanuqim saddan mushtarakan ma suriyyah ala al-asi wa-mahattat dakh ala dijlah' (Turkish minister: We will construct a shared dam with Syria on the Orontes and a pumping station on the Tigris), BBC Arabic, 21 June 2010, http://www.bbc.co.uk/arabic/middleeast/2010/06/100621_assaf_turkeysyria_tc2.shtml [accessed 4 October 2010].

'US increases pressure on Damascus', BBC, 17 February 2005, available at http://news.bbc.co.uk/2/hi/middle_east/4272719.stm [accessed 2010–08–30].

World Refugee Survey 2002 Country Report, 28 December 2002, available at www.refugees.com [accessed 11 October 2010].

Hiwar maftuh: suriyyah wa-l-milaff al-lubnani (Open Dialogue: Syria and the Lebanese Portfolio), Al-Jazeerah, 28 October 2004, http://www.aljazeera.net/programs/pages/82109d2a-e2f3–4b0b-b1b4-a9175206f403#L1 [accessed 30 April 2005].

Wathiqat al-wifaq al-watani – ittifaq taif (The National Pact Document: The Taif Agreement), http://www.lp.gov.lb/SecondaryAr.Aspx?id=13 [accessed 10 December 2010].

'Wafd al-kashafah al-turkiyyah yazur al-ladhiqiyyah' (Turkish Scout delegation visits Lattaqiyyah), *Tishreen*, 27 October 2010, www.tishreen.info [accessed 28 December 2010].

Ya Erdoğan samahnakum bi-liwaiskandarun wa alan sanutalibukum bihi (Erdoğan, we let you have Hatay and now we will demand it from you) date not given, uploaded on YouTube 29 March 2013, http://www.youtube.com/watch?v=K45ipsKXypc [accessed 15 April 2013].

UN material (available through the DagDok database at Dag Hammarskjöld Libarary, www.ub.uu.se)

A/31/251 Note Verbale dated 25 February 1976 from the Permanent Representative of the Syrian Arab Republic to the United Nations addressed to the Secretary-General.

A/41/184 Letter dated 3 March 1986 from the Permanent Representative of the Syrian Arab Republic to the United Nations addressed to the Secretary-General.

A/42/208 Letter dated 3 April 1987 from the Chargé d'affaires a.i. of the Permanent Mission of the Syrian Arab Republic to the United Nations addressed to the Secretary-General.

A/43/985 Letter dated 88/12/19 from the Permanent Representative of the Syrian Arab Republic to the United Nations addressed to the Secretary-General.

A/44/515 Lettre datée du 7 septembre 1989 adressée au Sécretaire Général par le representant permanent de la Syrie auprès de l'Organisation des Nations Unies.

A/45/333 Letter dated 28 June 1989 from the Permanent Representative of Syria to the United Nations addressed to the Secretary-General.

A/46/284 Letter dated 3 July 1991 from the Permanent Representative of Syria to the United Nations addressed to the Secretary-General.

A/46/475 Letter dated 16 September 1991 from the Permanent Representative of the Syrian Arab Republic to the United Nations addressed to the Secretary-General.

A/47/255 Letter dated 3 June 1992 from the Chargé d'affaires a.i. of the Permanent Mission of the Syrian Arab Republic to the United Nations addressed to the Secretary-General.

A/52/202 Note verbale dated 20 June 1997 from the Permanent Representative of the Syrian Arab Republic to the United Nations addressed to the Secretary-General.

A/53/876 Letter dated 24 March 1999 from the Permanent Representative of the Syrian Arab Republic to the United Nations addressed to the Secretary-General.

A/58/670 Identical letters dated 5 January 2004 from the Permanent Representative of the Syrian Arab Republic to the United Nations addressed to the Secretary-General and the President of the Security Council.

A/58/879 Identical letters dated 30 August 2004 from the Permanent Representative of Lebanon to the United Nations addressed to the Secretary-General and the President of the Security Council.

A/58/883 Identical letters dated 1 September 2004 from the Permanent Representative of the Syrian Arab Republic to the United Nations addressed to the Secretary-General and to the President of the Security Council.

A/61/953 Identical letters dated 12 June 2007 from the Chargé d'Affaires of Lebanon to the United Nations addressed to the Secretary-General and the President of the Security Council.

A/64/614 Letter dated 15 December 2009 from the Permanent Representative of the Syrian Arab Republic to the United Nations addressed to the Secretary-General.

A/64/619 Letter dated 5 January 2010 from the Permanent Representative of the Syrian Arab Republic to the United Nations addressed to the Secretary-General.

References

A/AC.145/R.51 Report by the Governorate of Quneitra on Israeli violations of human rights in the occupied Syrian Arab Golan in 1998/ Governorate of Quneitra, Syrian Arab Republic, Ministry of Local Administration.

E/CN.4/1982/22 Letter, dated 25 February 1982, addressed to the President of the Commission on Human Rights at its thirty-eighth session from the Permanent Representative of the Syrian Arab Republic.

E/CN.4/1982/25 Letter dated 3 March 1982 from the Permanent Representative of Syrian Arab Republic addressed to the Chairman of the Commission on Human Rights.

E/CN.4/1982/28 Letter dated 12 March 1982 from the Permanent Representative of Syrian Arab Republic addressed to the Chairman of the Commission on Human Rights.

S/11302/Add.1 (30 May 1974) Report of the Secretary-General concerning the Agreement on Disengagement between Israeli and Syrian Forces,

S/2157 Security Council Resolution of 18 May 1951.

S/8742 Letter dated 9 August 1968 from the Permanent Representative of Syria to the United Nations addressed to the Secretary-General.

S/8749 Letter dated 16 August 1968 from the Permanent Representative of Syria to the United Nations addressed to the Secretary-General.

S/8857 Letter dated 15 October 1968 from the Permanent Representative of Syria to the United Nations addressed to the Secretary-General.

S/8893 Letter dated 7 November 1968 from the Permanent Representative of Syria to the United Nations addressed to the Secretary-General.

S/8904 Letter dated 21 November 1968 from the Permanent Representative of Syria to the United Nations addressed to the Secretary-General.

S/8928 Letter dated 12 December 1968 from the Permanent Representative of Syria to the United Nations addressed to the Secretary-General.

S/8971 Letter dated 16 January 1968 from the Permanent Representative of Syria to the United Nations addressed to the Secretary-General.

S/9042 Lettre datée du 4 mars 1969 adressée au Secrétaire Général par le representant permanent de la Syrie auprès de l'Organisation des Nations Unies.

S/9131 Letter dated 4 April 1969 from the Permanent Representative of Syria to the United Nations addressed to the Secretary-General.

S/9139 Letter dated 8 April 1969 from the Permanent Representative of Syria to the United Nations addressed to the President of the Security Council.

S/9150 Letter dated 11 April 1969 from the Permanent Representative of Syria to the United Nations addressed to the Secretary-General.

S/9220 Letter dated 23 May 1969 from the Permanent Representative of Syria to the United Nations addressed to the Secretary-General.

S/9299 Letter dated 1 July 1969 from the Permanent Representative of Syria to the United Nations addressed to the Secretary-General.

S/9489 Letter dated 28 October 1969 from the Permanent Representative of Syria to the United Nations addressed to the Secretary-General.

S/9643 Letter dated 9 February 1968 from the Permanent Representative of Syria to the United Nations addressed to the Secretary-General.

S/9823 Letter dated 5 June 1970 from the Permanent Representative of Syria to the United Nations addressed to the Secretary-General.

S/10213 Letter dated 28 May 1971 from the Permanent Representative of Syria to the United Nations addressed to the Secretary-General.

S/10300 Letter dated 25 August 1971 from the Representative of Syria to the United Nations addressed to the Secretary-General.

S/11219 Letter dated 12 February 1974 from the Permanent Representative of the Syrian Arab Republic to the United Nations addressed to the Secretary-General.

S/11220 Letter dated 14 February 1974 from the Permanent Representative of the Syrian Arab Republic to the United Nations addressed to the Secretary-General.

S/11234 Letter dated 14 February 1974 from the Permanent Representative of the Syrian Arab Republic to the United Nations addressed to the Secretary-General.

S/11238 Letter dated 20 March 1974 from the Permanent Representative of the Syrian Arab Republic to the United Nations addressed to the Secretary-General.

S/11283 Letter dated 6 May 1974 from the Permanent Representative of the Syrian Arab Republic to the United Nations addressed to the Secretary-General.

S/11330 Letter dated 8 July 1974 from the Permanent Representatives of the Syrian Arab Republic to the United Nations addressed to the Secretary-General.

S/11533 Letter dated 9 October 1974 from the Permanent Representative of the Syrian Arab Republic to the United Nations addressed to the Secretary-General.

S/14239 Note Verbale dated 27 October 1980 from the Permanent Mission of the Syrian Arab Republic to the United Nations addressed to the Secretary-General.

S/14383 Note Verbale dated 24 February 1981 from the Permanent Mission of the Syrian Arab Republic to the United Nations addressed to the Secretary-General.

S/14411 Note Verbale dated 17 Mars 1981 from the Permanent Mission of the Syrian Arab Republic to the United Nations addressed to the Secretary-General.

S/14569 Note verbale dated 22 June 1981 from the Permanent Mission of the Syrian Arab Republic to the United Nations addressed to the Secretary-General.

S/14791 Letter dated 14 December 1981 from the Permanent Representative of the Syrian Arab Republic to the United Nations addressed to the President of the Security Council.

REFERENCES

S/14808 Note verbale dated 18 December 1981 from the Permanent Representative of the Syrian Arab Republic to the United Nations addressed to the Secretary-General.

S/14876 Letter dated 18 February 1982 from the Permanent Representative of the Syrian Arab Republic to the United Nations addressed to the Secretary-General.

S/14893 Letter dated 2 March 1982 from the Permanent Representative of the Syrian Arab Republic to the United Nations addressed to the Secretary-General.

S/17889 Letter dated 9 October 1974 from the Permanent Representative of the Syrian Arab Republic to the United Nations addressed to the President of the Security Council.

S/18782 Letter dated 3 April 1987 from the Chargé d'Affaires a.i. of the Permamnent Mission of the Syrian Arab Republic to the United Nations addressed to the Secretary-General.

S/22654 Letter dated 30 May 1991 from the Permanent Representative of the Syrian Arab Republic to the United Nations addressed to the Secretary-General.

S/22654 Letter dated 3 June 1991 from the Permanent Representative of the Syrian Arab Republic to the United Nations addressed to the Secretary-General.

S/1996/959 Report of the Secretary-General on the United Nations Disengagement Observer Force 18 November 1996.

S/2000/443 Letter dated 19 May 2000 from the Permanent Representative of Lebanon to the United Nations addressed to the Secretary-General.

S/2000/460 (22 May 2000) Report of the Secretary-General on the implementation of Security Council resolutions 425 (1978) and 426 (1978).

S/2001/180 Note verbale dated 28 February 2001 from the Permanent Representative of the Syrian Arab Republic to the United Nations addressed to the Secretary-General.

S/2001/699 Letter dated 16 July 2001 from the Chargé d'affaires a.i. of the Permanent Mission of the Syrian Arab Republic to the United Nations addressed to the Secretary-General.

S/2002/920 Letter dated 12 Augusti 2001 from the Permament Representative of the Syrian Arab Republic to the United Nations addressed to the Secretary-General.

S/2004/205 Identical letters dated 15 March 2004 from the Permanent Representative of the Syrian Arab Republic to the United Nations addressed to the Secretary-General and the President of the Security Council.

S/2004/777 (1 October 2004) Report of the Secretary-General pursuant to Security Council resolution 1559.

S/2005/203 (24 March 2005) Report of the Fact-finding Mission to Lebanon inquiring into the causes, circumstances and consequences of the assassination of former prime minister Rafik Hariri.

S/2005/627 Identical letters dated 30 September 2005 from the Permanent Representative of the Syrian Arab Republic to the United Nations addressed to the Secretary-General and the President of the Security Council.

S/2005/662 (20 October 2005) Report of the International Independent Investigation Commission established pursuant to Security Council resolution 1595.

S/2006/6 Identical letters dated 4 January 2006 from the Permanent Representative of the Syrian Arab Republic to the United Nations addressed to the Secretary-General and the President of the Security Council.

S/2006/947 Identical letters dated 5 December 2006 from the Permanent Representative of the Syrian Arab Republic to the United Nations addressed to the Secretary-General and the President of the Security Council.

S/2007/325 Note verbale dated 31 May 2007 from the Permanent Mission of the Syrian Arab Republic to the United Nations addressed to the Secretary-General.

S/2007/406 Note verbale dated 3 July 2007 from the Permanent Mission of the Syrian Arab Republic to the United Nations addressed to the United Nations Secretariat.

S/2007/511 Letter dated 27 August 2007 from the Permanent Representative of the Syrian Arab Republic to the United Nations addressed to the Secretary-General.

S/2007/630 Letter dated 23 October 2007 from the Permanent Representative of the Syrian Arab Republic to the United Nations addressed to the Secretary-General.

S/2008/582 (26 August 2008) Report of the Lebanon Independent Border Assessment Team II.

S/2008/161 Letter dated 3 March 2008 from the Permanent Representative of the Syrian Arab Republic to the United Nations addressed to the Secretary-General.

S/2008/752 (28 November 2008) Eleventh Report of the International Independent Investigation Commission established pursuant to Security Council resolution 1595 (2005), 1636 (2005), 1644 (2005), 1686 (2006), 1748 (2007), 1815 (2008).

SC/6878 (18 June 2000) Security Council Endorses Secretary-General's Conclusion on Israeli Withdrawal from Lebanon as of 16 June.

SC/8696 (21 April 2006) Lebanon's historic transition not yet complete, but important progress made towards self-governance, stability, Security Council told.

SC/8723 (17 May 2006) Security Council strongly encourages Syria to respond to Lebanon's request to delineate border, establish diplomatic relations.

S/RES/242 (22 November 1967) Security Council resolution.

S/RES/338 (22 October 1973) Security Council resolution.

S/RES/425 (19 March 1978) Security Council resolution.

S/RES/497 (17 December 1981) Security Council resolution.

S/RES/1559 (2 September 2004) Security Council resolution.

S/RES/1664 (24 March 2006) Security Council resolution.
S/RES/1680 (17 May 2006) Security Council resolution.
S/RES/ 1701(11 August 2006) Security Council resolution.
S/RES/1595 (7 April 2005) Security Council resolution.
Security Council Report: Monthly Forecast July 2007, 26 June 2007. http://www.securitycouncilreport.org/atf/cf/%7B65BFCF9B-6D27-4E9C-8CD3-CF6E4FF96FF9%7D/July%202007%20Forecast%20PDF%20version.pdf.

Unpublished sources

Al-jawlan, muhafazat Qunaytrah (Golan, the province of Qunaytrah).
Document handed to me at the Baath Regional Command Headquarters in Damascus 18 July 2003.
Atiyah, Wadih Nayla, *The Attitude of the Lebanese Sunnis towards the State of Lebanon*, PhD thesis, University of London (1973).
Bandazian, Walter C, *The Crisis of Alexandretta*, PhD thesis, American University (1967).
Damali Stefflbauer, Nakeema, *An Analysis of Syrian-Lebanese Informal Trade: 1943–1993*, PhD Thesis, Harvard University (1999).
Drysdale, Alastair, *Center and Periphery in Syria*, PhD Thesis, University of Michigan (1977).
Goldsmith, Leon T., *The Politics of Sectarian Insecurity: Alawaite Asabiyya and the Rise and Decline of the Asad Dynasty of Syria*, PhD Thesis, University of Otago (2012).
Khutab wa-kalimat wa-tasrihat al-sayyid al-rais Hafez al-Asad 1966–2000 (Speeches, announcemnet and statements by President Hafez al-Asad 1966–2000).
Landis, Joshua M., *Nationalism and the Politics of Za'ama*, PhD thesis, Princeton University (1997).
Mufti, Malik, *Pan-Arabism and State Formation in Syria and Iraq*, PhD thesis, Harvard University (1993).
Mufti, Malik, 'Turkish-Syrian Relations at the Turn of the Century', unpublished paper (2003).
Velud, Christian, *Une expérience d'administration régionale en Syrie durant le mandat français: conquête, colonisation et mise en valeur de la Ĝazira 1920–1936*, Université Lumière Lyon (1991).
Özden Oktav Alantar, Zeynep, *Turkey on the Agenda on the League of Nations*, PhD Thesis, Boğazaçi University (1992).

Interviews

Altunışık, Maliha, Department of International Relations, Middle East Technical University, Ankara, 29 April 2002.

Anon Professor at Damascus University, interviewed on the condition of anonymity, Damascus, 12 March and 8 July 2003
Anon Telephone interview with two high-level officials at the Turkish Ministry of Foreign Affairs, 8 and 9 April 2008. Both interviewed on the condition of anonymity.
Baydas, Lana, Legal Advisor ICRC, Damascus, 18 March 2003.
Conneally, Paul, Deputy Head of the ICRC delegation in Israel and the occupied territories, Tel Aviv, 12 November 2007.
Fawzi, Abu Jabal, Member of the Executive Committee of Golan Heights for Development, Majdal Shams, 14 November 2007.
Jabbour, George, advisor to President Hafez al-Asad 1971–1989, Damascus, 18 July 2003.
Al-Judah, Atiyah, Director of the Cultural Center of the Regional Command of the Baath party, Damascus, 8 July 2003.
Gökçen, Ufuk, First Secretary at the Turkish Embassy in Damascus, Damascus, 14 May 2002.
Kirişci, Kemal, Professor of International Relations, Department of Political Science, Boğaziçi University, Istanbul, 30 May 2002.
Moubayed, Sami, political analyst and journalist, Damascus, 15 March 2003.
Mazlum, Ibrahim, PhD Candidate, Department of International Relations, Marmara University, Istanbul, 27 March 2002.
Onhan, Ömer, Head of Middle East Department, Turkish Ministry of Foreign Affairs, Ankara, 24 April 2002.
Safadi, Asad, ICRC representative on the Golan Heights, Majdal Shams, 15 November 2007
Saleh, Medhat, ICRC Syrian liaison officer, Damascus, 22 March 2003.
Suvarierol, Semin, Project Manager for TESEV's Turkish-Syrian project, Turkish Economic and Social Studies Foundation, Istanbul, 30 May 2002 (telephone).
Al-Taqi, Samir, General Director of the Orient Center for International Studies, informal talk, St. Andrews, 7 July 2011.
Wranckler, Bo, Force Commander of the UNDOF, Damascus, 18 March 2003.
Yılmaz, Şuhnaz, Associate Professor of International Relations, Koç University Istanbul, informal talk in Athens, 21 April 2008.

INDEX

8 March Coalition, 74, 80–81
14 March Coalition, 74, 78–81,
    84, 138

Abdullah I, King of Jordan, 25
Abdullah, King of Saudi Arabia, 50
Abu Nidal, 48
Acre, 11
Adana, 11
Adana Agreement, 99–100
Alawites,
    Alawite State, 19–20
    and the annexation of Alexandretta,
        93, 146
    and the army, 31, 38
    under Bashar al-Asad, 36–37
    compact minority, 18
    economic liberalization, 38
    fears of the future, 38
    and Ottoman rule, 18
    support of Greater Syria, 25
    and Syrian national identity, 39
    village on the Golan, 165 note 1
    and the Syrian uprising, 109
    victims of 1976–1982 assassination
        campaign, 33
Albright, Madeleine, 125
Aleppo, 15, 17–18

as an agro-city, 37
and Iraq, 25–26, 30
the state of, 19–20, 22, 89
Alexandretta,
    elections, 91
    French-Turkish negotiations,
        91
    and the League of Nations,
        90
    Legislative Assembly, 91–92
    possible partition of, 91
    renaming of, 91
Allenby, 11, 13
Amal militia, 69
Anjar, 93
Ankara, 92, 94, 101
Antalya, 92
Antioch, 91, 107
Aoun, Michel, 68–69
Aqaba, 60
Arab Democratic Solidarity Party,
    107
Arab-Israeli peace process, the,
    contents, 118
    negotiations over the Golan Heights,
        118 ff
    opening in Madrid, 48
    Syrian control of Lebanon, 72

Arab League, the
    and 1982 resolution on Lebanon,
        64–65
    and Deterrent Force in Lebanon, 64
    and Hatay, 143
    and Lebanese borders, 56
    resolution 314, 65
    and sanctions on Syria, 50
    'the three no's', 115
Arab Writers' Union, 124
Aramoun meeting, 62
Armenians,
    repression of, 41
    settling in Jazirah, 18
    and Syrian national identity,
        39–40
    and the Turkish annexation of
        Alexandretta, 92–93
Arslan, Adil, 93
Al-Asad, Bashar,
    2011 uprising and civil war, 34
    and armed struggle on the Golan,
        130
    and constitutional amendments in
        Lebanon, 74, 78
    and demarcation of the Lebanese
        border, 83–84
    and diplomatic relations with
        Lebanon, 81, 138
    economic policies, 36, 50
    and the EU, 50
    first visit to Turkey, 103
    and Hatay, 100, 103, 108
    inauguration speech, 72–73, 100,
        127
    and independence of Lebanon, 77
    and Iraq, 34, 44, 48, 142
    and the Lebanon portfolio, 72
    murder of Rafiq al-Hariri, 49
    new economic and political elite,
        33–34, 36
    and Sunni Islam, 42
    and UNIFIL, 82
    and the USA, 48–50
    and withdrawal from Lebanon, 75–78

al-Asad, Hafez,
    1970 coup, 31
    and the 1983 Israeli-Lebanese
        agreement, 65–66
    and the Arab League Deterrent
        Force, 64
    and clientelism, 32, 37
    and the Cold War, 46
    and diplomatic relations with
        Lebanon, 81
    domestic instability, 33
    domestic stability, 29, 31–32
    economic policies, 32, 36
    and Geographical/Greater Syria, 26
    and Hatay, 96, 100
    human rights, 32
    and Iran, 47, 49
    and Iraq, 44, 48–49
    land reform, 36
    and independence of Lebanon, 64
    invasion of Lebanon, 47
    and withdrawal from Lebanon,
        64–65, 68–69, 74
    the National Progressive Front, 32
    negotiations with Israel, 118 ff
    personality cult, 31
    and Saddam Hussein, 43
    and the Soviet Union, 46–47
    and strategic parity with Israel, 47
    and Suleiman Franjieh, 62
    and Sunni Islam, 42
    and the Taif Agreement, 70
    united front against Israel, 26, 47, 60
    and USA, 47
al-Asad, Maher, 78
al-Asad, Rifaat, 33
ASALA, 44
Assyrians,
    settling in Jazirah, 18
    and Syrian national identity, 39–40
al-Atasi, Hashim,
    and Alexandretta, 89
    and Lebanon, 56
al-Atasi, Nur al-Din, 114
al-Azmah, Bashir, 59

INDEX

Baalbek, 19, 53
Baath Party, the,
   and the 1954 elections, 30
   1963 military coup, 30
   1966 military coup, 46
   and the Constitution, 27, 31
   economic policies, 36
   ideology 24, 27, 31, 39
   intra-party struggle, 31, 36
   and Israel, 141
   land reform, 35
   state and nation building, 35, 37, 39
   and the United Arab Republic, 30
Baghdad Pact, the, 26, 43–44
Banyas, 109, 114, 122, 148
Barak, Ehud 119, 122–123, 125
Bayda, 109
Beirut, 15
   population, 53
Bedouins, 18–19
   Contrôle Bédouin, 19
Bilal, Muhsin, 127
Biqaa, 19, 53, 63, 69, 75, 92, 145
Blair, Tony, 50
al-Bunni, Muhammad Said, 101
Bush, George W., 50, 119

Camp David Accord, 63
China, 49
   and the Syrian uprising, 51
Christopher, Warren, 120
Cilicia, 15–16
Circassians,
   and Syrian national identity, 42
Clinton, Bill, 100, 123, 125
Constitution,
   Syria's first, 22
   1973 Constitution, 31, 42
   2012 Constitution, 27, 31, 42
Correction Movement, the, 31
Cyprus, 45, 96

Dakhlallah, Mahdi, 76–77
Damascus,
   the Damascus Agreement, 62, 68
   the Damascus program, 14
   Damascus Spring, 34
   the State of Damascus, 19–20, 22
Dayr el-Zor,
   as an agro-city, 37
   and the Baath Party, 30
   inclusion in Syria, 16
   and Iraq 16, 25
   the sanjak of, 19
Diyarbakır 13, 18
Doha Agreement, the, 80–81, 138
Dörtyol, 92
Druze,
   and the army, 31
   compact minority, 18
   the Druze state, 19–20
   under Ottoman rule, 18
   and pilgrimage to Zabadani, 132
   and Shukri al-Quwatli, 40
   support of Greater Syria, 25
   suppression by Adib al-Shishakli, 35
   and Syrian national identity, 39–40
   villages on the Golan, 165 note 1

Egypt,
   anti-Syrian activities in Lebanon, 59
   and the Hashemites, 43
   and Israel, 47
   and military alliance with Syria, 43
   President Naser, 27, 43
   tension with Syria, 43
   the United Arab Republic, 26, 30, 43
Erdoğan, Recep Tayyip, 45, 105, 107–109
Erzin, 92
Euphrates, 96
European Community, the,
   relations with Syria, 50

Faysal, 11–14
   expulsion from Syria, 15
   as King of Iraq, 151 note 1
   and Mount Lebanon, 53–54
   and Palestine, 14, 151 note 1
Fares, Issam, 76

Fatah al-Islam, 82
France,
   divide and rule strategy, 19
   High Commissioner, 90
   negotiations with the National Bloc, 55
   negotiations with Turkey over Alexandretta, 91, 93
   Treaty of Friendship with Turkey, 90
Franjieh, Suleiman, 62–63
Frank-Bouillon Agreement, 16
French Mandate, *see also* Lebanon
   elections for the Constitutional Assembly, 22
   external borders, 15–17
   French divide and rule strategy, 19
   imposition of, 15
   internal borders, 17–21
   Syrian-French 1936 Treaty, 23, 89
Friendship dam (Syria-Turkey), 105, 110, 139

Gaziantep, 92
Geagea, Samir, 72
Gemayel, Amin, 65, 67, 157 note 30
Golan, the,
   Area of Separation, 115, 129
   demilitarized zones, 114, 122
   demographical changes after the Israeli annexation, 113
   'the deposit', 120, 122, 126–127
   disengagement agreement, 115–116
   ICRC activities, 131–132
   Israeli annexation of, 117, 126, 143
   Palestinian guerilla activity, 115
   refugees from 113, 129–130
   and the Syrian civil war, 131
   Syrian villages remaining, 165 note 1
   Syrian-Israeli negotiations, 118 ff
   United Nations Disengagement Observer Force (UNDOF), 115–116, 129, 131–132
Gorbatchev, Michail, 48

Great Revolt, the,
   as watershed in nationalist politics, 22
Greater Lebanon,
   border demarcation of, 59
   creation of, 19–20, 53–54

Haddad, Ibrahim, 105
Haifa, 54
Hama, 33, 37
Hamas,
   relations with Syria, 49
al-harakah al-tashihiyyah, 31
al-Hariri, Rafiq,
   assassination of, 49, 74, 78–79, 142
   resignation of, 74
al-Hariri, Saad,
   and the disarmament of Hizbullah, 80
   and improved relations with Syria, 81
   and the Rafiq al-Hariri murder investigation, 78–79, 81
Hasbaya, 19, 53
Hassa, 92
Hatay,
   autonomous within the French mandate, 91
   demarcation of the border with Syria, 101, 105, 110
   demographical changes after annexation, 92
   indirect recognition of the border, 105
   nationalised property, 104
   students in Syria, 98, 102
   on Syrian maps 95–101, 105–106, 107, 109, 111, 137, 139, 142, 146, 149
   and the Syrian uprising, 106–108, 139, 147, 149
Hatay Devleti, 91
Hawran, 18
   and the Baath Party, 30
Hejaz, 11

Index

Hinnawi affair, the, 48
Al-Hinnawi, Sami,
  and Hatay, 94
Hizbullah,
  and the 2006 war with Israel, 79, 130
  and the 2008 take-over of West Beirut and Beirut sit-in, 80
  and the Chouf, 80
  disarmament of, 80
  relations with Syria, 49, 129, 138, 145, 148
  as suspect in al-Hariri murder investigation, 79
  and the Taif Agreement, 69
Hrawi, Elias, 71
Hula,
  the lake, 114
  the valley, 114
Husayn-McMahon Correspondence, 10, 13
Hussein, Saddam, 43

Idlib, 105
Infitah, 32–33
Intérêts Communs, 21, 57, 144
International Committee of the Red Cross (ICRC), 130–134
Iran,
  relations with Syria, 49, 129
  and the Syrian uprising, 51
  war with Iraq 47
Iraq, 16, 18
  and Bashar al-Asad, 34, 44
  and coup attempt in Syria, 43
  and Hafez al-Asad, 44, 49
  and invasion of Kuwait, 48
  as mediator of Turkish-Syrian deal over Hatay, 93, 143
  as Syria's arch enemy, 43
  and unification with Syria, 23, 25, 30
  and water negotiations, 96, 100
Iskenderun 13, 17, 56, 91, 94, 97, 146
Ismailis,
  and the army, 31
  and Syrian national identity, 39

Israel,
  and the 1948–1949 war, 25, 95
  1983 agreement with Lebanon, 65, 84
  annexation of the Golan Heights, 117, 126, 143–144
  and Egypt, 47
  and Hizbullah, 79
  and Husni al-Zaim
  and the Oslo Accords, 48
  retaliation against Lebanon, 60
  and Russia, 49
  and the Soviet Union, 48
  Syrian-Israeli disengagement treaty, 47
  Syrian-Israeli negotiations, 118 ff
  and Syrian withdrawal from Lebanon, 48, 64
  and Turkey, 44–45
  water, 122
  withdrawal from Lebanon, 65, 73, 83

Jabbour, George, 102
al-jabhah al-shaabiyyah li-tahrir liwa iskandarun, 98, 109, 147
al-jabhah al-wataniyyah al-taqaddumiyyah, 32
al-Jabiri, Saadallah,
  and Alexandretta, 90
Jazirah, 17–18, 25
  imposition of direct French rule, 21
  nation building 18, 40
  the sanjak of, 19
  sedentarisation of, 19
Joint Military Committee, 76
Jordan 12, 17
  and Geographical/Greater Syria, 25, 43
  and Hatay, 143
  and peace with Israel, 48, 132
  the river, 115, 122, 125, 148
Junblatt, Walid, 81

Karami, Omar, 71
Karami, Rashid, 59

Al-Kayali, Ali, 109
Khaddam, Abdul Halim
  and a possible partition of Lebanon, 61–62
  and presidential elections in Lebanon, 68
al-Khoury, Faris, 56
Killis, 17
King-Crane Commission, 13–14
Kuftaro, Ahmad, 42
Kurds,
  arabisation of Kurdish territories, 40–41
  assimilation of Kurds 40–41
  autonomy, 41
  citizenship, 40; hopes for independence 17
  and Hatay, 98
  and the invasion of Iraq, 41, 45
  settling in Jazirah, 18
  and Syrian national identity, 39–40
al-kutlah al-wataniyyah, 22

Lahhoud, Émile, 71, 73–74, 78, 80
Lataqiyah, 18
  as an agro-city, 37
  and the Baath Party, 30
  and the Syrian uprising, 107, 109
Lausanne Treaty, the, 16, 89, 143
League of Nations, 15–16
  and Alexandretta, 90–92, 142
  and the Syrian Nationalist Movement, 54
Lebanese Arab Army, 67
Lebanese Constitutional Bloc, 55
Lebanese Forces militia, 72
Lebanese National Accord, 66
Lebanese National Army, 67, 82, 84
Lebanese National Movement, the, 61–62
Lebanese National Pact of 1943, 55–59, 85, 137
Lebanese-Syrian Treaty of Brotherhood, Cooperation and Coordination, 70

Lebanon, *see also* French Mandate
  8 March Coalition, 74, 80–81
  14 March Coalition, 74, 78–81, 84, 138
  the 2008 unity government, 80
  and the Arab-Israeli peace process, 72, 125, 145
  bilateral agreements with Syria, 60, 70, 81–82
  civil war 1958, 58
  civil war 1975–1990, 60 ff
  constitutional amendments, 71, 74, 78
  demarcation of the border, 59, 83–84, 86
  diplomatic relations with Syria, 59, 81, 138
  opposition to Syrian presence, 73–74
  Syrian arrests of Lebanese, 67, 72, 79
  and the Syrian civil war, 82
  Syrian demands for sanctions, 65
  Syrian formal recognition of independence, 56–57
  Syrian interference in elections, 68, 71, 73, 80
  and the United Arab Republic, 58
Lebanon Independent Border Assessment Team (LIBAT), 82–83
Lebanon-Syria Defence and Security Agreement, 71

Majdal Shams, 133
Mardam, Jamil,
  and Alexandretta, 90
  and Hatay, 94
  and the Lebanese National Pact, 55, 137
Maronite Christians, 53, 55
  Maronite-Maronite war, 69
  opposition to Syrian presence in Lebanon, 73–74
  the Patriarch, 55
al-Mekdad, Faysal, 81, 83
Menderes, Adnan, 95

INDEX

Mersin, 11
Minorities,
   overrepresentation in the army, 31
Mofaz, Shaul, 128
Moon, Ban-Ki, 80–81
Mosul, 15
Moubayed, Sami, 146
Mount Hermon, 148
Mount Lebanon, 14, 18–19, 53
al-Muallim, Walid, 79, 97, 126–127
Musa Dağ, 92
Muslim Brotherhood, the,
   confrontation with the regime, 36
   execution of prisoners, 33
   Hama, 33
   and Hatay, 149
   support in Aleppo and Hama, 36

Nahr al-Bared, 82
Naser, Gamal Adbul, 27, 43
   and Hatay, 95
National Bloc, the,
   and Alexandretta, 91, 139
   attitude towards Greater Lebanon, 23, 54–56, 144
   attitude towards Palestine, 23
   composition of, 22
   creation of, 22, 54
   negotiations with France, 55
   post-independence lack of program, 35
   post-independence split, 29; rhetoric, 39
   'Syria first' strategy, 23, 54–55, 139
   Syrian-French 1936 Treaty, 23, 55
   territorial priorities, 23–24
   and Tripoli, 55
National Coalition for Revolutionary and Opposition Forces, 51, 107
National Party, 29
National Progressive Front, 32
National Union Front, 66, 68
National Union Party, 95
Netanyahu, Benjamin, 118, 122

Obama, Barack, 50
October Crisis, the, 44, 99, 139–140
October War, the, 46
Organisation of Islamic Cooperation,
   and sanctions on Syria, 50
Orontes, 96–97, 101, 105, 110, 139
Oslo Accords, 48
Ottoman Empire,
   Arab revolt, 10–11
   post-World War I geographical divisions, 11–13, 15
   pre-World War I administrative divisions, 15, 53, 151 note 3
Öcalan, Abdullah, 109

Palestine, 11, 14–15, 17–18
   attitude of Faysal, 14
   attitude of the National Bloc, 23
   and the Oslo Accords, 48
   as 'Southern Syria', 23
Palestinians,
   the Arab-Israeli peace process, 118
   operating from Golan, 116
   Nahr al-Bared clashes 2007, 82
   Palestinian refugees in Syria, 40
   Syrian arrests of Palestinians in Lebanon, 67, 72
   Syrian hosting of militant Palestinian groups, 47–48
   Syrian support for Palestinians in Lebanon, 60–62, 145
Palestinian Liberation Army, 62, 65
Pan-Arabism,
   the Baath Party, 24, 27, 30
   decreasing importance, 26
   as part of Syrian discourse, 24
Payas, 17
People's Party, 25, 27, 30
Peres, Shimon, 118, 122
Permanent Mandates Commission,
   and Alexandretta, 17, 143
PKK, 44
   and Hatay, 99
   Syrian support for, 99, 109

PLO, 60, 69
Popular Front for the Liberation of
   Iskandarun, 98, 109, 147
Putin, Vladimir, 49

Qatar, 107
Qunaytrah,
   the 1974 disengagement agreement, 116, 129–130
   reconstruction of, 130
al-Quwatli, Shukri,
   and Geographical/Greater Syria, 25
   and Hatay, 93–95
   Independence Day speech, 23, 57
   and transfer of Druze, 40
   and unification with Iraq, 23

Rabin, Yitzhak, 116, 118, 120, 122
Rashaya, 19, 53
Reyhanlı, 109
Ross, Dennis, 123, 125
Russia, 49, *see also* Soviet Union
   and the Syrian uprising, 51

Saada, Antun,
   execution of, 26
   and Husni al-Zaim, 57–58
   ideas, 25
Sadat, Anwar, 46
al-Saghur, 19
Saleh, Medhat, 130
Salman, Muhammad, 99
Sarkis, Elias, 63, 157 note 29 and 30
Sarkozy, Nicolas, 50
Saudi Arabia, 11, 30, 68
   and the Hashemites, 43
   and Hatay, 143
   relations with Syria, 50
Shamir, Yitzhak, 119
al-Shara, Farouq,
   and early warning stations on the Golan, 123
   and Hatay, 100, 101
   opening speech in Madrid, 118–119, 130
   opening statement December 1999, 124
Sharif Husayn, 10
al-Shaqfa, Muhammad Riad, 149
al-Shawkat, Assef, 78
al-Shishakli, Adib,
   and Geographical Syria, 25
   and Hatay, 95
   suppression of minorities, 35, 40
Shebaa Farms, 59–60, 83–84
Sidon, 19, 53
Sinai Accord, 63
Siniora, Fuad, 79, 83
Six Days War, 46
Soviet Union, the, *see also* Russia,
   and the Cold War, 44–45
   and relations with Syria, 45–46, 48, 142
   as sponsor of the Arab-Israeli peace process, 48
   Treaty of Friendship and Cooperation, 47
Special Tribunal for Lebanon, 79
Suleiman, Michel, 80
al-Sulh, Riyad, 56
Sunni Islam,
   Bashar al-Asad, 42
   Hafez al-Asad, 42
   political and social elite, 29, 32, 35–37
   purges of Sunni Muslim officers, 31
   and Syrian national identity, 39–40
Sykes-Picot Agreement, 11, 15
Syria,
   the federation, 20
   and Iraqi/Jordanian/Egyptian rivalry, 43
   the Kingdom of, 14
   and Lebanese elections, 68, 71, 73
   and Lebanese media, 6, 58, 66–67, 71–72, 82
   national identity, 40–41

post-1970 political stability, 29
pre-1970 political instability, 28
the State of, 20–22, 90
Syria Accountability and Lebanese
   Sovereignty Restoration Act, 75
Syriacs,
   and Syrian national identity, 39
Syrian-Lebanese Higher Council, 70
Syrian National Congress, 13–15
Syrian Nationalist Movement, the,
   and the creation of Greater
      Lebanon, 54
Syrian Patriotic Youth Party, 108
Syrian Socialist National Party,
   banning in Syria, 26
   and Geographical/Greater Syria, 25
   and Husni al-Zaim, 57

Taif Agreement, the, 67–70, 138
   Lebanese reactions to, 69
   and Syrian withdrawal, 69, 86
Al-Taqi, Samir, 106
Tartous, 18
Tiberias, 114, 122–125, 148
Tigris, 96
Tlas, Mustapha, 97
Tripartite Agreement (1985), 66–68, 71
Tripartite High Commission, 68
Tripoli, 19, 53–54, 82
   as compensation for Iskenderun,
      56, 91
Turkey,
   border with Syria, 16–17, 89
   and coup attempt in Syria, 43
   Declaration of Principles, 100
   Frank-Bouillon Agreement, 16
   improved relations with Syria,
      44–45, 147
   and Israel, 44–45, 147
   Lausanne Treaty, 16
   negotiations with France over
      Alexandretta, 91, 93
   tension with Syria, 44–45
   Treaty of Friendhip with France, 90

and the Syrian uprising, 45, 50, 107
water, 44, 96–97, 101, 104–105, 146,
   148
Turkish National Security Council,
   97–98
Turkmen,
   and Syrian national identity, 39–40
   and the Syrian uprising, 107
Turkish Nationalist Forces, 15
Tyre, 11, 19, 53

United Arab Emirates, 107
United Arab Republic, 26–27, 43
   and Hatay, 95, 139
   land reform, 35
   and Lebanon,
   national identity, 40
United Nations Fact Finding Mission
   report, 78
United Nations Interim Force in
   Lebanon (UNIFIL), 75, 82, 84
United Nations International
   Independent Investigation
   Commission (UNIIIC) reports,
   63, 78
United Nations Disengagement
   Observer Force (UNDOF),
   115–116, 129, 131–132
United Nations Security Council
   Resolution 242, 118–119, 142
United Nations Security Council
   Resolution 338, 115
United Nations Security Council
   Resolution 497, 118, 144
United Nations Security Council
   Resolution 1559, 73–75, 77, 78
United Nations Security Council
   Resolution 1595, 78
United Nations Security Council
   Resolution 1664, 79
United Nations Security Council
   Resolution 1680, 83
United Nations Security Council
   Resolution 1701, 80, 82, 83

Uprisings,
  1976–1982, 33
  Kurdish autonomy, 41
  Kurdish citizenship, 41
  initial demands 2011, 27
  and Turkey, 45, 50
Ural, Miraç, 109
Uruba, 39
USA,
  and the 1973 October War, 45
  and the Cold War, 45
  and relations with Syria, 47–50, 75, 107, 142
  as sponsor of the Arab-Israeli peace process, 48
Al-Utri, Naji, 81, 105

Weizmann, Chaim, 14

World War I,
  Arab revolt, 10–11
  Paris Peace Conference, 11, 13–14
  San Remo Conference, 15
Wranckler, Bo, 129
Wye River, 121–122

Yeltsin, Boris, 49
Yılmaz, Masut,
  and Hatay, 99

Zabadani, 132
al-Zaim, Husni,
  and Hatay, 94, 110
  and Israel, 94
  and Jazirah, 40
  and Lebanon, 57–58

www.ingramcontent.com/pod-product-compliance
Ingram Content Group UK Ltd.
Pitfield, Milton Keynes, MK11 3LW, UK
UKHW021833220426
470268UK00007B/136